Bach and the Pedal Clavichord

Eastman Studies in Music

Ralph P. Locke, Senior Editor
Eastman School of Music

(ISSN 1071–9989)

Other titles on the History of Theory and Early Music

*Analyzing Wagner's Operas: Alfred
Lorenz and German Nationalist
Ideology*
Stephen McClatchie

*The Chansons of Orlando di Lasso and
Their Protestant Listeners: Music, Piety,
and Print in Sixteenth-Century France*
Richard Freedman

*Concert Music, Rock, and Jazz since
1945: Essays and Analytical Studies*
Edited by Elizabeth West Marvin
and Richard Hermann

*French Organ Music from the
Revolution to Franck and Widor*
Edited by Lawrence Archbold and
William J. Peterson

*The Gardano Music Printing Firms,
1569–1611*
Richard J. Agee

*Music and Musicians in the Escorial
Liturgy under the Habsburgs, 1563–
1700*
Michael Noone

Music Theory in Concept and Practice
Edited by James M. Baker, David W.
Beach, and Jonathan W. Bernard

*Theories of Fugue from the Age of
Josquin to the Age of Bach*
Paul Mark Walker

A complete list of titles in the Eastman Studies in Music series,
in order of publication, may be found at the end of this book.

Bach and the Pedal Clavichord

An Organist's Guide

Joel Speerstra

Foreword by Hans Davidsson

Ⓡ University of Rochester Press

First published 2004
by the University of Rochester Press

The University of Rochester Press
668 Mt. Hope Avenue, Rochester, NY 14620, USA
Boydell & Brewer, Ltd.
P.O. Box 9, Woodbridge, Suffolk IP12 3DF, UK
www.urpress.com

ISBN 1–58046–135–2
ISSN 1071–9989

Library of Congress Cataloging-in-Publication Data

Speerstra, Joel.
    Bach and the pedal clavichord : an organist's guide / Joel Speerstra.
        p. cm. — (Eastman studies in music, ISSN 1071-9989 ; [26])
    Includes bibliographical references and index.
        ISBN 1-58046-135-2 (hardcover : alk. paper)
    1. Pedal clavichord. 2. Bach, Johann Sebastian, 1685-1750. Organ music. 3. Organ music—Interpretation (Phrasing, dynamics, etc.) 4. Performance practice (Music)—18th century. I. Title. II. Eastman studies in music ; v. 26.

ML651.S642 2004
786.3'092–dc21   2003024587

British Library Cataloguing-in-Publication Data
A catalogue record for this book is available from the British Library

Designed and typeset by Straight Creek Bookmakers
Printed in the United States of America
This publication is printed on acid-free paper

John Barnes
in memoriam

Frontispiece. Photograph of a copy of the J. D. Gerstenberg pedal clavichord built by John Barnes and Joel Speerstra in 1995. Photo by Su Dunthorne. Reproduced with permission.

Contents

Lists of Figures, Tables, and Music Examples   viii
Acknowledgments   x
Foreword by Hans Davidsson   xi

Introduction   1

Part One: Source Studies
Prelude to Part One   13

1. The Historical Pedal Clavichord   17
2. J. S. Bach's Trio Sonatas: A Reception History of a Rumor   32
3. Reconstructing the Gerstenberg Pedal Clavichord   52
4. J. S. Bach and the Clavichord: A Reception History of a Technique   69

Part Two: Performance Practice Studies
Prelude to Part Two   91

5. Performance Practice at the Pedal Clavichord   95
6. Musica Poetica and Figural Notation   114
7. J. S. Bach's Passacaglia in C Minor, BWV 582: A Case Study   129
8. The Pedal Clavichord and the Organ in Dialogue   149

Appendix: Friederich Conrad Griepenkerl's Preface to J. S. Bach's
Chromatic Fantasy and Fugue (1819)   161
Notes   172
Bibliography   187
Index   199

Figures

Photograph of a copy of the J. D. Gerstenberg pedal
clavichord built by John Barnes and Joel Speerstra in 1995.   *frontispiece*

1.1. Pedal Clavichord from *Flores Musicae* (after 1467).   21
3.1a. The parts of the Gerstenberg Pedal Clavichord.   55
3.1b. The parts of the manual.   56
3.1c. The parts of the pedal.   57
3.2. The lower manual soundboard well with cross-brace.   58
3.3. A mysterious hole.   58
3.4. 16–foot stop mechanism.   59
3.5. Gerstenberg manual with the golden section and square root
      of five construction lines.   60
3.6. String tension's relationship to technique.   62
3.7. Edinburgh stringing on a string-tension scale.   65
5.1. Contact between string and tangent.   96
5.2. Historical and nonhistorical clavichord keylevers.   98
5.3. Good and bad notes at the clavichord.   104
5.4. J. S. Bach, Applicatio, right hand, first two measures.   104
5.5. Fulcrum points on the manual and pedal keys.   106
5.6. Kittel's alternating toe pedaling.   107
5.7. Kittel's alternating heel and toe pedaling.   107
5.8. Original Gerstenberg and modern standard organ sharp heights.   110
5.9. Pedaling in triple time.   111
5.10. Pedaling.   112
6.1. *Figura corta* at the clavichord.   115
6.2. *Figura suspirans* at the clavichord.   116
6.3. Traditional brush strokes in Chinese calligraphy.   119
6.4. Inventio 1, C Major, BWV 772a, in J. S. Bach's hand.   124
6.5. Inventio 1, C Major, BWV 772a, in figural notation.   125
6.6. Inventio 8, F Major, BWV 779, in J. S. Bach's hand.   126
6.7. Inventio 8, F Major, BWV 779, in figural notation.   127
8.1. Key-position measurement by triangulation.   151
8.2. Force characteristics of Gerstenberg lower manual c^1.   152
8.3. Key characteristics for North German Organ Hauptwerk c^1.   153
8.4. The new North German organ in Göteborg.   154
8.5. The keyboards of the North German organ in Göteborg.   156

Tables

3.1. Comparison of the plain string gauges of three eighteenth-
     century clavichords with the Gerstenberg copy.   66
5.1. Comparison between arm and leg at the clavichord.   107
6.1. Brief dictionary of notational figures.   121–123
6.2. The three steps in the execution of calligraphic characters
     and rhetorical figures at the clavichord.   128
7.1. Figural notation for the Passacaglia.   139
8.1. Great Organ at Alkmaar (NL): Initial resistance of key
     measured in grams.   150

Music Examples

7.1. Johann Pachelbel, *Ciacona* in D Minor, mm. 144–45.   132
7.2. Dieterich Buxtehude, Passacaglia BuxWV 161, mm. 84–85.   133
7.3. Johann Sebastian Bach, Passacaglia BWV 582, mm. 120–21.   133

Acknowledgments

There are many people to thank for their generous help and support of this work. Both Hans Davidsson, founder of the Göteborg Organ Art Center (GOArt), and Jan Ling, Professor of Musicology when this project started and later Rector of Göteborg University, made this project possible in the first place and saw it through to its end. John and Sheila Barnes in Edinburgh made it possible to realize the dream of building the instrument copy. The Bank of Sweden Tercentenary Foundation financially supported GOArt's first six-year research project, "Changing Processes in North European Organ Art: 1600–1970," of which this study was a part. Pamela Ruiter-Feenstra provided constant encouragement and developed a dialogue between clavichord technique and her ongoing research at GOArt into improvisation in historical styles. Because this project grew out of, and was nurtured by, the organ research workshop at GOArt, I want also to thank particularly Munetaka Yokota and Per Anders Terning for sharing their time, their knowledge, and their patience.

Then there is the entire family of international performers, researchers, and builders, too numerous to mention here, who provided the unique interdisciplinary atmosphere at GOArt, where this project took shape. For many aspects of the technical documentation, I thank Carl Johan Bergsten, as well as Eszter Fontana and the staff of the Leipzig University Musical Instrument Museum for their generous support during several study trips to see the original instrument. Dr. Gerhard Stradner, my dissertation examiner, along with Dr. Laurence Libin, provided valuable insights, as did the rest of the dissertation committee: Hans Ola Ericsson, Gunnar Ternhaug, and Sverker Jullander. Then there was the small army of people who read and proof-read various drafts of this work and gave invaluable feedback. These include Hans Davidsson, Olle Edström, Jan Ling, Karen Speerstra, Kerala Snyder, William Porter, Robin Blanton, Ibo Ortgies, Pamela Ruiter-Feenstra, Dale Carr, and Gregor Detzler. Ralph Locke, senior editor of the series Eastman Studies in Music, was most helpful in bringing the book into publication. And also, at the University of Rochester Press, I would like to extend my heartfelt thanks to Louise Goldberg and Timothy Madigan, as well as to the careful and thorough critique received from the Press's anonymous reader.

Finally, I also wish to thank all of the students at the School of Music in Göteborg and at the Smarano Organ, Clavichord, and Improvisation Academy who participated in the technique reconstruction experiments, and without whose seriousness, curiosity, and enthusiasm this project would not have developed as it did.

Foreword

Hans Davidsson

Bach and the Pedal Clavichord: An Organist's Guide is the first serious, many-faceted study ever published of the pedal clavichord. How Joel Speerstra's book came to be is a tale worth briefly telling and also helps explain why the instrument was so crucial to the organist's art in past centuries and is becoming so again today.

Exactly a decade has passed since the Bank of Sweden Tercentenary Foundation accepted a proposal to allow an international group of researchers to begin a new kind of work in the musical arts in Göteborg. Their belief in supporting truly interdisciplinary research between the sciences and humanities made this network of projects possible. The proposal was for a six-year research program to lead us to a better understanding of four hundred years of what we chose to call the "organ art" of Northern Europe. In the early days of the project we struggled to find a better translation for the term "organ art." In Swedish, *Orgelkonst,* and in German, *Orgelkunst,* is a powerful shorthand symbol for the matrix of disparate things that organs are (architecture, musical instrument, historical craft process, science experiments, sounding documents of the past) and what they generate around them (musical literature; connections and communities between artists, composers, architects, musicians, scientists, and handcraft persons; and bridges between high and low culture in many ages and contexts). So "organ art" it is, and it has been a special kind of pleasure to begin to hear that term used in wider contexts in English to define this new, broader, and more interdisciplinary view of all that fascinates us about the organ tradition.

The largest case study within this program is introduced at the end of this book: the reconstruction of a monumental Hanseatic City church organ from the mid- to late-seventeenth century. None of these organs survive in their original state, and the challenge to reconstruct not only the building methods, but the sound-world of the originals involved legions of instrument builders and dozens of scientific studies: everything from analyzing seventeenth-century metal to constructing new computer-modeling techniques in order to understand a wind system with three or four times as many giant wedge bellows as modern organs tend to have. The new organ in Göteborg is now being used by performers and students alike as a piece of "research equipment" to better understand the performance practice of that era.

The main thrust of the book is the project's smallest case study, or perhaps it could be better described as its most self-contained one. Our research program prioritized finding out as much as possible about the keyboard instruments that were most related to various phases of organ culture over the four-hundred-year period of our study. These related keyboard instruments are also part of organ art. For instance, exciting work was done in introducing a whole new generation to the importance of the French harmonium for the study and understanding of French Romantic organ culture. It was not a toy or a practice instrument, but an inspiration and a kind of ideal sound-world that influenced and inspired organbuilding to become more expressive, and it taught a generation of organ performers a mode of expressivity that is documented in our favorite organ works from that period. But in the harmonium study, we did not have to begin by reconstructing the harmoniums. Many instruments of the finest quality still exist and could be used.

In the case study described in this book, Joel Speerstra explores the pedal clavichord as a related instrument to better understand the organ culture of Central and Northern Europe in Johann Sebastian Bach's time and before. But there were no surviving historical pedal clavichords in playable condition to work with, so Speerstra had to be the instrument builder, the musicologist, the performer, and with some help, the scientist, to reconstruct the "pedal clavichord art." When the instrument was built, he also took on the role of teacher to help himself and others begin to explore this newly built old instrument's relationship to the craft of playing the organs, like the newly built old North German organ in Göteborg. Like the harmonium, the pedal clavichord also turned out to be far from the toy or cheap instrument of convenience that later generations have assumed. It turned out to be a powerfully expressive instrument that opened new musical windows on the Baroque organ literature and challenged us to be more technically careful and more passionately engaged in our art as organ performers.

Some of the important aspects described in this study involve a new awareness of how materials in clavichords were treated acoustically in the building process to enhance their resonance and create a coherent-sounding whole. The study also explores Baroque figuration, which at other instruments of the period can be experienced visually and temporally. But at the clavichord, there is an important third dimension: these figurations can be played with variations in dynamics. Perhaps most important, playing the pedals of the clavichord generates a new level of awareness of body balance in the organ student. When one suddenly is faced with having to take responsibility for the dynamic nuance of a pedal line, one experiences the necessity of creating and controlling the placement of musical accents within larger pedal figures. And when one does this, the production of these important impulses in the legs can be coordinated between pedal and manual playing, and the work of shaping the figures themselves in the pedals and manuals grows organically together into a single dance.

I take great pleasure in reporting to you that, as I write this, the pedal clavichord is becoming a fully integrated part of the organ performance curriculum at the Eastman School of Music in Rochester, N.Y. For the first time in two hundred years, an effective tool for building technique, technical proficiency, and expressive musicianship is returning and fulfilling its natural role in the education of young organists. I am convinced that this study will nurture an even wider interest in exploring the fascinating potential that this keyboard instrument offers us. In fifteen years, I would not be surprised if the pedal clavichord has become an integral part of organ education at leading institutions around the world; together with other organ-related keyboard instruments, the pedal clavichord will be enriching and reinvigorating the multi-faceted global organ art of the twenty-first century.

January 2004

Introduction

Musicology is for musicians what ornithology is for the birds.
                                                    —Charles Rosen

When I was a first-year undergraduate student at Oberlin College, a writing teacher assigned us a small research project. It was simple enough: choose a research topic, formulate a question about it, and produce a short paper. I chose to write about the *chekker,* the English term for a common Renaissance keyboard instrument which may or may not have been an early clavichord. Nobody knows exactly what it was and no one will probably ever resolve the issue completely. It introduced me to a long and interesting debate that had been carried on in places like the *Galpin Society Journal,* and introduced me, before I ever met them, to people like John Barnes, the English instrument researcher who would become indispensable to this work. An equally important experience was my introduction, through this lively debate, to the concept of an historical keyboard instrument as something between a treasure hunt and a mystery novel, and that sense of historical adventure has never left me.

The immediate mystery about the chekker led to questions about a larger mystery. Where were all the clavichords? Oberlin Conservatory, one of the premiere schools for early music in the country, had a half dozen harpsichords of different historical styles in the mid 1980s and even a virginal, but not a single clavichord, and Oberlin was not alone in this regard. The importance of clavichords seemed to be obvious in the historical sources I had been reading for my research paper. Carl Philipp Emanuel Bach (1714–1788) wrote in 1753, right at the beginning of his introduction to Part One of his famous *Essay on the True Art of Playing Keyboard Instruments*: "A good clavichordist makes an accomplished harpsichordist, but not the reverse."[1] Were we missing something relevant? I smelled a mystery as interesting as the great chekker debate, perhaps one in which I could somehow directly participate.

As an organist and harpsichordist at Oberlin I remember spending quite a bit of time trying to reconcile the two techniques. The French music I studied on the harpsichord seemed to need a technique that left the fingers as free as possible to work as independently as possible. And as I concentrated on the individual fingers' movement I didn't notice how my shoulders and elbows were rising ever higher and higher. We worked on small-scale movements of the fingers and how varying speeds of attack and release created different colors of sound. Fascinated by how much control it was possible to achieve with this attention to the individual finger's movement, I tried to find this same world at the organ. The conservatory owned a two-manual-and-pedal practice organ with a suspended action and only one flute stop per keyboard. The action, the small volume of sound, and the light flexible wind all combined to make the shape of the beginnings and ends of each note as controllable as possible. I vowed to practice the Bach trio sonata for my upcoming exam exclusively on this practice instrument and tried as much as possible to achieve this world of varied tone color and articulation that I had discovered on the harpsichord. But the exam itself was in the main concert hall on a large three-manual Flentrop organ built in North German style. It had a much heavier and relatively deeper action, of course, and much more resistance in the pallet box because of a higher wind pressure and stronger pallet springs. The distances between manuals and bench were larger and the pedalboard was also proportionally larger. At the time I didn't analyze the situation this clearly, and if I had, I would have understood the consequences of spending all of my practice time on a single instrument so unlike the performance experience I was about to have. The exam was from memory and one aspect of playing from memory is body memory: repeating shapes that the body itself has learned, both distances traveled and amount of pressure applied when you arrive. Needless to say, the performance experience was less than pleasant! But it was more valuable in the long run than all of the many subsequent and much more pleasant experiences I would have performing on that instrument. The experience led me to stop trying to force direct connections between the technique of the French historical harpsichord and the North European historical organ.

What was the historical practice instrument for the historical North European organ? The experience I had at Oberlin led me to question whether practicing exclusively on a light-actioned "house organ" was necessarily that helpful when it came to performing on a large North European organ. If, according to C. P. E. Bach, the clavichord was used in the "study of good performance" for the harpsichord, was the pedal clavichord used in the same way for the organ?[2]

After graduating from Oberlin, I was fortunate enough to be awarded a year-long grant to study the organ and clavichord with Prof. Harald Vogel at the North German Organ Academy and another grant from the Watson Foundation, for which graduating seniors have to propose an independent research project. I proposed to study the current clavichord scene in Europe. I met John Barnes, Curator Emeritus of the Russell Collection of Historical Keyboard Instruments at the University of Edinburgh. I came for tea one afternoon in September and left at Christmastime with a new clavichord and many new friends.

During this study time, by happy accident, I met Hans Davidsson in North Germany, who was looking for an English text editor for his dissertation on Matthias Weckmann; without him none of this work would have seen completion. The English text-editing brought me to Sweden several times, and on one of those occasions I met the University's Professor of

Musicology, Jan Ling, and told him about my studies and about this dream, as yet unrealizable, of building a pedal clavichord and having it somewhere where it could be tested by organ students to find out whether or not the instrument really could provide a new dimension in the "study of good performance" at the organ.

When I arrived in Sweden with the first copy of the Gerstenberg pedal clavichord built with John Barnes in Edinburgh in 1994, I found my project had become a small part of a much larger research project and an exciting new research environment. The Göteborg Organ Art Center had been founded that year at Göteborg University to administer a six-year research project focusing on the history of the North European organ from 1600 to 1970. The project was to be as interdisciplinary as possible, involving scientists from Chalmers Technical University in Göteborg, as well as instrument builders, musicologists, performers, documentation experts, and students. One of the main focuses of the project was the construction of a new four-manual organ in the style of the seventeenth-century North German masters, and the pedal-clavichord project would be part of a study of the keyboard instruments that were related to the giant North German organs. It became the ideal situation to test what the relationship between the two instruments might have been, physically, musically, and technically. The new North German organ would have a strictly reconstructed action that would be much heavier and louder and more difficult to control than many of the modern restoration actions of similar historical instruments.

Pedal clavichords were exactly like manual clavichords, but fitted with pedal keyboards like those of an organ. They appear in two forms historically: those with pedalboards attached to an independent clavichord and those with a pull-down mechanism attached to the keys of a manual clavichord. Both types made use of a variety of solutions, from simple strings to more complex organ-like actions which included wooden trackers and even rollerboards.

The practical nature of the pedal clavichord is obvious: the convenience of having a practice instrument at home at a time when churches were colder and darker than they are today and where the organist needed a trained (and normally paid) bellows pumper in order to practice. Apart from this level of economics and creature comfort, another subtler level of practicality is also clear. The North European organist often has the worst seat in the church to properly hear the organ. The soundscapes of the North European organ are often designed to be heard best well away from the keyboard, and so the divisions of the organ—the *Hauptwerk*, the *Brustwerk*, the *Oberwerk*, the pedal towers, the *Rückpositiv*—are placed above and behind and on top of the player, creating illusions of their relative strength and balance that are very different from those perceived by the listener in the church. The pedal clavichord creates exactly the opposite performance situation. The best seat from which to hear the clavichord is the player's.

This must have afforded the player a clear and intimate perspective of the music while preparing it for performance at the organ, not unlike the modern practice keyboards that are made for the convenience and education of carilloneurs.

Much of the twentieth-century commentary on the pedal clavichord as a *historical phenomenon* was written in a kind of vacuum, since the building tradition died with the rapid development of the piano in the early nineteenth century. The present study was designed to address the lack of physical experience of the instrument, by finding a historical model of a pedal clavichord and documenting and reconstructing it.

The Authenticity Debate

We could have simply ordered a pedal clavichord for this study from one of the builders who had already copied the Gerstenberg, but I was eager to be part of the building process myself, and wanted the process of copying the instrument to be documented. In order to do that thoroughly, it was easier to build it, going step by step through both the documentation and copying. John Barnes generously agreed to guide this work in his own workshop in Edinburgh. The result is that this study closely parallels, in miniature, the process GOArt has gone through in producing the North German Organ inaugurated in August of 2000. The organ is meant to be used by the university's organ students as *research equipment* to learn more about the process of playing the North German Baroque organ repertoire. Only after the building project began was it really clear just how much original research was needed in order to build the research equipment.[3]

One central problem in a study of this kind is its relation to the debate over how *authentic* any attempt to reconstruct an historical music-making situation can be. The word *authentic* has been thoroughly problematized in a debate within musicology since the beginning of the 1980s and tends now to be avoided. This debate is documented, among other places, in Richard Taruskin's *Text and Act: Essays on Music and Performance* (1995). The insurgent historical performance movement of the 1970s and 80s has gradually been replaced by a firmly established historically *informed* performance culture that picks its way through a dizzying number of problematized issues, like authorial intention, the selective use of historical evidence, and the vagaries of an audience's changing perceptions from place to place and age to age. This is made more challenging by the tensions between scholarship, individual artistic expression, and the demands of the commercial marketplace. The introduction to *Inside Early Music: Conversations with Performers* (1997) by Bernard Sherman gives a valuable historical overview of the authenticity debate from many perspectives before allowing the performers to speak for themselves in wide-ranging interviews. The issues of the authenticity debate as they pertain to the reconstruction of historical instruments themselves are also complex, but many parameters are possible to reconstruct, and a study of the more problematic ones provides valuable insight into the issues that need further research.

How Do You Recreate a Musical Aesthetic?

Charles Rosen once gave a lecture entitled "Explaining the Obvious," in which he paraphrased Barrett Newmann: "Musicology is for musicians what ornithology is for the birds."[4] But he also turned on the birds themselves, specifically the early-music birds, when he said "A sense of crisis periodically justifies our attempts to reinvent the practice of music, to discover new styles of interpretation and carry out experiments compounded equally of despair and of imagination,"[5] and went on to tell the following story:

> I have witnessed—not heard—the Well-Tempered Clavier performed on the clavichord in a hall seating twelve hundred people although the ear can only faintly pick up the sounds of this instrument in a small concert hall or a good sized living room. This would tend to show that the effect of musicology on performance is often to inspire the more ambitious musicians to make a nuisance of themselves. I sometimes long for the days gone by when performers were supposed to be ignorant unthinking animals, like tenors—or, better like Plato's poets, who as Socrates maintained, produce their works through inspiration and understand neither how they are created nor what they mean![6]

Musicologists, in Rosen's lecture, walk a fine line between creating work that explains music and creating work that just creates more work, while the more ambitious musicians circle like buzzards, often misunderstanding what they manage to fly off with, leaving the long-suffering listeners, consumers of musicological thought and musicologically misinformed performance, at the mercy of all and sundry. This is clearly an entertaining overstatement, but the idea that performance and musicology have begun to inhabit separate realms has been discussed widely.

From its founding in 1995, GOArt, the Göteborg Organ Art Center, has been trying to develop models to bridge just these sorts of gaps in the musicologist-performer-listener chain in organ and related keyboard research. One of the most important bridges has been the inclusion of the organological perspective—the study of the historical instrument itself—to explore the historical aesthetic that helped produce both the music and the performance practice in the first place. If you begin with the assumption that it is worthwhile musically and artistically to try to explore an historical musical aesthetic, how do you go about doing it? Leo Treitler defined the problem this way:

A recurrent theme in this new round of questioning and defining, stems from a unique condition of historical studies in the arts. It is that the central object of study is an artifact born into a special, that is, an aesthetic, relationship with the culture of which it is a part and which continues through its survival to be both a historical record and an object of aesthetic perception.[7]

The central historical object in this study, the Johann David Gerstenberg pedal clavichord, once had a functional but complex aesthetic relationship to the culture that produced it; it was what anthropologists might call a piece of material culture that preserves non-material cultural values. Now it serves as an historical record. But when the pedal clavichord is faithfully reconstructed, it can also serve as a tool that can be used to broaden our understanding, and to debate our own aesthetic perceptions of the special relationship it once had to eighteenth-century organ culture.

Creating and Re-creating: A New Approach

In the following exploration of the use of the pedal clavichord, the goal has not been to recreate *authentically* every one of the historical aesthetic's particulars. Still, every attempt has been made to recreate as much of the system of particular relationships as is possible, in order to produce a result that is experientially organic. What rescues this experiment from becoming "compounded equally of despair and of imagination" is that these particulars have a certain hierarchy of importance. If one is restoring a Renaissance fresco and one uses egg tempera, the historical recipe is of particular importance. It is also important to have brushes that function in the same way as the Renaissance brushes in stiffness and volume and control. But the fact that it will be almost impossible to find any fifteenth-century eggs should not keep us from trying to recreate the paint. On the other hand, the balance between historical recreation and musical imagination will always contain individual decisions, each motivated by a complex of factors. The recreative process necessarily involves creative acts. There are parameters in the historical models that one can never be extrinsically sure of; but, within the *language* of the original building tradition, the creative imagination can engage itself, solving problems in a dialectical process with the working model.

Treitler went on to suggest that musicologists fall into two categories when describing a specific historical aesthetic period, such as the Baroque. One is either a *nominalist* like John Mueller, who thinks that Baroque, as a style category, is an invention of historians and its integrity can never be demonstrated. Or one is a *realist* like Manfred Bukofzer, who thinks that Baroque describes a collection of real attributes. A radical *essentialist* form of the latter is expressed by Paul Henry Lang who believes that "the Baroque stands vividly before us for its power to mold all the arts according to its own eloquent spirit."[8]

A middle way can be taken between these nominalist and realist poles, expressed in this pedal-clavichord experiment and the North German Organ project. These projects are not nominalist because they are unapologetically engaged with the "spirit" of the Baroque, the North European Baroque in particular, and their starting point is a belief that there is a coherent aesthetic there worthy of categorizing and describing and experiencing. But they are not realist either, because a realist like Paul Henry Lang would say that historically informed work is primarily an exercise in creation rather than re-creation, that we cannot, in any tangible way, experience first-hand that "eloquent spirit" of the Baroque. We can only create a new experience for ourselves. The middle way is phenomenological, and consists of constructing historically informed experiments by combining phenomena and observing what happens. Because these experiments are grounded in organological research, the new experience that results is demonstrably closer to the spirit of the Baroque on a spectrum that includes many alternatives that are farther away. For instance, a carefully reconstructed pedal clavichord is closer to the original in dimensions, touch characteristics, and tonal production than a "modern clavichord" from the middle of the twentieth century.

Kant and Eighteenth-Century Phenomenology

This phenomenological approach is grounded in the philosophy of Gerstenberg's own time. The late eighteenth century witnessed the flowering of the German Enlightenment. Immanuel Kant (1724–1804), the father of German idealism, was inspired to create his philosophical system in reaction to the work of the Scottish philosopher David Hume (1711–76). Hume said that causality could only be observed but never predicted with absolute certainty, and therefore there could never be absolute knowledge. Kant's answer was that the nature of the human mind can perceive only the phenomenology of things: their shapes and forms and attributes. Even though we can never have absolute knowledge about them, we can have relative knowledge, because all minds function alike. For example, "An analysis of time gives rise to arithmetic, that of space, to geometry."[9] The way a modern performer perceives the phenomena of a historically reconstructed clavichord—its dynamic capabilities, its touch characteristics, its quiet but intense and colorful volume of sound—may not necessarily be substantially different from the way an eighteenth-century performer experienced those same phenomena. It is then possible to depend upon the phenomenology of an historical instrument to help analyze and reconstruct an historical aesthetic. We cannot absolutely be sure of the historical clavichord, but we *can* be sure that the phenomena we experience at the historical instrument today are a dependable source of *relative* knowledge about the phenomena eighteenth-century clavichordists experienced themselves. This phenomenological approach has its parallel in musicology as described in the works of Lawrence Ferrara, for example his *Philosophy and the Analysis of Music* (1991).

Now, clearly, relying on our own bodies for information about how eighteenth-century bodies experienced phenomena can be seen as problematical. We are generally larger than our eighteenth-century counterparts and we cannot ever be sure if we perceive in the same ways that they did, either culturally or physically. Therefore, I need to define, very narrowly for the purpose of this study, what can be defended as unchanged from the eighteenth century. We still have five fingers on each hand, and more importantly, the tendons of our third and fourth fingers are connected to each other, whereas those of the other three fingers are not connected to others. This leaves the fourth finger in a position to move less independently than the first three. A simple experiment allows you to experience this phenomenon for yourself. Place all your fingertips on a tabletop and observe how high you can raise the second finger without lifting the others. Now try lifting the fourth finger without lifting the others. Lift the third and fourth fingers simultaneously. Note that this is easier but still not as easy as lifting the second finger. Now try lifting and striking down to see how much force you can apply to the tabletop with the second finger, then the fourth, then the third and fourth together. Chances are you will experience the force the second finger can deliver as almost unlimited, the fourth as next to impossible, and the third and fourth together as better, but not really helpful at the keyboard! Now try lifting and striking with the fifth finger. It can move independently, but is also weaker than the others by virtue of its relatively small size and position in the hand.

Johann Sebastian Bach (1685–1750) apparently developed a technique to overcome this biological shortcoming that we all share. The second half of this book explores whether this technique description makes more sense physically when explored on the clavichord, the instrument for which it was apparently developed. The experience was quite consistent for both genders and many different body types, some larger and many as small or smaller than the smallest eighteenth-century person. So the argument for a phenomenological approach is based on only one specific physical constant: human fingers strike with unequal strength.

The instrument is the anchoring thread of this interdependent web, and for a phenomenological experiment to generate valuable experiential results, the instrument needs to represent as closely as possible the qualities of the instrument in the historical web. The process of copying, on the other hand, can never be a strictly re-creative one. When we build we have no other choice but to create new. No matter how much we might like to re-create the objects of quality that we admire from past eras, it is only possible to create new ones which must be judged on their own merits. However, the close observation of historical objects can lead to a deeper understanding of the craft *processes* which created the historical object in the first place. Every historical object is a product of a once-living craft tradition. The study and application of these craft processes ought to lead to the creation of new objects of similar quality with similar properties. The goal of copying, therefore, is not to recreate the exact dimensions of an historical object by any means, but to gain insights about old methods and skills, so that we can learn to create new objects comparable in level of quality and functionality to those of the past.

This concept of *craft process* can also be broadened and applied to performance. Playing the North European Baroque organ was a craft process taught in a manner very similar to the guild system that produced the instruments themselves. Like traditional woodworkers who are limited by natural materials and the skills they have developed with hand tools, the organ performers' skill set was also dependent on the instruments that they had at their disposal. One of the tools they had at their disposal historically was the pedal clavichord.

When it first occurred to me to question the role of the pedal clavichord for organists, there were no modern examples to look at, but by the time John Barnes and I began building our research copy in 1994, there were several manual and pedal clavichords, one built by Jack Peters (Seattle), now at the University of California at Chico; one built by Michael O'Brien (Smithsonian Institute), now at the University of Nebraska; and one by Gary Blaise (San Francisco), now in private ownership, as well as the copy of the Johann David Gerstenberg pedal clavichord by Dick Verwolf of the Netherlands, and now there are more, including an instrument that GOArt has built for the Eastman School of Music in Rochester, N.Y. (U.S.A.) that is being used actively, at the time of writing, in Eastman's organ performance education program. I hope that this current work will encourage others to build and play more copies of this instrument.

Pitch names are given using the following system: C c c^1 c^2 c^3, where c^1 is middle C. All translations not otherwise attributed are the author's.

Part One

Source Studies

Prelude

Organology, Reception History, and Reconstruction

Clavicordo. . . . This well-known instrument is, so to say, every player's first Grammar.
—Johann Gottfried Walther

Many historical references point to the clavichord as a superior teaching instrument for the other keyboard instruments, but was the pedal clavichord equally valued by organists in their teaching? Were pedal clavichords just inexpensive practice instruments (an opinion voiced many times in the twentieth-century literature) or were they used in the same way that the eighteenth-century manual clavichords were, as study instruments and even *performance* instruments in their own right?

Juxtaposing J. S. Bach's *Clavier* technique with the pedal clavichord is a speculative endeavor at best, because so little information survives about both Bach's keyboard instruments and his teaching technique. One could be forgiven for asking, "Why try it at all?" We cannot prove conclusively that Bach had a pedal clavichord, although that is what his first biographer tells us. Nor can we prove that the pedal clavichord played a role in his teaching, although at least two of his students used them that way. We have some historical instruments that we can assume no longer play the way they did when they were new, and we have some written sources that describe how they should be played if they still worked.

This book is about a dialectical process between the historical material (both written and built) and information gleaned from a copy of one of the surviving instruments, involving my personal experience as a builder, teacher, and player. The structure of the book reflects this process. Part One presents the pedal clavichord in its historical context, using the tools of musicology, and also gives a brief history of the reconstruction of my first copy of the instrument, built under the direction of John Barnes, the Curator Emeritus of the Russell Collection of Keyboards Instruments at the University of Edinburgh. Part Two describes the teaching experiments with the instrument, and necessarily involves more of the personal than is common in a work of musical scholarship. The two halves of the book are divided for the sake of clarity, but in reality, the experience of such a process is more intertwined, not least through the presence of some additional historical information in the second half of the book (such as evidence, in chapter 8, suggesting that organ teachers regularly taught their students at home on pedal clavichords). Part Two also presents a new pedagogy for the pedal clavichord intended for students and others interested in beginning to play it.

Part One uses two of the primary tools of musicology: organology and reception history. In organology, we learn about the history and function of historical instruments from studying surviving examples, allowing us to make informed decisions about how to reconstruct them. Organological information, too, will be presented in places in the second half of the book, as it proves relevant. Reception history is generally concerned with the reception of a piece or a whole repertory of music in a different context than the one for which it was originally written: How was a Bach cantata perceived differently, for instance, sung by a mass choir in nineteenth-century America than in its first performance by a small Lutheran church choir in eighteenth-century Germany?

The reception histories in this book, however, follow how a little repertory of *ideas* concerning the pedal clavichord are received differently through time. Although they mostly appear in older secondary literature, the point is *not* to take up old arguments from outdated secondary sources, but rather to present a history of the published discussion on these points and compare it to the history of the clavichord itself. This proves to be a valuable comparison, because much of the discussion was written after clavichords stopped being built in their historical form.

Organology and Historical Context

In the Introduction, the interdisciplinary approach that informed this project was set in the context of the historical reconstruction methods developed at the Göteborg Organ Art Center, where this work was carried out. The overview in chapter 1 puts the reconstructed pedal clavichord in its historical context. There were several other kinds of domestic instruments with pedals in eighteenth-century Europe that are not discussed further in this book. There are, for instance, surviving claviorganums with pedalboards that variously combine harpsichords, fortepianos, or clavichords with organ pipes.[1]

The Pedal Harpsichord

There is also evidence—both written and organological—for the pedal harpsichord. Although no independent pedal instruments survive, there is no reason to doubt from written references that they existed in France,[2] and at least seven Italian harpsichords once had simple pull-down pedals.[3] Although the pedal harpsichord seems to have been more common in Italy and France than in Germany it existed side by side with the pedal clavichord, and Bach's biographer claims that Bach owned one of each (see chapter 2). But the clavichord is discussed consistently in the historical literature in terms of its pedagogical value in preparing for the other keyboard instruments. This study tries to answer what that often-repeated claim of *value* might have consisted of, and whether it also extends to playing the pedals of the clavichord. Furthermore, it tackles the question: does this process prepare a student differently to perform on the pedal harpsichord or the organ? Another kind of dialectical process existed historically among the keyboard instruments: students were encouraged to play the same literature on different instruments interchangeably.[4] They learned something different both technically and musically from each instrument type that contributed to the whole development of the musician.

Reception History

Part One ends with a brief reception history that establishes the likelihood that Johann Sebastian Bach owned a pedal clavichord, and that his students used them in their study and teaching. In this case, reception history is a valuable tool for identifying the possible meanings of the problematic term *Clavier*. The other two reception histories in this study also help to demonstrate that neither the early twentieth-century English attitude that *Clavier* always meant clavichord, nor the late twentieth-century opinion that it *always* means general keyboard is tenable from a close study of the eighteenth-century sources. In the present study, neither of these opposite poles is automatically assumed, and the term is treated on a case-by-case basis.

The frame for this entire work is marked out by two larger interrelated reception histories. The first one, in chapter 2, explores the changing perceptions of the role over time of the pedal clavichord, and the second, in chapter 4, follows the changing perceptions over time of the so-called Bach technique school. They define the ground that can be explored in Part Two, placing the intrinsic experiments in performance practice and teaching within the frame of historical boundaries.

While this may be a slightly unusual way of using reception history as a tool, it is not unlike the recent reception history of the transmission of Bach manuscripts by Russell Stinson:

As a branch of historical musicology [reception history] has chosen Johann

Sebastian Bach as its subject more often than any other composer. There are some obvious reasons why Bach's music has had such appeal to reception historians. Its "rediscovery" in the early nineteenth century, after all, "marked the first time that a great composer, after a period of neglect, was accorded his rightful place by a later generation" and as an early example of a new historicism, "eventually opened all periods of Western music to discovery and performance."[5]

The "rediscovery" of Bach was not limited exclusively to his music but also to accounts and speculations about his role as a teacher and performer. These anecdotes are also, of course, subject to changing receptions through time.

Instrument Reconstruction

The actual process of reconstructing an historical instrument often leads to new insights about the original. Chapter 3 discusses the decisions that John Barnes took in order to set the most important parameter of the historical clavichord, the tension of the strings. The evidence is presented for using higher string tensions in what has come to be known as the "Edinburgh stringing" theory, to which the copy of the Gerstenberg built for this study conforms. These string tensions provide the critical information for the performance practice discussed in Part Two.

1

The Historical Pedal Clavichord

Both are so common and well known: but so that nothing gets omitted from
Musica mechanica organœdi *that ought to belong to it, I will say something
about both of them.*
    —Jakob Adlung (on the clavichord and pedal clavichord in Germany)

Pedal Clavichords: The Historical Evidence

At least by the fifteenth century, the pedal clavichord was already being
used as a practice instrument for the organ with pedals. Because fairly few
historical examples survive and none of them are in their original playing
condition, it has been easy to ignore the full extent of the tradition of these
instruments that once existed in central and northern Europe. There are a
number of surviving instruments that still have, or once had pedals, all
dating from the eighteenth century.

Extant Historical Pedal Clavichords

Although the written evidence, presented below, shows that the pedal clavichord was found all over central and northern Europe, only German and
Swedish examples survive. As with an evaluation of any collection of historical instruments, some questions of methodology arise. In the following
inventory, there are three different categories of instruments: 1) instruments
presumed to be near their original state, 2) instruments which are no longer
pedal clavichords but show obvious traces of having been at one stage,
and, 3) instruments for which we now have only documentation.
    How do we tell that the instrument is in its original condition, and if
not, how do we judge what kinds of changes have been made to it? For the
pull-down pedal instruments missing their pedals, all that can be said for
certain is that the instruments had pedalboards at some point during their
working lives. If an instrument is part of a museum collection it may have
a written record of any restorations or changes made to it, and careful
examination can reveal modifications of various kinds. For instance, if the
layout of a clavichord has been radically altered, as on the Wolthersson
discussed below, the tangents will also have to be moved, and this leaves a

pattern of holes that can be used to try to reconstruct the original position of the tangents and thus the strings. Conversely, if there is no trace of previous holes for the tangents, and they still line up with their pairs of strings, the position of the strings is either original, or the whole keyboard has been replaced, something awkward enough to do that it is generally a much more unlikely option. Often many small open questions remain about an instrument's original state.

The first instrument discussed below served as the model for the clavichord used in this study, partly because it presents comparatively few questions about its original state. The Johann David Gerstenberg pedal clavichord has had a long museum provenance and has a carefully documented restoration report. The reasons for considering all three parts of the instrument to be original and by the same maker will be discussed in chapter 4.

Germany

In Germany a number of pedal clavichords survive, or survived long enough into the twentieth century to be documented. The most famous and well-preserved of them is Johann David Gerstenberg's two manual and pedal clavichord.[1] Dated 1760, it has two manuals each with a compass of C–e^3, and an independent pedal with a compass of C–c^1. An instrument with a similar pedal survived until WW II. There are still archival photographs (now in Nuremberg) of the Johann Paul Krämer & Söhne pedal clavichord dated ca.1800.[2] It had a single-manual instrument with a compass of FF–f^3, and an independent pedal with a compass of C–d^1. The pedal instrument was similar to Gerstenberg's construction. It had long pedal keys that pulled the keys inside the instrument down from the back using organ trackers.[3]

The pedal clavichord at the Bachhaus in Eisenach is composed of two separate instruments, probably by different builders.[4] Dated ca. 1815, it has a single manual instrument with a compass of FF–f^4 built by Johann Georg Marckert. It sits on top of an earlier independent pedal, probably by Johann Heinrich Stumpff. Unlike the pedal instruments in the Gerstenberg and the Krämer pedal clavichords, the Stumpff pedal instrument has a pedalboard with short levers that extend only a little way beyond the toeboard, like a normal organ pedalboard. Instead of wooden trackers, the Stumpff clavichord uses strings that pull down the keylevers at the front of the instrument, rather than at the back, like the Gerstenberg. The Stumpff pedal instrument has adjustment pegs in the pedal keys to tighten the strings that connect the pedal keyboard to the pedalboard just like the Gerstenberg pedal instrument.

At the Historical Museum in Bergen, Norway, an undated double-manual clavichord has evidence of pull-down pedals: hooks attached to the lowest keys of the lower manual and holes in the baseboard through which the pull-down strings once passed. This instrument has, like some Northern European organs, two different short octaves. The lower manual begins C D E F G A B , and the upper manual is missing only the bass C . Because it has these two different compasses this instrument might have been built as a practice instrument for a specific organ with the same keyboard layouts. The instrument by Adam Gottfried Oehme dated 1760 (now in The Hague), with a manual compass of C–d³, like the instrument in Bergen, was once a double-manual clavichord.[5] Both the Bergen clavichord and the Oehme clavichord have a case into which the upper manual is permanently built. The lower manual fits into the space underneath like a drawer and can be drawn out. The lower manual of the Oehme clavichord is missing but could have had the same pull-down pedal arrangement as the Bergen clavichord.[6]

Carl Ludwig Glück's clavichord has a single manual dated 1775, with a compass of C–f³, and an independent pedal with a compass of C–d¹.[7] The unusual feature of this instrument is that the independent pedal is upside down and attached to the underside of the manual baseboard. Both instruments share the same baseboard, spine, and left-hand case end. The pedal keys are outside of the case and strike upwards as in a normal clavichord. The pedal instrument is almost surely nineteenth-century, built by a piano builder.[8]

Sweden

Five clavichords have survived from the historical period with evidence of pull-down pedals; however, none of their pedal boards have survived.[9]

1. An unsigned and undated clavichord (now in Skara) with a single manual compass of C–d³ and holes for a pull-down pedal of 20 keys.[10]
2. A clavichord by Lars Kinström, dated 1748 (now in Östersund), with a single manual compass of C–d³, that once had pull-down pedals for the bottom 22 keys.[11]
3. An undated and unsigned single manual clavichord (now in Skellefteå) with a compass of C–d³, and pull-down pedal holes for the bottom 22 keys.[12]
4. A clavichord by the organbuilder Pehr Schiörlin, undated (now in Stockholm), with a single manual compass of C–f³, and pull-downs originally for the bottom 23 keys.[13]
5. A single manual clavichord by the organbuilder Gustaf Gabriel Wolthersson, dated 1759 (now in Göteborg), with holes for pull-downs for the bottom 22 keys[14] and a pantaleon stop that may or may not be original to the instrument.[15]

Some general observations can be made about the Swedish pedal-clavichord tradition. All five of the surviving clavichords are single-manual instruments, and they all have evidence of the same simple system of pull-downs. On the underside of each manual key to be pulled down, a U-shaped nail has been inserted as close to the front of the key as possible. Directly underneath these points, holes were drilled in the baseboard to allow the strings to pass directly between the manual keys and the pedal keys. Several of the instruments also had a life (perhaps as decorative furniture) after their practical life as pedal clavichords. The anonymous instrument in Skara and the Wolthersson clavichord in Göteborg both have decorative stands with drawers that now block the holes under the manual keys and could not have been original to the period when these instruments had pedals.

These surviving instruments are not necessarily representative of the Swedish pedal-clavichord tradition, however. There are many eighteenth-century references to independent pedal instruments in Sweden as well. "In 1752, Lars Kinström advertised in a Stockholm newspaper 'a new pedal clavichord with a special innovation and three stops, two of 8' pitch and one of 16' pitch that makes an excellent effect.'"[16]

Historical References to Pedal Clavichords

The Fifteenth Century

Paulus Paulirinus (1413–after 1463)

The invention of the pedal clavichord must be dated to sometime before 1460, but perhaps not much before this date. The first written reference to the pedal clavichord is found in Paulirinus's two-part encyclopedic work, the *Encyclopedia Scientarum*, or *Liber XX artium* and *Opus Magicum*, written between 1459 and 1463. According to Paulirinus: "The clavichord is the instrument of study for the organ and all other instruments . . . any well-trained musician acquires his science from it."[17] The text also records the earliest historical reference to a clavichord with a pedalboard.[18]

Egidius de Buolach 1464

The first iconographic evidence of the pedal clavichord is also from the second half of the fifteenth century. The *Flores musicae omnis cantus Gregoriani* manuscript by Hugo von Reutlingen (ca. 1285–1359) has notations at the end, which, as Bernard Brauchli notes, were "added by a certain scholar, Egidius de Buolach, in 1464, and on its last page is found the drawing of a pedal-clavichord, that very likely dates from the late fifteenth century."[19] (See figure 1.1.)

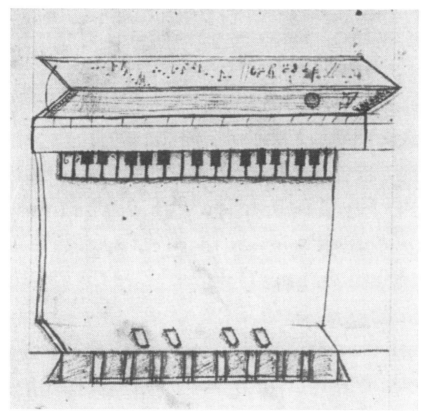

Figure 1.1. Pedal Clavichord from *Flores Musicae* (after 1467). Württembergische Landesbibliothek, Stuttgart (Cod. poet. et phil. 4° 52, fol. 65v). Reproduced with permission.

The Sixteenth Century

Sebastian Virdung (b. 1465)

Virdung's treatise on musical instruments and contemporary music making in Germany, *Musica getutscht*, was printed in Basel in 1511. Virdung's description of musical instruments gives a prominent place to the clavichord. In his account of the clavichord's recent development, Virdung reports:

> Then too, even though many newer clavichords are found nowadays that are even larger or longer—having four octaves or even more keys—still, these [keys] are nothing other than the equivalent of a repetition of the first pitches of the three octaves; and because of this, the majority [of these larger clavichords] are made in such a way that hanging pedals (pedalia) can be added to them, and [thus] of late another category of clavichords (*clavicordia*) [has been] made.[20]

In 1511, the pedal clavichord was apparently considered by Virdung to be a fairly new idea. It is difficult to know what we are to make of this, knowing as we do that the clavichord with pedals was known at least sixty years before the publication of *Musica getutscht*. Virdung's description stands, however, as a clear marker that the clavichord with pedals was an established fact at the beginning of the sixteenth century.

A Pedal Clavichord Tradition in the Czech Lands

Bohuslav Cizek reports that there are a large number of citations about pedal clavichords in the Czech lands from the sixteenth century. Apart from Paulirinus, he reports that a Bohemian organist's will from 1524 lists a "Clauicordium with Pedal." Cizek goes on to report that:

> At the turn of the sixteenth century the pedal clavichord appears in two versions of the inventory of the Lords of Rozmberk Band. Mention is also found in the inventories of the Monastery of Osek, the Collegium of the Piarists in Slany, the castle of Pecka, etc. While no instruments have survived, pedal clavichords were clearly a Czech peculiarity and were obviously well known in Bohemia.[21]

The Seventeenth Century

Michael Praetorius (1571–1621)

Praetorius published his *De organographia*, the second volume of his three-volume *Syntagma Musicum*, in 1619. It is a comprehensive work of scholarship describing musical instruments ancient and modern. Although *De organographia* never mentions the pedal clavichord specifically, in chapter 36, which is devoted to the clavichord, Praetorius confirms the clavichord's pedagogical connection to the organ as a commonly accepted practice:

> The clavichord is the foundation of all keyboard instruments—organ, clavicymbal, symphony, spinet, virginal, and so on. [Also] organ pupils receive their first lessons on the clavichord.[22]

Praetorius goes on to amplify this statement by saying that the reasons are mainly practical: that the clavichord is a more stable instrument for beginners, requiring less tuning and maintenance time than the other keyboard instruments.

Claas Douwes (ca. 1650–ca. 1725)

Unlike Praetorius, Douwes was an active instrument builder. His treatise *Grondig ondersoek van de Toonen der Musijk,* published in 1699, gives a very important and rare practical description of how to design and build a clavichord. In the section: "Of Clavichords," Douwes's description of the building process concludes with a final paragraph about how to build the pedals, giving the impression that Douwes considered the pedal to be such an integral part of the clavichord that the pedal clavichord didn't need a separate subheading. The final paragraph is worth reading closely:

> The pedals, if they have to be with a rollerboard, can be so divided that at the top, four, and at the bottom, three keys strike on one course of strings. In this way I have made manual and pedal clavichords that did not have more than eight courses of strings in the pedal and that comprise nevertheless two full octaves and a note, which is very easy because few strings are needed and it is very quickly tuned. There are also hooks in the ends of the pedal keys and holes in the stickers where the hooks fit in, so that one may push the said keyboard in and out which makes it very easy when travelling or when moving the instrument, because there is then no need for coupling or uncoupling. This is not, as far as I know, practiced by anyone else.

> De *Pedaalen,* alsoo de selve met een walsembord moeten sijn / konnen soo afgedeeldt worden / datter boven vier / en onder drie klauwieren aan een perk snaaren komen te staan; gelijk sodanigen *Manuaal* en *Pedâl* klavekordium door my is gemaakt / daar niet meer als acht perken snaaren in 't *pedâl* sijn / ende begrijpt nochtans twee volle *octaaven* ende een toon; het welke seer gemakkelijk is / alsoo daar weinig snaaren toe van nooden sijn / ende seer haast gestemt is: ook sijnder haaken in 't eindt van het *pedâl*-klauwier gemaakt / ende de *Extrakten* met gaten / daar die haaken in komen / soo datmen het selve klauwier daar uit en in schuiven kan; het welke mede seer gemakkelijk is / wanneer men het *instrument* vervoeren of versetten wil / om dat'er als dan geen af noch aankoppelinge van nooden is; het welke (mijns weetens) noch van niemant anders is gepractiseert.[23]

John Barnes pointed out that the motivation for this paragraph must have been economic; this description was effectively an advertisement for Douwes's own instruments, which had a special invention that allowed the pedal to be uncoupled quickly.[24] Douwes's description gives us a picture of the pedal clavichord as anything but an anomaly. The final sentence suggests that Douwes was operating in a market where enough other people were building pedal clavichords commercially to warrant this clearly competitive statement. Also, the finished instruments must have been real work horses and not just curiosities if they were used, moved, and tuned often enough that such time-saving inventions as reduced tuning time and ease of assembly were worth advertising.

The Eighteenth Century

Jakob Adlung (1699–1762)

Chapter 26 of Jakob Adlung's *Musica mechanica organœdi,* published in 1768, is entitled "Von dem Clavichord und Pedal." The title makes it clear that, like Douwes, Adlung made no organological distinction between the clavichord and the pedal clavichord. Along with this unambiguous title, the first sentence of the chapter makes it abundantly clear that the author considered the clavichord with a pedal to be as common as the single-manual clavichord: "Both are so common and well known: but so that nothing [relevant in Germany] gets omitted from *Musica mechanica organœdi* that ought to belong to it, so I will say something about both of them."[25]

Joseph Glonner (1753–72)

Glonner built "*ein dreifaches* Clavicord" for the Electress of Bavaria in 1756.[26] According to John Koster,[27] "this could mean three manual, but more probably triple strung." The other possibility is that the instrument is not "three manual," but "three-part," the third part being a pedal instrument. All of the surviving double-manual clavichords have an independent pedal instrument or evidence of once having been equipped with a pull-down pedal, and no three-manual clavichords survive. Double-manual clavichords need more vertical space between the keyboards than organs or harpsichords. For instance, the upper manual of the Gerstenberg pedal clavichord was designed using the minimum possible case depth in order to bring the upper manual as close as possible to the lower manual without compromising the sound of the upper manual, but still a double-manual clavichord presents an ergonomic challenge exactly like playing the first and third manuals of an organ. It would be difficult to imagine the practical use of a three-manual clavichord without pedals. There are descriptions of triple-strung clavichords in Virdung and Douwes, and Brauchli mentions two surviving examples of triple-strung instruments, so a triple-strung clavichord is certainly a possibility. However, "*dreifaches*" also could be translated "tripartite," or "three-part," and because the description does not mention strings, the instrument in question could have been a double-manual clavichord with an independent pedal case, hence an instrument in three parts.

The Bach Family

Several sources of extant information suggest that Johann Sebastian Bach also had and used a pedal clavichord.

Johann Nikolaus Forkel (1749–1818)

Johann Nikolaus Forkel, Bach's first biographer, published his work *Ueber Johann Sebastian Bachs Leben, Kunst und Kunstwerke* first in 1802, but had already started gathering material for the book in the 1770s by corresponding directly with Bach's two eldest sons, Wilhelm Friedemann (1710–1784) and Carl Philipp Emanuel Bach. Forkel is generally regarded as a careful curator of the information that W. F. and C. P. E. Bach entrusted with him. C. P. E. Bach wrote to Forkel about his father: "There are many wonderful stories about him. A few of them may be true and belong to his youthful pranks. The deceased never wanted anything known of them, so leave these comical things out,"[28] and Forkel did just that. Forkel also reports that Johann Sebastian Bach "liked best to play upon the clavichord."[29] But in two other places Forkel also talks about Bach and the pedal clavichord. In a description of Bach's love of extemporizing trios, Forkel reports that for these performances at home "he used two clavichords and the pedal, or a harpsichord with two sets of keys, provided with a pedal,"[30] and later in the biography Forkel makes a list of Bach's pieces, categorizing them by appropriate instrument and makes this curious pronouncement: "I add a very artificially composed Passacaglia, which, however, is rather for two clavichords and pedal than for the organ."[31]

Johann Sebastian Bach's Last Will and Testament

The inventory of instruments in Bach's estate as recorded in his last will and testament contains no pedal clavichord, but it does contain this curious appendix to the document by the family lawyer, labeled paragraph 8:

> The instruments specified under Cap. VI. (as they cannot be divided, and as no purchaser offers) are also set aside, with the hope that they may be sold before Estate. . . . But because Herr Joh. Christian Bach, the youngest son of the deceased, had received from his father during his lifetime three claviers with pedal, these have not been included in the specification, since he declares them to have been given to him as a present, and has brought witnesses to that effect, the widow and Herr Altnikol and Herr Hesemann, having known of it. The guardian, however, finds something suspicious in the matter, as do also the children of the first marriage, but they refrain from urging their objections, and on the contrary, the widow, the other heirs and their representatives acknowledge and admit the gift.[32]

> Sind die *Cap. VI. specific*irten *Instrumente*, weiln solche nicht füglich zu vertheilen, auch nicht gleich Liebhaber darzu zu finden, ausgesezt, und dieserhalben beliebt worden, daß man sich . . . solche ins Geld zu sezen bemühen wolle. . . . Und weil der jüngste Herr Sohn, Herr Johann Christian Bach 3. *Clavire* nebst *Pedal* von dem *Defuncto* seelig bey Lebzeitn erhalten und bei sich hat, solches auch um deßwillen nicht in die *Specification* gebracht worden, weil derselbe solche von dem *Defuncto* seelig geschenckt erhalten zu haben angeführet, und dieserwegen unterschiedene Zeügen angegeben, der Frau Wittbe auch sowohl als Herrn Altnickoln und Herr Hesemann solches wißend ist, der Herr Vormund auch daher diesen seinen | Mündel etwas darinne zu vergeben billig Bedencken gefunden, gleichwohl die Kinder ersterer Ehe solche Schenckung gedachten ihren

jüngsten Bruder zur Zeit nicht so gleich zugestehen wollen; So haben leztere ihre Rechte dießfalls wieder denselben auszuführen sich vorbehalten und der Ansprüche dießfallß an | selbigen sich begeben.[33]

Raymond Russell chose to translate the instrument in question as "three claviers with a set of pedals" but continues that "whether these were clavichords or harpsichords, and whether the pedals were simple pull-downs or a separate instrument is unknown, and speculation will not solve the problem."[34] But Robert Marshall has more recently concluded "that the '3. *Clavire* nebst *Pedal*' Bach gave to Johann Christian were, in all likelihood, so many clavichords, (not harpsichords) along with a pedal board."[35]

Odd as it may sound at first, the phrase "three claviers with [and, next to] a pedal" and "two claviers and the pedals" may have indicated the same instrument. The lawyer may have counted the pedal instrument as a separate and third "clavier" with the pedalboard "*nebst*" the rest of the instrument. Forkel's description includes the pedal instrument, its action, and its pedal board all under the description "and pedal." Forkel uses the term "two claviers and pedal" to describe the pedal clavichord in his description of the instruments in J. S. Bach's house that were fitted with pedals, "Zu solchen Künsten bediente er sich zweyer Claviere und des Pedals, oder eines mit einem Pedal versehenen Doppelflügels."[36] The *Flügel*, which means *wing*, always referred to the harpsichord because of the instrument's wing shape. From this single statement it is possible to deduce by the simple process of elimination, that "two claviers and pedal" must mean pedal clavichord. Forkel states that the piano was too much in its infancy to satisfy Bach, and no one would argue that the instrument in question is a double manual piano with pedals. Although it can be proven that the circle around C. P. E. Bach used *Clavier* sometimes to mean *clavichord,* it cannot be proven convincingly that Johann Sebastian Bach ever did. But the lack of written evidence on this point may very well be because Bach rarely committed anything to print. With Bach, a lack of written evidence cannot be taken as proof of a negative.

Some scholars have ignored Forkel's clear semantic distinction between a double-manual harpsichord (Doppelflügel) with pedals, and a double-manual clavichord, which has two entirely separate manual instruments, *zweyer Claviere,* with pedals. Charles Sanford Terry's biography of Johann Christian Bach describes Bach's gift to his youngest son by summarizing the appendix to Bach's will as follows: "Christian claimed three pedaled *claviers,* which, he declared, his father had given him before his death. His mother and Altnikol confirmed the statement, and the elder children, though grudgingly, admitted it. Thus Christian faced the world with three *claviers,* each valued at about fifty thalers."[37] Terry thus implies that Johann Christian began life with a financial edge that carried him all the way to fame and glory in London. But we can no more prove that the gift consisted of three separate instruments (of whatever kind—Terry does not translate), each with a separate pedal, than we can prove that the gift was a pedal clavichord made up of three clavichords with a pedal board. We can however return to Forkel's description of Bach's music-making at home. Bach's passion for trio and even quartet playing would certainly better be satisfied at the instruments Forkel describes than at three separate single-manual instruments, each with its own pedal board.

> [Bach] went so far, when he was in a cheerful humour and in the full conscious-ness of his powers, as to perform extempore to three single parts, a fourth part, and thus to make a quartetto of a trio. For these purposes he used two clavi-chords and the pedal, or a harpsichord with two sets of keys, provided with a pedal.[38]

Wanda Landowska assumed that the gift consisted of "three pedal-harp-sichords he personally gave to Johann Christian before his death. Anyone who wants to convince us that Bach's favorite instrument was the clavi-chord should reflect that there is no trace of that instrument in the inven-tory."[39] The reasoning is entirely circular: no trace of the pedal clavichord can exist in the inventory if it is misrepresented as three pedal harpsichords.

Heinrich Nikolaus Gerber (1702–1775)

If Bach was using the pedal clavichord not just to improvise trios but also to teach students, we would expect mention of it somewhere in the docu-ments pertaining to those students. Johann Gottfried Müthel (1728–88) was an avid clavichordist as was C. P. E. Bach, but no mention of the pedal clavichord has been found associated with either of them. If, however, the clavichord with pedal, according to Adlung, was so common that it was barely worth mentioning, a pedal clavichord in conjunction with a student of Bach's might conceivably only be mentioned if it were unusual in some way, or if it came to be built in an unusual way that was worth remarking upon. Both criteria are met in the case of Bach's student Heinrich Nikolaus Gerber, who was newsworthy both as an amateur instrument builder—unusual for an organist—and the inventor of an unusual pedal clavichord. Gerber's son Ernst Ludwig published an encyclopedic dictionary of musi-cians' biographies (*Historisch-biographische Lexicon der Tonkünstler*) in 1790–92. In his entry on "Students of Bach," he includes a biography of his father, in which he describes how his father came home from studying with J. S. Bach and built his own pedal clavichord in an unusual shape, with apparently ten different registers[40]:

> Before then, he had two clavichords (Klaviere) of the usual shape stacked one upon the other, which were fine, but he found this always annoying because of the difficulty of tuning and because of the large amount of space that they took

up. He worked then from 1742 onwards, with the help of a cabinetmaker, on a clavichord nearly in the shape of a pyramid, with 2 keyboards and pedal and 10 variations of tone, which was 9 feet high, 7 feet wide in the widest place, and 1 foot deep, not including the protruding keyboards and the pedalboard. From that point on, he began to dedicate all of his free time until 1749 to composition and to the education of young people who wanted to become organists or cantors.

Bisher hatte er zwei Klaviere von gewöhnlicher Form auf der Stube übereinander stehen gehabt, welche an sich zwar gut, aber ihm immer wegen ihrer beschwerlichen Stimmung und wegen dem großen Platze, den sie einnahmen, lästig fielen. Er arbeite(te) also seit dem Jahre 1742 mit Hülfe eines Schreiners, an einem Klavichord, fast in Gestalt einer Pyramide, mit 2 Klavieren und Pedal und 10 Veränderungen, welches 9 Fuß hoch, in der größten Breite 7 Fuß, und 1 Fuß Tiefe ist, der Raum ungerechnet, den die hervorragenden Tasten der Manualen und des Pedals einnehmen. Zugleich widmete er von dieser Zeit an bis 1749 alle seine Nebenstunden der Komposition und dem Unterrichte junger Leute, die sich zu Organisten oder Cantoren bilden wollten.[41]

Gerber thus probably already had a "normal" double manual clavichord in the house; it is not explicitly stated that this instrument was a pedal clavichord. The mention of the "large amount of space they took up" however, is given as the motivation for building a "new" pedal clavichord that took up less space. We can probably assume that the instrument was very much like the Gerstenberg, with the manuals stacked on top of one another "in the normal way" on a stand supporting the pedal instrument. This normal instrument is not mentioned in any of the twentieth century quotations of this story. New orthodoxies can be created just as effectively by selective omission of quotations as by their selective inclusion. Boalch, for instance, cites Gerber's construction of a new pedal clavichord, but fails to point out that there already was one in the house:

In 1727 Gerber returned to his father in the countryside and began to marshal the knowledge collected at Leipzig. He also started to make a small organ of 12 stops with pedals, with the help of a joiner. Next year he became organist at Heringen, and 3 years after that at Sondershausen. In 1742, according to his son, he began work, again with the help of a joiner, on a clavichord almost in the shape of a pyramid, with two manuals and a pedal keyboard and 10 variations of tone.[42]

In the *Bach Dokumente,* Neumann and Schulz publish an excerpted version of Gerber's biography of his father that eliminates the descriptions of his father's construction of both the organ and the new pedal clavichord.[43] The *Bach Reader* of 1966 and the *New Bach Reader* of 1998 both include the story about the organ, but also omit the paragraph about the pedal clavichord construction and the mention of the already existing pedal clavichord in Gerber's household. However, the *Bach Reader* does include an interesting paragraph not noted by Boalch:

The continual persecution at the hands of recruiting officers to which, on account of his youth, he was exposed almost until 1740 prevented him from getting to know the world outside his fatherland. He permitted himself but a single journey in 1737 to his beloved teacher Bach in Leipzig.[44]

Perhaps significantly, Gerber built this new pedal clavichord only after a second visit to "his beloved teacher Bach."

The original biography of Gerber, read in total, gives us a picture of a young, ambitious student who starts to build his own house organ after his first study trip to Johann Sebastian Bach is cut short. He attempted his own pedal clavichord after his second visit to Bach. Gerber doesn't report when or if either of these ambitious building projects was finished, but the clear inference of the complete text is that these projects were begun after being exposed to Johann Sebastian Bach's influence.

But an even more interesting picture appears in the original text. The only reason this pedal clavichord gets mentioned at all by Gerber's son is because it proves that his father was cleverer than average. Its unusual vertical shape, like the motivation behind Douwes's description of detachable pedals, is mentioned precisely because it is seen as a practical improvement over the normal pedal clavichords. A close reading of the original text makes it clear that this was not even Gerber's first pedal clavichord. Before he began to build his pyramid clavichord, he had the normal kind of pedal clavichord with two clavichords one on top of the other (like the Gerstenberg), which was fine, but it took a long time to tune and took up a lot of room in his house (also like the Gerstenberg). During this time, Gerber was also teaching students who wanted to become organists and cantors, using the training he had received from Bach. It must be assumed that these lessons took advantage of the instruments in Gerber's house: the house organ and the pedal clavichord.

The *Clavier* and the Clavichord

By choosing to eliminate an important reference to two pedal clavichords connected directly to any student of Johann Sebastian Bach, the 1966 *Bach Reader* (perhaps inadvertently) helped to support the mid-twentieth-century orthodoxy that the clavichord's role in Bach's musical life had become overstated. To some extent that orthodoxy was due for puncturing. *The Bach Reader*, for instance, rightly revised the translation of *The Well-Tempered Clavichord* to the *Well-Tempered Clavier*, but the pendulum swung, perhaps, too far in the opposite direction:

> Clavier means keyboard and was also used in Bach's time to designate any keyboard instrument, although usually the reference is particularly to the harpsi-

chord or clavichord, as distinguished from the organ. Later the meaning came to
indicate specifically the clavichord, but there is no indication that Bach ever used
the word in this sense or that the work was written exclusively for the clavichord. The common English name for the work—Well-Tempered Clavichord—
is therefore wrong.[45]

The new orthodoxy that *Clavier* must always mean general keyboard
until proven otherwise can be traced directly back to Wanda Landowska.
It was, for instance, she who convinced Kalmus Publishers to change *The
Well-Tempered Clavichord* back to *The Well-Tempered Clavier* around
1950.[46] But she also went further than necessary and after righting this
wrong, argued insistently over many years for the inherent qualitative value
of her nonhistorical harpsichord over and above the clavichord, based on
her own personal experience, in terms such as: "The vogue of the clavichord, like its sonority, had a sweet and discreet luster. Why attribute to it
soaring and haughty ambitions? Why not let its *Bebung* fade away under
the moonlight of adolescent romanticism?"[47] This sustained siege of rhetorical bravura finally convinced the musicologist Georg Kinsky that the
clavichord was completely irrelevant to the performance of Bach's music.
While preparing a book about the Heyer musical instrument collection in
Cologne, Kinsky writes: "The sentence about Bach in Volume I, third chapter, p. 23, is to be stricken out. Wanda Landowska's campaign, as artist
and musicologist, has proved that *The Well-Tempered Clavier* as well as all
great keyboard works of Bach were composed, not for the clavichord, but
for the harpsichord."[48] At the time, the collection in Cologne contained the
Gerstenberg pedal clavichord. As we shall see in the following chapter,
Landowska's influence extended to the point that Kinsky went out of his
way to construct an argument for the irrelevance of the *pedal* clavichord to
Bach's music as well. The question must be raised whether his argument is
based on personal working knowledge of the instrument, or on his documented belief in Landowska's word over Forkel's.

In this new orthodoxy, extending to the beginning of the twenty-first
century, *Clavier* must always be suspected of meaning *general keyboard*
until proven otherwise, an attitude that can be sustained only by a creative
reading of many eighteenth-century sources. One way out of this semantic
maze is to suggest that around Bach's time and among his circle of friends
and family, the word *Clavier* could and did refer specifically to the clavichord, but because it also literally means *keyboard,* it can also refer to the
keyboard of the harpsichord or the organ. Therefore, when *Clavier* appears in the titles of musical works, such as *Das wohltemperierte Clavier,* it
does indeed have the general meaning of "music for any keyboard," but
when used alone as a noun to describe a specific physical keyboard instrument, it can and often does refer to a clavichord.

It is understandable that *The Bach Reader*'s brief is to publish references from primary source material that contain the word "Bach," just as Boalch must prioritize space for references that mention *clavichord*, but the editorial policies result in a divorce of the concepts *Bach* and *pedal clavichord* that does not exist in the original source. The long tradition of the pedal clavichord in central Europe, the reference to it in Bach's will, and the fondness shown for the instrument by Bach's sons and at least one student, combined with the explicit reference to the pedal clavichord in Bach's household in Forkel's biography, make it possible to move forward under the assumption that Bach had the instrument and used it to play and teach. In the following chapter, several more curious references to the pedal clavichord from Forkel's biography will be examined closely.

2

J. S. Bach's Trio Sonatas: A Reception History of a Rumor

The fact is that this is one of those questions over which much ink is spilt to little purpose because no-one will admit that anyone else can be even partly right.

—Walter Emery

What is the Rumor?

There is a long-standing rumor that Johann Sebastian Bach's *Six Trio Sonatas* (BWV 525–530) were originally written for pedal clavichord and not for the organ. This rumor was kept alive in, among other places, the first two editions of the Schmieder *Catalog of Bach's Works* (BWV):

525–530 Sechs Sonaten
Besetzung. Orgel. In erster Linie für Pedalclavichord oder Pedalcembalo geschrieben.[1]

The idea that the *Six Trio Sonatas* were "written for pedal clavichord or pedal harpsichord in the first place" has been removed from the current edition. The first question to ask is, "Where did this idea come from?" And the logical answer is to begin with the literature list that Schmieder himself provides. The 1966 literature list has nothing that was published after 1937, because the pre-publication material was destroyed during the Second World War and it took Wolfgang Schmieder (1901–1990) many years to reconstruct the work.

The reception history in this chapter begins with the nineteenth-century German response to the rumor, preserved in the sources recorded by Schmieder, namely: Johann Forkel, Philipp Spitta, and Albert Schweitzer. This response is more complex than reported by later scholars. The English reaction to the rumor was influenced by the early twentieth-century revival of the clavichord in a nonhistorical form. The modern response is marked by a concerted effort to remove the idea of the pedal clavichord altogether.

The Rumor at the End of the Eighteenth Century

Johann Nikolaus Forkel (1749–1818)

Johann Nikolaus Forkel's large essay on the life of Johann Sebastian Bach is based in part on correspondence directly with Carl Philipp Emanuel Bach. It is the first extensive biography of Bach from the first real music historian in German. A professor at Göttingen University, and an organist himself, Forkel published his essay in 1802 and it first appeared in English in 1820. In Chapter III, Forkel reports the oft-quoted information that Bach

> liked best to play upon the clavichord; the harpsichord, though certainly suscep-
> tible of a very great variety of expression, had not soul enough for him; and the
> piano was in his life time too much in its infancy and still much too coarse to
> satisfy him. He therefore considered the clavichord as the best instrument for
> study, and, in general, for private musical entertainment. He found it the most
> convenient for the expression of his most refined thoughts, and did not believe it
> possible to produce from any harpsichord or pianoforte, such a variety in the
> gradations of tone as on this instrument, which is, indeed, poor in tone, but on a
> small scale extremely flexible.[2]

> Am Liebsten spielte er auf dem Clavichord. Die sogenannten Flügel, obgleich
> auch auf ihnen ein gar verschiederner Vortrag statt findet, waren ihm doch zu
> seelenlos, und die Pianoforte waren bey seinem Leben noch zu sehr in ihrer
> ersten Entstehung, und noch viel zu plump, als daß sie ihm hätten Genüge thun
> können. Er hielt daher das Clavichord für das beste Instrument zum Studiren, so
> wie überhaupt zur musikalischen Privatunterhaltung. Er fand es zum Vortrag
> seiner feinsten Gedanken am bequemsten, und glaubte nicht, daß auf irgend
> einem Flügel oder Pianoforte eine solche Mannigfaltigkeit in den Schattirungen
> des Tons hervor gebracht werden könne, als auf diesem zwar Ton-armen, aber
> im kleinen außerordentlich biegsamen Instrument.[3]

Forkel presents a journalistic voice, one that reports the facts, in his portrait of a man only recently deceased, particularly in his extensive cor-respondence with Bach's son Carl Philipp Emanuel. And as we shall see in chapter 4, Forkel's discussion of Bach's technique engages C. P. E. Bach's own writings about technique. Whether Bach's own view of the clavichord and the late eighteenth-century popularity of the instrument as a vehicle for the *Empfindsamkeit* movement were substantially different from one another will be explored further in chapter 4. Forkel's own description of Bach and the clavichord serves as the principal transmission of our rumor to the rest of the nineteenth-century writers.

Directly before the well-known passage mentioned above we get an in-sight into the possible purpose and performance practice of trio sonatas. Spitta does not choose to quote this, possibly because it represents a view of Bach, not as timeless genius, but as playful musician, engaged with the composers of his time, and the craft of playing, rather than the Art of Music:

> He had an equal facility in overlooking scores and executing the substance of them at first sight on the harpsichord. He even saw so easily through parts laid side by side that he could immediately play them. This he often did, when a friend had received a new trio or quartetto for stringed instruments and wished to hear how it sounded. He was also able, if a single bass part, often ill figured, was laid before him, immediately to play from it a trio or a quartet; nay, he even went so far, when he was in a cheerful humour and in the full consciousness of his powers, as to perform extempore, to three single parts, a fourth part, and thus to make a quartetto of a trio. For these purposes he used two clavichords and the pedal, or a harpsichord with two sets of keys, provided with a pedal.[4]

> Nicht minder groß war seine Fertigkeit, Partituren zu übersehen und ihren wesentlichen Inhalt beym ersten Anblick auf dem Clavier vorzutragen. Auch neben einander gelegte einzelne Stimmen übersah er so leicht, daß er sie sogleich abspielen konnte. Dieses Kunststück machte er oft, wenn jemand etwa ein neues Trio oder Quartett für Bogeninstrumente bekommen hatte, und nun gern hören wollte, wie es klinge. Er konnte ferner aus einer ihm vorgelegten, oft schlecht bezifferten einzelnen Baßstimme augenblicklich ein Trio oder Quartett abspielen; ja er ging sogar bisweilen so weit, wenn er gerade fröhlicher Laune und im vollen Gefühl seiner Kraft war, zu 3 einzelnen Stimmen sogleich eine vierte zu extemporiren, also aus einem Trio ein Quartett zu machen. Zu solchen Künsten bediente er sich zweyer Claviere und des Pedals, oder eines mit einem Pedal versehenen Doppelflügels.[5]

Forkel describes Bach's performance practice of trios as improvisatory, and playful to the point of showing off. Above all, Forkel places the practice of trio playing in the home, with an audience of friends and family and perhaps often for private entertainment. How different this immediate pastel sketch of Bach is from the oil portrait of Bach that will be presented by Philipp Spitta! The habit of performing and improvising trios and quartets for Bach's own pleasure was done interchangeably on either the harpsichord or clavichord with pedals.

The fourth sentence of this story seems to come almost verbatim from a letter received from C. P. E. Bach in December of 1774: "Thanks to his greatness in harmony, he accompanied trios more than once and, since he was in high spirits and knew that the composer of these trios would not be offended, he composed a complete fourth part on the spur of the moment and from the sparsely figured bass part set before him, which astonished the composer of these trios."[6] But, while Forkel talks about playing trios or quartets at the keyboard, C. P. E. Bach's letter clearly refers to when "he accompanied trios," which may or may not infer a more formal setting than Bach's living room. Forkel's allusions to sightreading trio parts and to playing them on the pedal harpsichord or pedal clavichord at home do not appear in this letter, raising the question of whether Forkel conflated two separate stories or embroidered upon one of them. The general question also remains: how much can we trust what Forkel has done with the stories that were entrusted to him? Too little corroborating evidence survives to make a comprehensive judgment, but the possibility must be considered that some of Forkel's material for the biography comes from direct conversations with C. P. E. Bach. In the same letter, C. P. E. Bach charges Forkel to "leave the comical things out"[7] about Bach's youthful pranks, and it is some mark of Forkel's respectfulness as a biographer that he follows this wish. C. P. E. Bach signals his own trust of Forkel as a biographer as he closes the letter, encouraging Forkel to use his memories of his father "as you please and put them in better order."[8]

But the *Six Trio Sonatas* themselves, according to Forkel, are not only for pleasure but also for a pedagogical purpose, designed to complete Wilhelm Friedemann's education as a performer. In chapter 9 of his book, Forkel reports:

> Six Sonatas, or Trios, for two sets of keys and an obbligato pedal. Bach composed them for his eldest son William Friedemann, who, by practising them, prepared himself to become the great performer on the organ that he afterwards was. It is impossible to say enough of their beauty. They were composed when the author was in the full vigour of his mature age, and may be considered as his chief work of this description.[9]

> 3) Sechs Sonaten oder Trio für zwey Claviere mit dem obligaten Pedal. Bach hat sie für seinen ältesten Sohn, Wilh. Friedemann, aufgesetzt, welcher sich damit zu dem großen Orgelspieler vorbereiten mußte, der er nachher geworden ist. Man kann von ihrer Schönheit nicht genug sagen. Sie sind in dem reifsten Alter des Verfassers gemacht, und können als das Hauptwerk desselben in dieser Art angesehen werden.[10]

Because this text appears in Forkel's list of Bach's *Organ Pieces,* there is a built-in tension between the description of the *Trio Sonatas* as practice pieces and the label of the section as organ performance pieces. It does not help matters that under the organ section there also appears this:

> I add a very artificially composed Passacaglia, which, however, is rather for two clavichords and pedal than for the organ.[11]

> Zu diesen setze ich noch eine sehr kunstreich gearbeitete Passacaglia, die aber mehr für zwey Claviere und Pedal als für die Orgel ist.[12]

In this case it seems clear that the instrument Forkel refers to is a pedal clavichord. In the case of the trio sonatas there is ambiguity because the same term can *also* be used to describe the two manuals and pedals of an organ necessary to play the piece. It cannot be doubted that this term for the pedal clavichord was in general use at the end of the eighteenth century. Was Forkel merely reporting what appeared on his manuscript page of the trio sonatas? Or was he advocating for the pedal clavichord, in the same way as with the *Passacaglia*? Or was he stating that the pieces are intended for any instrument with two manuals and pedal? Or was he simply saying that they are organ pieces for two manuals and pedal? If only he had been specific on this point in the way that he was specific with the *Passacaglia*, most of the ink would still be in the bottle; instead, this ambiguity opened the way for Philipp Spitta to offer an interpretation that suited purposes of his own.

The Rumor in the Nineteenth Century

Philipp Spitta (1841–94)

Throughout Philipp Spitta's extensive biography of Bach[13] his relationship to the clavichord is particularly complex; it is worth looking at closely. Spitta adopts the term "Clavier" to refer to general keyboard even though among the late eighteenth-century clavichordists like C. P. E. Bach, when discussing a *specific* instrument (as opposed to music for general keyboard, for instance) they used the term *Clavichord*. Spitta reports C. P. E. Bach's belief that the clavichord was his father's favorite instrument:

> Even though it had not much strength, the tone was wonderfully capable of light and shade, and comparatively persistent. It was possible to play *cantabile* on it, and this *cantabile* style was regarded by Bach as the foundation of all Clavier playing.[14]

> Besaß es auch nur geringe Stärke, so war der Ton doch außerordentlich schattirungsfähig und verhältnißmäßig andauernd. Man konnte singen darauf und das gesangreiche Spiel legte Bach aller Clavierkunst zu Grunde.[15]

But Spitta uses the concept of the clavichord for his own purposes. The clavichord is a symbol for him of a romantic sound world in embryo, as it were, and a clever tool used to win the reader gently to his particular point of view regarding Bach's genius. The clavichord is, for Spitta, an entrée to discuss what is really important to him, which is that Bach's genius transcends the ages and therefore his music should transcend all historical keyboard instruments:

> Nowhere can we see more strikingly than here how a great genius can contain within itself the aim and end of a long process of historical development, and

foresee it across the lapse even of centuries. The ideal instrument which floated in the mind of Bach for the performance of his *Inventions* and *Sinfonias,* of his suites and Clavier fugues, was not altogether the clavichord; the ideas brought down by him from the sublime heights of the organ were too ponderous, and weighed too heavily on its delicate frame. But it was not the organ either. From the organ, no doubt, emanated that craving for more abundant alternations of feeling which sought its satisfaction in chamber-music, just as the endeavor after definition of feeling gave rise to the main idea of the church cantata as proceeding from the organ chorale . . . The harpsichord could not here satisfy him.[16]

Nirgends läßt sich überzeugender darthun, wie große Geister die Ziele geschichtlicher Entwicklungen im eignen Thun beschlossen tragen und prophetisch oft über Jahrhunderte hinwegblicken, als hier. Das Idealinstrument, das Bach für seine Inventionen und Sinfonien, Suiten und Clavierfugen vorschwebte, war nicht ganz das Clavichord: zu wuchtig lasteten die aus der erhabenen Alpenwelt des Orgelreiches herabgebrachten Gedanken auf dem zarten Baue desselben. Aber die Orgel war es auch nicht. Aus ihrem Gebiete emanirte eben das Bedürfniß nach reicherem Gefühls-wechsel, das in der Kammermusik Befriedigung suchte, ähnlich wie das Streben nach Gefühlsbestimmtheit aus dem Orgelchoral den Kern der Kirchencantate hervorgehen ließ: aus der erhabenen Ruhe und träumereichen Einsamkeit trieb es herunter in blühende Thäler und zu redenden Menschen. Das Cembalo konnte die Ausgleichung nicht herstellen.[17]

This rhetoric sounds like logic, but it is really a catechism of the nineteenth century faith in the cult of the genius. Spitta's belief allows him to assume that he knows "the ideal instrument which floated in the mind of Bach." We are caught up in the atmosphere of the nineteenth century in this prose and can almost believe that "A great genius can contain within itself the aim and end of a long process of historical development."[18] There follows a curious syllogism: If the process of historical development across centuries can be accomplished in a single man, then this process should also be true for the man's keyboard instrument. After rhetorically eliminating the clavichord, the harpsichord, and the organ, Spitta says:

No instrument but one which should combine the volume of tone of the organ with the expressive quality of the clavichord, in due proportion could be capable of reproducing the image which dwelt in the master's imagination when he composed for the Clavier. Every one sees at once that the modern pianoforte is in fact just such an instrument.[19]

Erst ein instrument, das die Klangfülle der Orgel mit der Ausdrucksfähigkeit des Clavichords in richtigen Verhältnissen vereinigte, war im Stande, dem Erscheinung zu geben, was in des Meisters Phantasie erklang, wenn er für Clavier componirte. Daß unser moderner Flügel dieses Instrument ist, sieht ein jeder.[20]

In the two previous quotations Spitta consistently uses *Clavichord* to describe the clavichord, and uses *Clavier* to indicate a general keyboard.

This is important to note, because later Spitta will be accused of inventing the confusion about these two terms, an ambiguity that exists in the eighteenth-century sources themselves but one that does *not* seem to have been invented or even encouraged by nineteenth-century scholars. Spitta is not even a proponent of the clavichord itself. Having used it to lead his readers to the piano bench, he has no qualms at all about ritually sacrificing the clavichord:

> Nothing can be more perverse than to wish to have the old clavichord restored in order to play Bach's Clavier pieces—or even the harpsichord, which, indeed was of the very smallest importance in Bach's musical practice; this might do for Kuhnau, for Couperin, and Marchand; Bach's grander creations demand a flowing robe of sound, an inspired mien and expressive motions.[21]

> Nichts kann verkehrter sein, als zur Ausführung Bachscher Clavierstücke sich das Clavichord zurückzuwünschen, oder gar das Cembalo, das für Bachs Kunstübung überhaupt die wenigst selbständige Bedeutung gehabt hat; dies mag für Kuhnau, für Couperin und Marchand passen, Bachs Gestalten verlangen ein wallendes Tongewand, seelenvollen Blick und sprechende Mienen.[22]

It is interesting to note that Spitta is aware of the possibility that some literature from the eighteenth century may be more aptly suited to the historical clavichord and harpsichord. Spitta argues that Bach's music has a different quality altogether from that of his illustrious contemporaries and that Bach is such an exception that his keyboard music demands a nonhistorical sound resource.

It is in this light that Spitta's view of the concept of the pedal clavichord must be judged. Having climbed out on a limb about the organ's limitations as a musical instrument, he is forced to uphold the view that the pedal clavichord can bring something of his ideal sound world for Bach to the trio sonatas:

> That form in three movements which Bach vainly attempted to produce as long as he tried to insert a contrasting middle movement between the prelude and the fugue, he discovered in the six so-called organ sonatas. These are compositions in which the forms of the Italian chamber sonata, as developed by Bach, and of the instrumental concerto, appear united. . . . Bach produced this form under the influence of his chamber music, and it holds a central position between the style of organ and chamber music; it is accordingly best suited to an instrument which would give expression to this medium character. That instrument is the pedal Clavier with two manuals. The original MSS. distinctly state them to be for that instrument, and the title of "Organ Sonatas" now in use is, strictly speaking, incorrect.[23]

> Jene dreisätzige Form, welche Bach vergeblich suchte, als er zwischen Praeludium und Fuge einen contrastirenden Mittelsatz einschob, hat er in den sechs sogenannten Orgelsonaten gefunden. Es sind dies Compositionen, in denen die

Formen der italiänischen Kammersonate, wie sie Bach ausbildete, und des Instrumentalconcerts combinirt erscheinen. . . . Von seiner Kammermusik ausgehend ist Bach zu dieser Form gelangt. Die Musik, welche uns in ihr geboten wird, hält zwischen Orgel- und Kammerstil die Mitte und gehört sich demgemäß auch für ein Instrument, welches diese mittlere Stellung zum Ausdruck bringt. Es ist das PedalClavier mit zwei Manualen. Die Originalmanuscripte bestimmen sie ausdrücklick dafür und die jetzt übliche Benennung "Orgelsonaten" ist genau genommen unrichtig.[24]

Spitta uses the pedal clavichord in the same way as he used the clavichord: to argue that Bach's genius was searching for expressions that lay in the land between forms, between the cantata and the organ chorale, between organ and chamber music. This realm between established forms eventually craved an instrument like the piano to explore it. He needs historical proof in order to take this stand, and the proof he cites is the title of the "original" manuscripts, although neither of them is, in fact, an original manuscript, since they are not composing scores. There are two main manuscript sources for the trio sonatas: P 271 and P 272.[25] P 271 is in Bach's own hand and is the older of the two. The first half of P 272 was copied out by Wilhelm Friedemann Bach and the rest probably by Anna Magdalena Bach.[26] In both manuscripts each Sonata begins with the "title" *Sonata à 2 Clav: et Pedal,* which Spitta interprets as referring to the pedal clavichord. There is, however, no title page for the original manuscript. Spitta bases his comments on the information available in Forkel's work. He might even have deliberately confused the two distinct uses to which Forkel puts the term "Zwey Claviere und Pedal" (sometimes as an instrument designation for pedal clavichord and sometimes as a description of the number of keyboards necessary to perform a piece), in order to argue that Bach's *Trio Sonatas* looked forward toward the piano in the same way that his single-manual keyboard pieces did.

Early Twentieth-Century Germany

Albert Schweitzer (1875–1965)

Albert Schweitzer's biography, *J. S. Bach,* takes up the ambiguity that was introduced by Spitta and adds a new level of confusion:

> Actually it is false to speak of Bach's organ sonatas. The two manuscripts that have come down to us, the one in Friedemann's estate, the other in Emmanuel's, state that they concern works for "Klavizimbel" with two keyboards and pedals. This instrument was in that time, common far and wide.

> Eigentlich ist es falsch, von Orgelsonaten Bachs zu reden. Die beiden Handschriften, die sie uns überliefern—die eine aus dem Besitze Friedemanns,

die andere aus dem Emmanuels—besagen, daß es sich um Werke für das
Klavizimbel mit zwei Klavieren und Pedal handelte. Dieses Instrument war damals
allgemein verbreitet. [27]

Where does the concept of the *Klavizimbel* (pedal harpsichord) come
from in Schweitzer's book? Schweitzer published this work originally in
1905 with the help of a colleague at his University in Strasbourg, where the
instrument is already referred to as a pedal harpsichord: "un clavecin à
deux claviers avec pédale."[28] In the original French, Schweitzer also assumes the pedal harpsichord was Forkel's choice for the *Passacaglia*: "Forkel
fait remarquer, précisément, à son propos, qu'elle aussi appelle plutôt le
clavecin à pédale que l'orgue."[29] It is interesting to note that while in the
original French, Schweitzer is content to suggest that Bach must certainly
have also played the Passacaglia on the organ, in the expanded German
edition, Schweitzer gives more explicit aesthetic reasons for playing the
Passacaglia on the organ rather than a stringed keyboard instrument:

Also the Passacaglia (Peters I, S. 75; B:G: XV, S. 289) was written in the first
place for the harpsichord with pedal, and is only secondarily written for the
organ. However, because of its polyphonic construction it is so suitable for the
organ that we can today no longer hardly understand how one could play it on
a stringed keyboard instrument. Also, there is no other organ piece that makes
more demands on the art of registration than this. Every one of the twenty movements built upon the continuously returning theme, should have its own charac-
teristic tone color, but cannot be glaringly different from the previous and following variations, or else the piece becomes a picture of discontinuity.

Auch die Passacaglia (Peters I, S. 75; B:G: XV, S. 289) ist in erster Linie für das
Cembalo mit Pedal und erst in zweiter für die Orgel geschrieben. Freilich ist sie
durch ihren polyphonen Aufbau so für die Orgel geeignet, daß wir es heute
kaum mehr verstehen, wie man es wagen konnte, sie auf einem Saiteninstrument
auszuführen. Andrerseits gibt es kein Orgelstück, das an die Registrierkunst solche
Anforderungen stellt wie dieses. Jeder der zwanzig Sätze, die sich über dem immer
wiederkehrenden Thema aufbauen, soll seine charakteristische Klangfarbe haben,
darf sich aber nicht grell von dem vorhergehenden und folgenden abheben, da
sonst das Stück nur das Bild der Zerrissenheit bietet.[30]

As has been shown, Forkel states, "I add a very artificially composed
Passacaglia, which, however, is rather for two clavichords and pedal than
for the organ."[31] Schweitzer conflated the two specific names of the pedal
harpsichord and the pedal clavichord from Forkel and confused them with
the indication for "two keyboards and pedal" from the trio sonata manuscripts, translated the result into French and back into German, and it's a
marvel we are not further afield than "Klavizimbel." It is perhaps no won-
der that confusion about the term "Clavier" begins to be a serious issue for
twentieth-century readers.

Georg Kinsky

The argument in Georg Kinsky's 1936 article, "Pedalklavier oder Orgel bei Bach?" summarizes, in a paragraph, all of the important sources then known about the existence of the pedal clavichord in everyday musical life in Germany. Kinsky suggests that Friedemann first practiced the *Trio Sonatas* at home on the "Pedalklavier" and then, after a full technical understanding of the pieces, was allowed to play them on the organ.[32] Kinsky blames Spitta, among others for manufacturing the idea that the title page of the *Trio Sonatas* suggests that they are for pedal clavichord and notes that this had led to subsequent misunderstandings. Kinsky noticed the difference, noted earlier in this chapter, between Forkel's clear statement that the Passacaglia was "more for pedal clavichord" and his ambiguous description of the *Trio Sonatas*, for "2 Claviers and pedal," and he comments on Spitta's misrepresentation of the information. Kinsky also reviews the history of the manuscript P 271 but does not note that the manuscript was assembled after C. P. E. Bach's death and that the title page of the manuscript (including mention of the organ chorales) postdates C. P. E. Bach.

Kinsky is the only musicologist in this reception history who has actually engaged with the phenomenology of the pedal clavichord directly. He knew the Gerstenberg pedal clavichord in 1936 and he says that he experimented on it, but, as we saw in chapter 1, Wanda Landowska had already convinced him that the clavichord was irrelevant to Bach's music, so it is difficult to accept the notion that this experiment with the Gerstenberg pedal clavichord was unbiased:

One needs for this purpose only to make a test on the well-preserved pedal clavichord in the Heyer collection in Leipzig . . . and try any part of the Passacaglia. How weak and monotonous the great work will become on this instrument, that on the organ—for which it was created—achieves its greatest effect! Already the dominant basso-ostinato theme of the piece with its long-held half-notes is antithetical to the nature of a stringed keyboard instrument: it is implicitly organ-like and calls for the Prinzipalbass 16' strengthened by the Oktavbass 8' of a Silbermann organ. Schweitzer drives home the point that "Furthermore, there is no other organ piece that makes more demands on the art of registration than this," a demand that cannot be met on the normal pedal clavichord that has no stops at all and only two 8' manuals.[33]

Man braucht zu diesem Zwecke nur die Probe auf's Exempel zu machen und auf dem trefflich erhaltenen Pedal-Clavichord der Heyer-Sammlung in Leipzig . . . einen beliebigen Teil der Passacaglia zu versuchen. Wie matt und eintönig wird sich auf diesem Instrument das großartige Werk ausnehmen, das auf der Orgel— für die es geschaffen ist—zu stärkster Wirkung kommt! Schon das als basso ostinato das ganze Stück beherrschende wuchtige Thema mit seinen lang auszuhaltenden halben Noten widerspricht durchaus dem Wesen eines besaiteten Tasteninstruments: es ist unbedingt orgelmäßig empfunden und verlangt nach dem durch Oktavbass 8' verstärkten Prinzipalbass 16' der Silbermann-Orgel. "Andrerseits gibt es kein Orgelstück, das an die Registrierkunst solche Anforderungen stellt wie dieses," fährt Schweitzer fort: eine Aufgabe, die auf dem aller Register entbehrenden üblichen Pedal-Clavichord mit seinen zwei 8' Klavieren ebenfalls unlösbar ist.

According to Kinsky, all one has to do is try *any part* of the Passacaglia on the Gerstenberg and one will be immediately convinced that it is better on the organ. Reading this description closely reveals how the experiment may have been biased from the beginning. It is unlikely that the pedal clavichord was in playing order in 1936. The instrument was either in an unrestored state or a badly restored state.[34] Let us grant Kinsky the benefit of the doubt that he spent enough time with the instrument to discover how to get the best tone from it, in spite of his statement that the experiment need only be brief in order to prove his point. Still, Kinsky's critique seems to be based solely on the opening unaccompanied pedal statement of the theme. Given that the pedal part of the instrument is the only part still playable, is it possible that this is all that Kinsky tried before judging the instrument?

Kinsky also misappropriates Schweitzer's comment. Schweitzer admits the possibility that an instrument capable of dynamic variation could play the Passacaglia without having to worry about registering twenty successive variations in a way that gave each its own character without producing a disjointed performance. Schweitzer argues that the piece might *not* have been intended for the organ. Kinsky turns this around and uses Schweitzer to argue that the Passacaglia cannot have been intended for an instrument incapable of registration changes.

Finally, Kinsky is the only writer who has commented on the actual texture of the trio sonatas, specifically the long tied notes and the long notes without any trill signs, as evidence that they couldn't have been "performed" on the pedal clavichord. He also points out that two of the middle movements were used by Bach as middle movements of organ preludes and fugues.

Early Twentieth-Century England

George Bernard Shaw (1856–1950)

The English rediscovery of the clavichord at the beginning of the century centers around two figures: a piano technician and a music critic. The critic is none other than George Bernard Shaw, who did more through his writings to shape the British national idea of the clavichord than anyone else. Shaw chronicled at first hand the direct result of London's Great Exhibition in August of 1885, which included a large exhibition of historical keyboard instruments. In Shaw's occasional writings about the clavichord one can also trace the sea change from Spitta's mid-nineteenth-century romantic piano to the fascination with *historical* keyboard instruments in the twentieth century. In August of 1885 Arnold Dolmetsch had not yet built his first replicas of Hass clavichords when Shaw covered the opening of the Musical Instruments at the Inventions Exhibition: "A harpsichord with a glass lid on the keyboard is disappointing; but a clavichord similarly secured is downrightly exasperating, for if there is one instrument that every musician would like to try, it is the *Wohltemperirte Klavier* of Sebastian Bach."[35]

But it wasn't until he first heard the piano technician Alfred James Hipkins (1826–1903)[36] play a recital on an historical clavichord that Shaw became a champion of the clavichord. Perhaps Shaw must shoulder most of the blame for convincing the English-speaking world of the translation, *The Well-Tempered Clavichord.* The concept of the clavichord and of early instruments in general seems to have appealed to the eccentric free-thinker in Shaw. Shaw formed the following opinion, thirty years before Kinsky and Schweitzer:

> Hipkins's proficiency as a player on the harpsichord and clavichord is an old story upon which I need not dwell. If any swaggering pianist is inclined to undervalue that proficiency, let him try his hand on a clavichord and see what he can make of an instrument which depends for its "action" not on the elaborate mechanism of Erard or any modification thereof, but on the dexterity of the player.[37]

The Late Twentieth-Century Perspective

Walter Emery

Near the end of Walter Emery's 1957 study of the *Trio Sonatas* comes a short essay called "Organ or Domestic Instrument?"[38] The essay summarizes Emery's thoughts about the pedal clavichord as a performance instrument for the trio sonatas in sixteen numbered paragraphs with an introduction that acknowledges that the famous "2 Clav. & Pedal" title presents a problem:

> The word Clavier may mean: keyboard instruments in general, including the organ, clavichord, manual. There are thus two ways in which the heading can be interpreted: (I) for an organ with two manuals and pedal, (2) for two clavichords with a pedal attachment. The latter interpretation is perfectly reasonable. Pedal clavichords were cheap and not uncommon; organists found the expression 'two Claviers and pedal' was sometimes used. But strangely enough, it was not until the nineteenth century, when the pedal clavichord was a thing of the past, that anyone associated Bach's Sonatas *unambiguously* with that instrument. . . . The fact is that this is one of those questions over which much ink is

spilt to little purpose because no-one will admit that anyone else can be even partly right. To deny that the Sonatas are organ music is just about on a par with refusing to believe that Friedemann practised them on a pedal clavichord. It is to be hoped that students of Bach will let the matter drop, and devote their surplus energy to something useful, such as identifying copyists' hands or compiling a proper bibliography of Bach editions before 1850.[39]

Why the fun questions in musicology are always of the ink-spilling sort is a topic for another conversation, but this particular trail of spilt ink has made a series of Rorschach blots down through history that can be interpreted individually and as a whole. This reception history has concentrated so far on the specific agenda and historical contexts behind the scenes of each writer's remarks, rather than accepting each as an objective expression of the truth. The latter is presumably the kind of attitude that led Emery to lament that "no-one will admit that anyone else can be even partly right." Forkel is dismissed by Emery as a less than reliable source of information: "Whatever his opinion about the Sonatas may have been, it carries no more weight than his opinion about the Passacaglia; and the latter is absurd."[40] Absurd according to whose criteria, one is tempted to ask? Emery and Schweitzer are in agreement on this matter. They cannot conceive of Bach playing the grand Passacaglia on an instrument at home.

A wry comment like, "It is to be hoped that students of Bach will let the matter drop, and devote their surplus energy to something useful," could not be more different from Spitta's nineteenth-century style. But it is not just the rhetoric that has changed. The battleground has moved too. There is so much more written about Bach in 1950 than there was in 1870, that Emery is engaged in a far different kind of work than Spitta was. While Spitta had the luxury of speculating about Bach's ideal keyboard instrument, Emery is in service to a large volume of facts already known. The rumor about the trio sonatas is no longer a tool in itself, used to promote Spitta's ideal of the modern piano sound or Schweitzer's idolization of the modern piano's action. The belief in progress that leads Spitta and Schweitzer to romanticize about the clavichord's role and call what they write historical accuracy is a luxury Emery cannot indulge in. But it is tempting to suggest that his own equally strong belief in objectivity, the desire to have all of the known facts arranged neatly so that we can finally lay a problem or two to rest, holds its own pitfalls and traps. It encourages us to dispense with imagination and to refrain from looking at old patterns of information for new insights, and it closes our eyes to possible clues that may have been there all along.

Lady Susi Jeans

Emery engages Lady Jeans in his argument when she suggests that everything by Johann Sebastian Bach that was designated in the manuscript as *à*

2 *Clav et pédale* was originally intended for pedal clavichord. However Jeans's own argument is much closer to the original sources than Emery intimates. Jeans gives the first wide-ranging well-researched history of historical keyboard instruments fitted with pedals to appear in English. She also presents a close reading of Forkel. Unfortunately she assumes that Forkel said the trio sonatas "were written for two Claviers and obbligato pedal,"[41] without elaborating on the ambiguity concerning this statement. Jeans makes the argument that Forkel's biography clearly identifies at least two two-manual instruments with pedals in the Bach family home. In Jeans's presentation to the Royal Music Association, she dares to take an intrinsic approach to the facts that are known about the pedal clavichord during Bach's lifetime. She comments, for instance:

> There is no doubt that music was especially written for the pedal house-Claviers. One of Adlung's remarks supports this view, when he asks for the inclusion of the *d* in the pedal compass of the pedal clavichord 'because it is needed more at home than on the Church organ.[42]

Jeans is more interested in arguing that the pedal clavichord must have been in general use than in identifying specific repertoire for the instrument, but when she tries to identify pieces that can be labeled exclusively for pedal clavichord she is criticized on all fronts. It is impossible to prove extrinsically that the title *à 2 clav. e pedal* referred to the pedal clavichord, rather than simply the number of keyboards required to play the piece.

Peter Williams

Peter Williams tries to set the rumor to rest once and for all: "Despite assertions still made, there is no clear indication that '2 Clav. & Pedal' suggested pedal harpsichord or pedal clavichord, as Kinsky has shown."[43] But Georg Kinsky wrote the article in 1936, and as we have seen, admitted that he was primarily influenced by Landowska's rhetoric about an admittedly nonhistorical harpsichord and a shamelessly misrepresented clavichord. The obvious concerns about Kinsky's actual grasp of the phenomenology of the pedal clavichord have already been addressed in this chapter. Williams does, however, also go over some of the same material that Emery presents: for instance, Forkel's entry on the *Trio Sonatas* is included in the "organ pieces" section. Williams repeats the assertion that the *Trio Sonatas* could have been studied on organs of one manual and pedal with 4' register and the left hand down an octave. Williams also reviews all of the sources where the terms "trio" and "for organ" were used in references to the sonatas including the anonymous obituary of 1754, which was written by C. P. E. Bach with Johann Friedrich Agricola, where they are referred to as *Sechs Trios für die Orgel mit dem obligaten Pedal*.[44] He concludes:

The two traditions of music to practice and music to admire explain the accounts about these pieces, but the nineteenth-century editors and commentators began to equate *Clavier* with clavichord and thence to speculate on the purpose in domestic music-making of both the Sonatas and the Passacaglia (e.g. Griepenkerl preface to Peters I, 1844). It is not known who told Forkel that the Six Sonatas were compiled for W. F. Bach—perhaps C. P. E. Bach, who corresponded with Forkel and who seems to have owned [manuscript] P 271.[45]

The question of the term *Clavier* in the context of this reception history is confusing, but not impossibly so. Forkel uses *Clavier* to describe a specific keyboard instrument within the context of the name of the pedal clavichord: "Zwey Claviere und Pedal," wheras Spitta uses it very consistently to mean general keyboard. It is C. P. E. Bach himself, however, and other musicians like Johann Friedrich Reichardt (1752–1814) and Gerber, not nineteenth-century commentators, who used the term freely to mean both clavichord and keyboard.

Robert Marshall

Robert Marshall reports that the original Schmieder catalog suggested that no fewer than nineteen different Bach pieces were for house instrument with pedals rather than for organ.[46] These indications have now been removed from the latest edition of the Schmieder catalog. Marshall makes a thorough survey of all of the appearances of *2 Clav. et Pedal* in the music scores of J. S. Bach, and finally untangles the confusion about the *Trio Sonatas* that Spitta and Schweitzer managed to introduce. At the same time, Marshall confirms that the instrument described as *3. Clavire nebst pedal* in Bach's will is in all likelihood a pedal clavichord. Marshall concludes his discussion of the role of the pedal clavichord with: "As for Bach's use of the contraption, Forkel reports in chapter 3 of his biography that the composer used it for such private purposes as sight reading ensemble pieces at the keyboard(s) and improvising upon them."[47] However, Marshall has managed to clarify two points that still stand in opposition to one another. On the one hand, he makes it clear that there is no evidence from instrumental prescriptions in scores that *2 Clav. et Pedal* can mean that a piece was intended exclusively for the pedal clavichord. On the other hand, he confirms that *3. Clavire nebst pedal* in the case of the instrument mentioned in Bach's will is probably the common term to describe a pedal clavichord. This leaves Forkel's description of the Passacaglia as meant more for pedal clavichord standing unscathed, despite the fact that Marshall glosses over this fact rhetorically:

> In sum, the proposition entertained, if not quite advocated, in the pages of the BWV that any composition of Johann Sebastian Bach's could have been seriously intended for—as distinct from merely tolerated on—a pedal harpsichord or clavichord is surely nothing but a red herring.[48]

The Rumor in the Twenty-First Century?

One thread running through the twentieth-century argument about this rumor is the notion that Wilhelm Friedemann Bach was *merely practicing* on the pedal clavichord. The more generous authors allude to building technical proficiency on the "contraption." The 1966 *Bach Reader* goes so far as to say, "These instruments, however, were only substitutes for the organ, and even if Wilhelm Friedemann was forced to do some of his practicing on such instruments, the pieces were still Organ Sonatas."[49] However, it must be pointed out that all of the twentieth-century authors in this chapter, with the exception of George Bernard Shaw and Georg Kinsky, exhibit no direct experience of the instrument in question and its peculiar phenomenology. Shaw and Kinsky represent the two extremes of using phenomenological experience with an historical instrument to justify a musicological point. The insight into the possible technical and musical demands and rewards of the clavichord exhibited in Shaw's writings—comments that are nearly indistinguishable from historical descriptions of the instrument— are all but absent among the musicologists who have written on the subject since. Kinsky, the only musicologist with any physical experience of the historical instrument, was biased against the instrument in the first place.

But if we can trust C. P. E. Bach as any guide at all about his father's feeling for the clavichord, the pedal clavichord was not intended to be only a substitute for getting a chance to practice in church. Perhaps the twenty-first-century rumor about the *Trio Sonatas* will be closer to the eighteenth-century one. The argument in the eighteenth century was never about either/or clavichord or organ. The clavichord was a training instrument, yes, but, as Forkel reports, it was also the place where Bach went to have some musical fun, to create trios out of bass lines, and to create quartets out of trios. If we begin with Forkel's assumption that the trios were the culmination of Wilhelm Friedemann's clavichord training, is there any evidence that it was C. P. E. Bach who gave this impression directly to Forkel? Did C. P. E. Bach communicate about the trios directly with Forkel? Williams, as we have seen, concluded his discussion of this topic with the same question.

Stephen Clark's complete translation of the letters of C. P. E. Bach[50] is full of the loaning of manuscripts, the discussion of manuscripts, and of details of his late father's life, all for the benefit of Forkel's ongoing biography project. Turning to Letter 71:

> To Johann Nikolaus Forkel. In haste I have the pleasure of sending you, best friend, the rest of my Sebastianoren, namely 11 trios, 3 pedal pieces, and Vom Himmel hoch, etc. If you should already have this last chorale then send it back again at your convenience. The 6 Clavier trios which belong together in their numbered order, are among the best works of my late father.

They still sound very good now, and give me much pleasure, despite the fact that they are over 50 years old. There are a few Adagios in them that to this day are unexcelled in their later cantabile qualities. Please take good care of them, since they are very tattered. Emanueliana will follow in the future. It was not possible now.[51]

In a footnote, Clark suggests that the six trios discussed in this letter may be Bach's Sonatas for obligato keyboard and violin (BWV 1014–1019). But the rest of the letter mentions only keyboard music. Although C. P. E. Bach's *Nachlassverzeichniss* describes these pieces as trios,[52] one cannot exclude the possibility that Bach is referring to the *Six Trio Sonatas*. Once admitted as a possibility, the rest of the letter provides a considerable number of clues that lead in this direction. Consider the following:

1. The six pieces are in numbered order 1 to 6, as are the trios in MS P 271, which C. P. E. Bach owned and which was still a separate manuscript from the organ chorales in 1774.
2. The pieces are more than 50 years old in October of 1774 as are the trios, barely, if they were in fact written in 1723, the earliest possible date hypothesized. (The violin sonatas also fit the bill, as they were written while Bach was in Cöthen between 1717 and 1722).
3. They contain adagios of the highest quality that represent Carl Philipp Emanuel Bach's ideal of "modern" *cantabile* playing. *Cantabile* is a word C. P. E. Bach associates again and again with the clavichord. Referring once more to the beginning of this chapter, Spitta records: "Even though it had not much strength, the tone was wonderfully capable of light and shade, and comparatively persistent. It was possible to play *cantabile* on it, and this *cantabile* style was regarded by Bach as the foundation of all Clavier playing."[53]
4. They rank among the best work of the late Johann Sebastian Bach in his son's estimation. This certainly does not exclude the trio sonatas and in fact sounds very much like the language with which Forkel chose to describe them. "It is impossible to say enough of their beauty. They were composed when the author was in the full vigour of his most mature age and may be considered as his chief work of this description."[54]

    Forkel also reports on the *Six Keyboard and Violin Sonatas*. He says they "may be reckoned among Bach's first masterpieces in this field. They are throughout fugued; there are also a few canons between the Clavier and the violin which are extremely singing and full of character."[55] But Forkel does not refer to them as trios, nor does he single out their adagios for mention.
5. The six pieces in question are explicitly described as trios. Although Spitta refers to the *Six Keyboard and Violin Sonatas* BWV 1014–1019 as trios, Forkel does not.

6. They are for *Clavier*. Forkel refers to the violin sonatas as sonatas "for the Clavier with the accompaniment of a violin obligato." It is certainly conceivable that C. P. E. Bach simply dropped the violin from the description, and, on the other hand, if he is discussing the trio sonatas, then he dropped the mention of the two Claviers and pedal. Either way he is speaking quickly, as is clear from the rest of the tone of the letter, and in a form of short-hand. The rest of the music mentioned in the list, however, consists exclusively of "pedal pieces."

7. C. P. E. Bach probably wants this manuscript back. "Please take good care of them, since they are very tattered." P 271 was part of C. P. E. Bach's estate when he died, as were the violin sonatas.

Assuming that Bach cannot possibly be referring to vocal works or organ works based on chorale material, a brief tour of the rest of the Schmieder catalog produces only the following seven suspects that meet the first criterion: that they belong together in their numbered order.

Among the *Klavier* works:
 BWV 825–830 Sechs Partiten
 BWV 933–938 Sechs kleine Präludien
Among the *Kammermusik* works:
 BWV 1001–1006 Sechs Sonaten und Partiten für Violine allein
 BWV 1007–1012 Sechs Suiten für Violoncello allein
 BWV 1014–1019a Sechs Sonaten für Violine und Klavier
 BWV 1046–1051 Die Sechs Brandenburgischen Konzerte
And finally among the Organ works:
 BWV 525–530 Sechs Sonaten
 BWV 592–597 Sechs Konzerte nach verschiedenen Meistern

But when the other six criteria from C. P. E. Bach's letter to Forkel are applied, most of these can be eliminated. The *Sechs Partiten* (BWV 825–830) have no adagios. They are from the right time period, 1725, but they have no trio texture and so these can be dismissed. *Sechs kleine Präludien* (BWV 933–938) are from around 1720, and written for Clavier, but they obviously have no adagios either and are mostly written in two part texture. *Sech Sonaten une Partiten für Violine allein* (BWV 1001–1006) are for solo violin with no Clavier. *Sechs Suiten für Violoncello allein* (BWV 1007–1012) are pieces for solo cello with no Clavier, and there are no adagios either, because the pieces are suites of dance music. The *Sechs Brandenburgische Konzerte* (BWV 1046–1051) are obviously not Clavier pieces, nor are they trios, and equally easy to eliminate. *Sechs Konzerte nach verschiedenen Meistern* (BWV 592–597), are not by Bach.

It is clear why Clark, in his edition of C. P. E. Bach's letters, suggests *Sechs Sonaten für Violine und Klavier* (BWV 1014–1019a); seeing no other likely candidate among the Clavier works, he looked farther afield and found a possible candidate in the *Kammermusik* section. These pieces are numbered 1 to 6, were written around 1720, and contain some adagios. They might even be described as some of Bach's best work, as that is certainly a subjective comment on C. P. E. Bach's part. But what about the final two criteria?

However, C. P. E. Bach is discussing *trios* with Forkel. He says that of the eleven trios he is sending to Forkel for his perusal, six of them are numbered and belong together in order. Either trios have to have a consistent three voiced texture or they have to be written for three instruments. The *Sonatas for Violine und Klavier* are written for two instruments and the texture of the keyboard writing is rarely limited to two voices.

C. P. E. Bach clearly says these pieces he is sending Forkel are for *Clavier*. Does C. P. E. Bach used *Clavier* to be short-hand for "Clavier and Violin"? It is perhaps relevant that in a previous letter Bach had just complained bitterly to Forkel that he would love to write more complex *cantabile* pieces for Clavier but his public and his publisher were forcing him to turn out Clavier solos with obligato violin parts, which he clearly disapproves of. That doesn't mean to suggest that he couldn't have highly respected his father's work for Clavier and violin. It is simply worth noting that he currently had no great love for this combination of instruments.

And so we return to the *Trio Sonatas* (BWV 525–530). They are clearly numbered 1 to 6 in the surviving manuscript. They were written in 1723 or possibly 1727, making them, as noted earlier, about fifty years old when the letter was written. They contain some stunning adagios that are remarkably similar to the writing style which C. P. E. Bach himself considers to be good *cantabile* writing for the clavichord. They still enjoy a reputation as being among Bach's finest works for keyboard. They are clearly trios in the strictest sense of the word. They are three-part sonatas written consistently in three voices. Are they for *Clavier*? If we take C. P. E. Bach's word literally, they are for a keyboard instrument alone.

All in all, the trio sonatas fit C. P. E. Bach's first five clues very well. Clark's suggestion fits only four of the six. What about the final clue? If we accept that the trio sonatas are being discussed in this letter, then this is perhaps the moment when Forkel gets the idea in his head that these pieces are intended for pedal clavichord rather than organ. If only we had the letter after this one, the one that contained their discussion of the pieces once Forkel had received the shipment of manuscripts, we might be able to say something definitive.

A Final Thought

Finally, reading backwards in C. P. E. Bach's letters to Forkel, we come to Letter 66, written only six weeks before Letter 71, on 26 August, 1774. In it, together with a shipment of musical scores to Forkel, Bach also comments: "Nearly a dozen trios by J. S. and several more pedal pieces by him are available."[56] The original German reads: "Beynähe ein Dutzend Trii von J.S: u. noch einige Pedalstücke von ihm stehen zu Dienste."[57] It is difficult to doubt that these were the same pieces that were sent in the next shipment with letter 71: "namely 11 trios, 3 pedal pieces, and Vom Himmel hoch etc."[58] What can we infer from "and several more (*und noch einige*) pedal pieces"? It cannot be excluded that Bach used the phrase in the sense of "and several more pieces that are also for obligato pedal."

If one is to argue that *Clavier* means something other than clavichord in the context of Letter 71, one has to explain why C. P. E. Bach wrote a "Farewell to my Silbermann Clavier" which was a clavichord, and why he so often equates the concept of *cantabile* with the experience of playing the clavichord in his keyboard treatise. The possibility exists that in Letter 71, C. P. E. Bach is discussing the *Trio Sonatas*, referred to in a letter six weeks earlier, not as organ pieces but as "pedal pieces."

But in the end, this argument breaks no new ground either, because, clearly the Sonatas were also organ music. Only experiential work with the pedal clavichord could shed new light on whether the instrument itself has something phenomenologically relevant to bring to the trio sonatas *and* their performance at the organ. And the only way to do that was to build a copy of a pedal clavichord. The following chapter discusses the process of building that copy.

3

Reconstructing the Gerstenberg Pedal Clavichord

Some say that if a soundboard is not installed at dawn, when the sun rises, it will not sound as well as others.

—Jakob Adlung

Introduction

Not one of the surviving historical pedal clavichords is in its original playing condition, making it necessary to build a copy of one of them in order to learn about how it might have worked when it was new. Focusing on the Bach family and *Clavier* technique made the Johann David Gerstenberg (1716–96) pedal clavichord in the Leipzig collection the only logical choice.[1] Of the surviving instruments, documented in chapter 1, his is the only one with two manuals and an independent pedal, making it possible to play Bach's trio sonatas on it. Also, the Gerstenberg is representative of the tradition around Leipzig: he was a clavichord and organbuilder in Geringswalde, in Saxony. The instrument probably dates from 1766[2] and is also very similar in design to the single-manual clavichord by Christian Gottfried Friederici (1714–77) of Gera in the Leipzig collection, built in 1765.[3] The Friederici family produced some of C. P. E. Bach's favorite clavichords. He owned one at the time of his death, on which he had composed most of his Hamburg keyboard works.[4] C. P. E. Bach wrote to Forkel that the Friederici clavichords had a great advantage over the Barthold Fritz and Johann Adolph Hass clavichords because the action was better, and because they did not have the four-foot octave strings in the bass, which he "couldn't stand."[5] This instrument was built by Christian Gottfried's brother Christian Ernst Friederici (1709–80), who was also an organbuilder. The brothers worked together closely, and it must be assumed that their instrument building styles were similar. So by sheer good luck both the Gerstenberg and the Friederici clavichords survive in the same collection, and it is possible to state with some certainty that C. P. E. Bach would have approved of the Gerstenberg clavichord because it is so similar in design to the Friederici.

How close would J. S. Bach's clavichord have been to these instruments from the 1760s? There is still speculation about whether J. S. Bach could have owned an unfretted instrument, because we do not have any example from his lifetime, but the Friederici brothers were only about 20 years younger than the senior Bach and the instrument preserved in Leipzig is a mature design, not an experiment.

An unfretted instrument has a pair of strings for each note on the keyboard and can play overlapping legato between any two notes, whereas on a fretted instrument, the same pair of strings may be used to produce two or more notes. The tangents strike the strings in different places, just like fingers on the fretboard of a guitar, creating a different sounding length, and consequently a different pitch. Because the same pair of strings cannot sound more than one note simultaneously, there are places in the *Well Tempered Clavier* that are very difficult to play on a fretted clavichord, hence the debate about what kind of instrument J. S. Bach might have had.

Even though large unfretted clavichords were being built in Hamburg at least by the 1720s,[6] there are no surviving unfretted instruments for the same period around Weimar and Leipzig. Faced with an unsolvable problem, one can only speculate that the Gerstenberg is probably closer to J. S. Bach's local clavichord instrument-building tradition than the Hamburg instruments, even if the latter are closer to him in time. One can at least cite the early unfretted Hamburg tradition as proof that the possibility of an unfretted instrument in J. S. Bach's home cannot be excluded. In Part Two, the investigation of the Clavier technique texts related to Bach will depend, in any event, more on the touch characteristics of the instrument than on its fretting pattern.

The Parts of the Gerstenberg Pedal Clavichord

The Gerstenberg pedal clavichord has two independent unfretted manual clavichords (both C–e³) that fit into a box like a chest of drawers (the original box was lost during the war), resting on an independent pedal instrument that stands on three legs connected to each other with runners and wedges. The pedal instrument is also unfretted with a compass of C–c¹ and has two 16' and two 8' strings per key. The keys in the pedal instrument have organ trackers that hang from them and connect to the back ends of the keys in the pedalboard below (see figure 3.1).

My first copy, built in Edinburgh in 1994 under the guidance of John Barnes, is now at the School of Music at Göteborg University. John Barnes, Curator Emeritus of the Russell Collection of keyboard instruments at the University of Edinburgh, was a pioneer historical keyboard instrument builder and researcher, and was invaluable to the vision and realization of this project. In three separate study trips to Leipzig, twice by myself and once with John

Barnes, we documented the three separate instruments and the related case parts that make up the pedal clavichord and also the single Friederici clavichord. The original instrument was documented by Hubert Henkel.[7] A few comments to add about our own study of the instrument follow.

Interior Case Construction

Using a boroscope to look under the soundboard, I could establish that the lower manual has a downward-slanting bar wedged from the bass end of the wrestplank to the center of the bellyrail (see figure 3.2).

This bar follows the angle of the string band and is evidently meant to counteract the tendency of clavichord cases to twist. This construction method was also identified at the same time to be a design feature of the C. G. Friederici clavichord of 1765. Because the wrestplank of the lower manual is, as Henkel describes, on small pylons like a bridge,[8] the entire air cavity under the soundboard is active. There is no mousehole in the bellyrail of the upper manual so it was not possible to look under the upper manual soundboard.

A Mysterious Hole

There is a rectangular hole in the front of the pedal case above the 8' bellyrail and just to the right of the pedal keys. It is noticeable in the photograph dating from the Heyer Collection and is therefore probably original (see figure 3.3). On close examination it could be seen to have been expertly cut on two sides. A scribe line running up onto the molding on the right hand side probably marked the original width of the hole. It had been enlarged to the right of this scribe line competently but with less care.

We were forced to accept it as original and to conclude that it had some importance since it needed to be enlarged during the period when the instrument was in use. It seemed most likely that the hole was cut for a register knob, probably operating a means of silencing the 16' strings so that the 8' strings could be played alone. The mechanism for damping the 16' strings must have been simple, because we could find no trace of it except some lines of wear on the soundboard molding just behind the hole. The hole is in the perfect position for the stop knob to be operated by the player with ease while seated at the bench.

John Barnes designed a mechanism for silencing the 16' strings by means of a stop knob positioned according to the hole we had found, shown in figure 3.4. When the stop knob is pulled out, the 16' strings strings sound unimpaired, and when the knob is in, the sound from the 16' strings is completely absent except for a small transient which blends with the 8' sound.

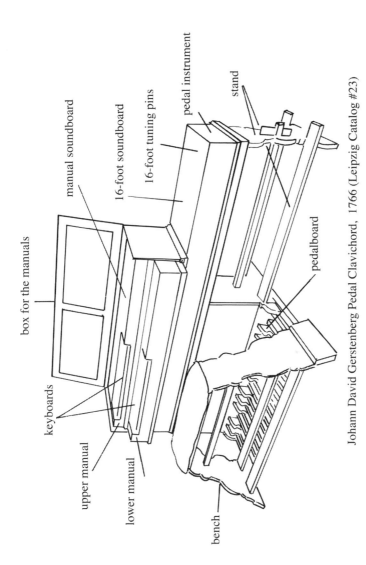

box for the manuals

manual soundboard

16-foot soundboard

16-foot tuning pins

pedal instrument

stand

keyboards

upper manual

lower manual

bench

pedalboard

Johann David Gerstenberg Pedal Clavichord, 1766 (Leipzig Catalog #23)

Figure 3.1a. The parts of the Gerstenberg Pedal Clavichord.

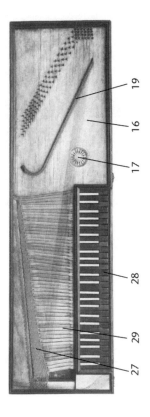

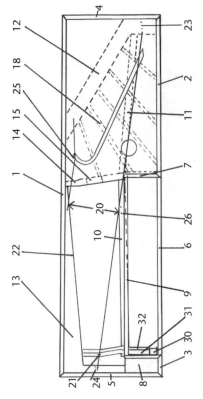

Figure 3.1b. The parts of the manual.

Manual:

Case: 1. back; 2. right front side; 3. left front side; 4. treble side; 5. bass side; 6. keyboard well; 7. key cheek; 8. toolbox; 9. nameboard; 10. balance rail; 11. cross-brace; 12. wrestplank; 13. hitchpin rail; 14. bellyrail; 15. mousehole.

Action: 16. soundboard; 17. soundboard rose; 18. soundboard ribs; 19. bridge; 20. stringband; 21. tangent; 22. rack; 23. tuning pins; 24. hitchpins; 25. bridge pins; 26 balance pins; 27. listing cloth; 28. keyboard; 29. keylever; 30. key head; 31. key tail; 32. sharp.

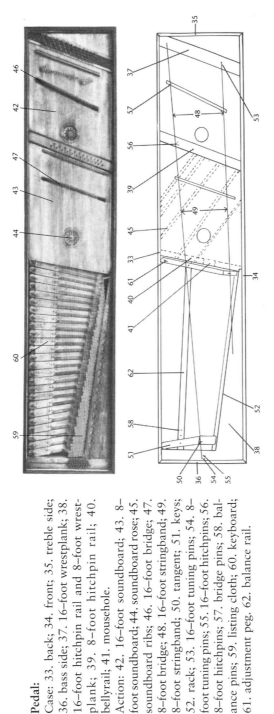

Figure 3.1c. The parts of the pedal.

Pedal:

Case: 33. back; 34. front; 35. treble side; 36. bass side; 37. 16–foot wrestplank; 38. 16–foot hitchpin rail and 8–foot wrestplank; 39. 8–foot hitchpin rail; 40. bellyrail; 41. mousehole.

Action: 42. 16–foot soundboard; 43. 8–foot soundboard; 44. soundboard rose; 45. soundboard ribs; 46. 16–foot bridge; 47. 8–foot bridge; 48. 16–foot stringband; 49. 8–foot stringband; 50. tangent; 51. keys; 52. rack; 53. 16–foot tuning pins; 54. 8–foot tuning pins; 55. 16–foot hitchpins; 56. 8–foot hitchpins; 57. bridge pins; 58. balance pins; 59. listing cloth; 60. keyboard; 61. adjustment peg. 62. balance rail.

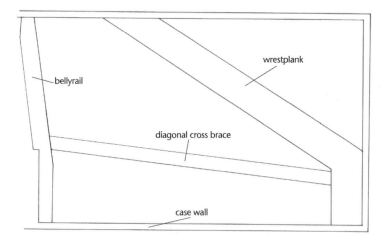

Figure 3.2. The lower manual soundboard well with cross-brace.

In our copy the only major change made from the original design was to add c♯^{1} and d^1 in the pedal in order to make it possible to play all of J. S. Bach's trio sonatas. There is ample room in the pedal design, and it was possible to add eight strings in the treble without changing the scaling of the rest of the instrument.

Clavichord Design

Because the Gerstenberg is really three separate instruments, all built at the same time by the same builder, it offers an unusual opportunity to study a

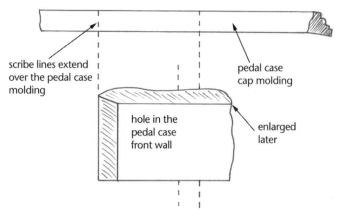

Figure 3.3. A mysterious hole.

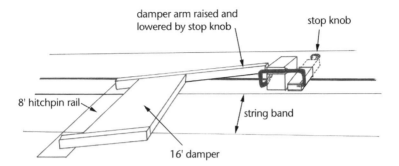

Figure 3.4. 16–foot stop mechanism.

builder's working methods. How was it designed? How was the pedal adapted from the manual design? What unit of measure did Gerstenberg use? There were many different local foot measurements in Germany in the eighteenth century. The Gerstenberg was built using the Leipzig foot, where 1 inch = 26.240mm.[9] In Leipzig inches, for instance, some of thedesign choices become clear. The pedal instrument is exactly two inches wider and two inches higher than the lower manual, and the upper manual case has a height to width ratio of 4 inches to 16 inches (1:4). But these kinds of proportions don't really tell us how the instrument was designed in the first place. Stephen Birkett and William Jurgenson suggest that instruments in this period were designed geometrically, using a language of basic proportions like the square root of 2, the square root of 5, and the golden section. These can all easily be derived from a single modular unit that didn't *necessarily* have to be the local foot measure.[10]

The first task was to find if there was a modular unit from which the rest of the instrument could be generated geometrically, and it turned out to be the width of the stringband, that is, the width of all of the strings on the clavichord measured perpendicularly to themselves. The manual stringband is exactly 8 Leipzig inches wide, while the pedal stringband is exactly 9. Gerstenberg might simply have doubled this modular unit to determine the width of both the manual and the pedal cases. The placement of the treble end of the keyboard could have been designed using the golden section of the case side (0.618 x 16 inches), and the most important diagonal line that determines the rack guiding the backs of the keys could have been drawn with a simple construction using the square root of five of the case side (2.236 x 16 inches; see figure 3.5).

Variations on the same simple geometrical constructions can explain the placement of all of the major pieces of the pedal instrument as well, providing confirmation that the entire instrument could have been designed geometrically in a way that could be taught easily and reproduced accurately.[11]

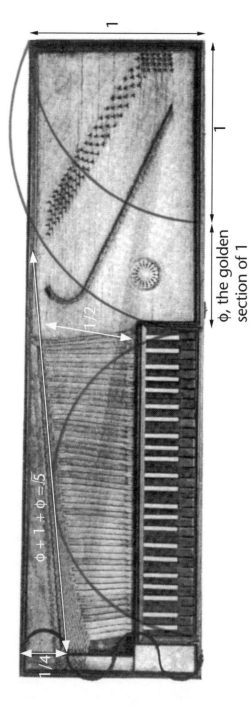

Figure 3.5. Gerstenberg manual with the golden section and square root of five construction lines.

Clavichord Stringing

The most important aspect of reconstructing the Gerstenberg was the question of how to string it. The exact tensions for the strings of a historical clavichord are very difficult to determine from written historical evidence, and, because their tension depends on the pitch to which they are tuned, they are also impossible to guess exactly from historical models. Of all historical keyboard instruments, this is a problem unique to the clavichord, because the tension of the strings determines how the instrument can be played. C. P. E. Bach said:

> Taut strings keep the tone of a vibrato pure; yet they should not be too taut or they will sound strained and the performer will be unable to achieve any volume; on the other hand, if they are too loose, they will sound impure and unclear if they sound at all.[12]

His comment, however, is descriptive rather than prescriptive. Rather than giving the correct string tensions in numbers, Bach describes the process for finding the right tension for the strings. It is practical for Bach to give this kind of process-oriented description, because these instruments were most likely built proportionally, and every clavichord builder's work might need slightly different stringing to produce the same touch. A description like this, however, is really practical only for the eighteenth-century player who was already acquainted with what that touch was supposed to be.

There is some evidence that even C. P. E. Bach found proper string tensions for a clavichord difficult to explain clearly. He added the comment that taut strings keep a vibrato pure in a footnote in the 1787 edition of the *Versuch*.[13] The original German 1753 edition reads:

> in einem Falle die Sayten überschreien und der Spieler kan seine Stärcke nicht brauchen; im andern Falle wird es entweder gar nicht oder unrein und undeutlich ansprechen.[14]

The 1949 English translation, above, also leaves out the important concept that it is the player's own "Stärcke" that needs to be allowed to work. A new translation might be:

> in the first case, the strings will "over-screech" and the player cannot apply any force; in the other case they will either sound not at all, or the attack will speak uncleanly and unclearly.

Überschreien is an archaic German word, but an intuitively descriptive one. There is an acceptable range of string tension somewhere in between these two phenomena that allows the player to apply some force to the strings but where the strings are not so tight that the tangents only bounce back from them and make an unclean sound.

It is clear from the original German that it is the *player* who needs to be able to apply differing degrees of "force" to the instrument, not the strings that passively "achieve . . . volume," and it is important not to leave this concept out of the description in English, because it will be an important clue about appropriate technique in Part Two.

Force is probably a good translation of *Stärcke* in this context. When talking about the same issue of string tensions at the clavichord, instead of *Stärcke,* Jakob Adlung even uses the word *Force,* set in Latin typeface to indicate that it is being used as a foreign word in German: "Denn man kann das forte und piano darauf einigermaaßen haben durch die *Force* des Spielers."[15] This can be translated: "Then one can have, to some extent, the forte and piano through the player's *Force.*"

The tension of the strings limits the kinds of technique that can be applied to the clavichord. If the strings are too loose, in order to keep from actually playing out of tune, the only technique possible is to hold the natural weight of the arm off the keyboard and play with the fingers only. If the strings are too tight, it is impossible to play even with the natural weight of the arm. Taking our cue from C. P. E. Bach, a scale representing the relation between technique and string tension at the clavichord might look like that shown in figure 3.6.

Figure 3.6. String tension's relationship to technique.

Historical descriptions of technique, such as Griepenkerl's in the Appendix of this book, make it clear that both finger-based and natural weight-based techniques were in common use. Both extreme ends of the scale shown in figure 3.6 can be eliminated as historical possibilities, because they decide conclusively *for* the player what technique is possible. Also, the loosest possible stringing produces a very impure sound, and the tightest possible stringing stretches strings so close to their breaking point that one spends more time replacing strings than playing.

Beyond that, the range of options on this scale that the historical tradition (or traditions) actually occupied cannot be determined exactly. Even with the correct historical string gauges and using the proper density of string material, there is still the question of pitch. Tuning an instrument up just a half a step increases the hardness of touch by 12 percent.[16] Since information about exact local pitch standards in the eighteenth century is difficult to find, this most important parameter for technique at the clavichord also presents some of the most difficult problems. It has been suggested by John Koster[17] that late-eighteenth-century German clavichords with a c^2 speaking length of about 250 to 275 mm long were probably strung in brass and also approximately tuned to chamber pitch, $a^1 = 415$ Hz, commonly referred to as *Kammerton*. The longer scalings based on c^2 of approximately 290 mm, commonly found on Scandinavian clavichords, seem to have been for lower density and longer-length iron strings, also tuned to *Kammerton*. The Gerstenberg has a c^2 speaking length of 275 mm and seems to fall easily within the South German brass-strung *Kammerton* tradition. At the Yale meeting of the American Bach Society in 1998, Koster presented a paper on keyboard instruments surrounding the Bach family in which he argued that the Gerstenberg could also have been strung in iron at the higher *Chorton* pitch, to agree with the normal pitch of Thuringian organs. Its extant set of strings are iron, but that is no guarantee that the original strings were.

The Gerstenberg may very well have been an iron-strung instrument, but the pitch of *Chorton* organs might not have been the only determining factor. Seventeenth- and eighteenth-century church musicians would have been used to hearing music at different pitch levels. The Schnitger organ at Hamburg St. Jacobi, for instance, had one stop in the *Hauptwerk,* a Gedackt 8-foot that was tuned to *Kammerton* pitch so that it could be used to accompany low-pitch instruments in the balcony. In central Germany the presence of one or two *Kammerton* registers or whole organs tuned in *Kammerton* was not unusual—for example, in Dresden and Merseburg.[18]

It seems more likely that whatever the absolute pitch, performers were more concerned that the practice clavichords were musically inspiring to play and, perhaps, replicated the action of the organ as much as possible. Jakob Adlung suggests that a deeper key movement at the clavichord would allow students to transfer technique more easily to the organ[19] but mentions nowhere the importance of coordinating the pitch levels of practice and performance instrument.

Many other factors go into determining the player's experience of the hardness of touch at the clavichord, but most of these can be controlled through careful copying of an historical model.[20] Some of the most important parameters are: the correct balance point in a key, the amount of mass of the key itself, the distance between the top of the tangent and the strings, and the so-called "after-length" of the string—the distance between the point where the tangent strikes the string and the string's left-hand end. The kind of material used for the listing cloth and how tightly it is woven between the strings also directly affects the player's perception of hardness of touch, but as it is so easily redone or replaced, it is considered one of the instrument's *ephemera*, that is, material that disappears from an instrument through use or over time.

Edinburgh Stringing

It was not possible to construct a complete stringing schedule for the Gerstenberg manuals based on information from the original instrument. There are only nine gauge numbers in total for both keyboards. Four of them are possibly original, according to Hubert Henkel. The other five, all in the bass, are clearly non-original.[21] Many keys of the original manuals have been replaced over the years, so the record is incomplete, and it has to be questioned how Henkel could be sure of the originality of any of the numbers. With an incomplete picture of the original stringing schedule from the historical model, we needed to find other references to design a stringing schedule for the copy.

A clavichord stringing theory developed in Edinburgh by Grant O'Brien and Lance Whitehead grew out of a study of the harpsichords and clavichords of the Hamburg Hass family. This study strongly suggests that the Hass family clavichord stringing practice was exactly like their harpsichord stringing practice. Although a logical possibility, there had been no previous evidence for it. They have identified three Hass clavichords whose 4' strings in the bass change from brass to iron where harpsichords from the same tradition also change from brass to iron: when the scalings exceed about 288 mm. Other contemporary Hamburg clavichords, like the Gerlach instrument cited in table 3.1, confirm that the Hass stringing tradition was not unique to the family. O'Brien argues that this high-tension stringing practice was carried on unchanged by the Hass family for many years, indicating that the customers for these instruments did not find them unusually difficult to play.[22]

In addition, the 1785 Gottfried Joseph Horn clavichord has a complete set of gauge numbers written on the keylevers and represents a very close link to the Friederici/Gerstenberg tradition.[23] Horn was a student of Friederici, and it can be assumed that the Horn gauge numbers represent the stringing tradition of the master. John Barnes designed a stringing scale for his copy of the Friederici in 1991 using the tensions of the Hamburg Hass tradition as a guide and the Horn gauge numbers as direct references, adjusting the string gauges for the slightly longer scaling of the Friederici. Because of the many design similarities between the Friederici and Gerstenberg instruments, the Barnes stringing schedule was taken directly over to the manuals of the Gerstenberg. Table 3.1 compares the string thicknesses of two reference instruments from the Hamburg school and the gauge numbers, plus theoretical thicknesses for the Horn instrument in Leipzig, with the schedule created by Barnes for the Gerstenberg. The Hamburg instruments have c^2 scalings of 288 mm and the Horn has a slightly shorter scaling than the Gerstenberg and Friederici, $c^2 = 256$ mm, compared to 272 mm for Friederici and 276 mm for Gerstenberg.

O'Brien cites the advantages of applying the historically correct Hass stringing to other clavichords:

- pitch stability—heavy taut strings resist the pressure of the player's fingers and are harder to put out of tune
- greater dynamic range—because the strings do not go out of tune, a greater amount of force can be used to extend the forte range of the instrument
- greater volume—thicker strings are louder strings because the sound produced by a string increases at the fourth power of the string diameter[24]

He concludes with a challenge to both players and builders to experiment with these higher string tensions and resist the urge to be put off by the initial higher level of technical difficulty that they create. Barnes's stringing places the Gerstenberg somewhere to the right of the middle point of the scale (see figure 3.7), into territory where a weightier technique is absolutely necessary in order to produce a good sound at the instrument, where, as C. P. E. Bach recommends, the strings are tight enough that it is possible to attack them and not put them out of tune, but still loose enough that they can be caressed.[25]

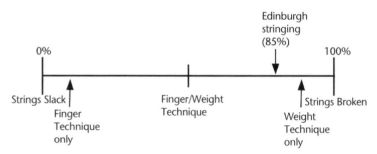

Figure 3.7. Edinburgh stringing on a string-tension scale.

The jury is still out as to how far to the right on this scale it is possible to move. Hardness of touch will remain, to some extent, a matter of personal taste and may be directly related to the natural amount of mass the player has in his or her arm, but the attempt has been to confine the Gerstenberg copy's pitch and stringing within the narrowest possible frame that can be historically determined, based on the well-documented Hass tradition and the Horn clavichord. String tension is the single most valuable parameter for the technique discussion in Part Two of this book.

Source Studies

Table 3.1. Comparison of the plain string gauges of three eighteenth-century clavichords with the Gerstenberg copy.

	1756 Gerlach	1763 Hass	1785 Horn[1]	1994 J. Barnes
g^3			0.283	
$f\sharp^3$				
f^3	0.284	0.254		
e^3				0.27
$d\sharp^3$		0.254		
d^3	0.284	0.284		0.27
$c\sharp$				0.30
c^3				
b^2			0.283	
$b\flat^2$			0.298	
a^2				
$g\sharp^2$				0.30
g^2				0.33
$f\sharp^2$				
f^2			0.298	
e^2			0.314	
$d\sharp^2$				
d^2				
$c\sharp^2$			0.314	0.33
c^2	0.284	0.284	0.331	0.36
b^1	0.318	0.318		
$b\sharp^1$				
a^1				
$g\sharp^1$			0.331	
g^1			0.349	
$f\sharp^1$				
f^1			0.349	
e^1			0.367	0.36
$d\sharp^1$				0.40
d^1			0.367	
$c\sharp^1$			0.387	
c^1	0.318	0.318	0.387	
b	0.355	0.355	0.407	0.40
$b\flat$			0.407	0.44
a			0.429	
$g\sharp$			0.429	
g			0.452	
$f\sharp$			0.452	0.44
f	0.355	0.355	0.476	0.48
e	0.397	0.397	0.476	
$d\sharp$			0.501	0.48
d			0.501	0.52
$c\sharp$			0.528	0.52

[1]From an unpublished manuscript by John Barnes, "Bass covered strings in clavichords by G. J. Horn 1785 and J. P. Krämer 1803" (February 1998), 3. Barnes uses O'Brien's information about string gauges, presented in *De Clavicordio I*, (1993), 129, to extrapolate numbers for the half gauge values on the Horn clavichord. "The . . . diameters are a compromise between columns two and three [of O'Brien's table in *De Clavicordio*] and are extrapolated at each end to cover all the gauges used on the Horn and Krämer clavichords."

Clavichord Soundboards

The Gerstenberg clavichord has four separate soundboards, two separate manuals and two in the pedal, all prepared by the same builder. A soundboard's thinning pattern is one of the most important design factors of a stringed-keyboard instrument, but historical descriptions of soundboard preparation such as Jakob Adlung's "It is customary to make the soundboard somewhat thicker in the bass, for the sake of sonorousness"[26] are process-oriented: interesting but impossible to copy exactly. They do, however, some-times serve the important function of alerting us to issues of which we were unaware. For instance, Adlung also mentions in passing that a clavichord may turn out to be unsuccessful because the sound post is in slightly the wrong place.[27] We would not otherwise even know that experimenting with sound posts under clavichord soundboards was a possibility. He adds, "Some say that if a soundboard is not installed at dawn, when the sun rises, it will not sound as well as others," and, although he himself dismisses "such astrological opinions,"[28] it gives us a glimpse of the mystery instrument builders created around soundboard preparation, surely in part to please their customers. They might, however, simply have been taking advantage of the daily cycle of relative humidity in the workshop. It is possible that what they hid from their customers were the true tricks of the trade. Per-haps not much is written about soundboard preparation because the gen-erative ideas behind the work were hard-earned secrets passed on from master to apprentice within the traditional guild mentality of seventeenth- and eighteenth-century Northern Europe. The Gerstenberg provided a unique opportunity to compare several soundboards that were produced by the same builder at the same time. A simple rubbing test on the surface of the soundboard produced a coherent pattern of pitches that suggests that clavichord soundboards may have been tuned the way guitars and violins were tap-tuned.[29] These pitches were defined by rubbing gently on the surface of the soundboard at various points and comparing the pitches produced. Rubbing works better than tapping on the soundboard, as the latter introduces too much energy into the soundboard and one hears too many areas of it at once. Both manual soundboards of the Gerstenberg have exactly the same pitch relationships between the areas around the bass and treble ends of the bridges. These areas are, in both cases, a minor third apart. The minor third was often used historically in tuning bells, so the concept of the minor third tuned in the material of an instrument would not have been foreign to the eighteenth-century mind.[30] The minor third seems to naturally promote complexity of overtone production, possibly because the interval is so high in the overtone series. It does not appear until the eighteenth overtone above the fundamental, long after overtones corresponding to most of the other harmonic intervals—the octave, the fifth, the major third, the major seventh, the second, and so on. Even when it does appear, it is slightly narrow, precisely speaking, a 48/57 integer proportion with the fundamental rather than a pure 5/6 minor third.[31] In this chapter we have seen that the stringing for the Gerstenberg pedal clavichord copy was designed within the frame of the Hamburg clavichord stringing tradition, using the Horn instrument in the Leipzig collection as a southern German reference because of its close relationship to the Friederici/ Gerstenberg building tradition. There is a closer relationship between string tension and technique on the clavichord than on any other stringed keyboard instrument. The perception of hardness of touch on a clavichord is affected by many factors. Even the quality of the sound has a psychological influence on our perception of its hardness of touch. An instrument was built purposefully tuning the soundboard to a pure fifth between the treble and bass ends instead of a minor third that strengthened the fundamental and lowest overtones and damped many of the higher overtones. Even though the stringing schedule and the keyboard were the same, the general impression of this experimental instrument from many players who tried it was that it was more difficult to play and that the touch was harder. This must have been a psychological reaction; players were not noticing that they were subconsciously working harder to produce the sound response they were used to from other instruments that produced a wider range of overtone response in the sound. This suggests that the quality of the soundboard must also be critical to the performer's experience of the instrument's touch.

4

J. S. Bach and the Clavichord: A Reception History of a Technique

Keyboardists can be heard, who after torturous trouble have finally learned how to make their instrument sound loathsome to an enlightened listener. Their playing lacks roundness, clarity, forthrightness, and in their stead one hears only hacking, thumping, and stumbling.

—C. P. E. Bach

Bach's Clavichord Technique

In this chapter, as in chapter 2, reception history is used as a tool to follow the reception of an abstract concept (rather than reception of a "musical work") through time. Was the clavichord central to J. S. Bach's technique and, if so, how? There are many good modern surveys of keyboard technique,[1] and many treatises dating from the late Baroque.[2] Some of them will be discussed here, but many of them will not, because our focus is on the immediate Bach family and instruments as close to that family as possible. Of all of Bach's children C. P. E. Bach was the great proponent of the clavichord, not only in his own writings but also in accounts of his contemporaries. Johann Friedrich Reichardt wrote about C. P. E. Bach in 1774:

> Bach's manner of playing would not have been devised without the clavichord, and he devised it only for the clavichord. But he who once masters this instrument plays the harpsichord quite differently from those who never touch a clavichord.[3]

Bachs Spielart konnte ohne Clavier gar nicht erfunden werden, und er hat sie auch nur fürs Clavier erfunden: derjenige aber, der diese einmal inne hat, der spielt auch ganz anders den Flügel, als jener, der nie ein Clavier berühret.[4]

It is clear from the context in Reichardt's original letter that "Clavier" refers to the clavichord. The prceding sentence reads: "Die Italiäner haben nie das Clavier bey sich im Gebrauch gehabt, sondern bedienen sich allein des Flügels" (The Italians have never used the clavichord, but rather use only the harpsichord).[5] The wing-shaped harpsichord, the Flügel, was more popular than the clavichord in eighteenth-century Italy, although he exaggerates when he says the clavichord never existed there. According to Reichardt, C. P. E. Bach's technique is closely related to the clavichord. The question remains whether his father's was equally closely related.

The problem is that J. S. Bach himself recorded nothing about his philosophy of technique. Reichardt's statement postdates J. S. Bach by a quarter century and coincides with a documented late blooming of the clavichord as a serious performance instrument and a symbol of the whole *Empfindsamkeit* period. Because this technique chain is missing its first link (information directly from J. S. Bach himself), there is a great deal of debate about the next links in the chain of information from musicians such as Reichardt, C. P. E. Bach, and Forkel. Did Forkel and his generation inflate the importance of the role that the clavichord played for J. S. Bach in order to justify their own passion for the instrument? Lack of written evidence from J. S. Bach himself cannot completely be equated with proof of a negative, and it is just as logical to assume in the absence of evidence that J. S. Bach's biographer, students, and children developed their passion for the clavichord *because* of the Master rather than *despite* him. What can be documented in the secondary literature is how the reception of Bach's technique changes over time, especially after the historical clavichord itself has disappeared.

The Bach Technique Thread

Information about Bach's technique is transmitted in three texts: Carl Philipp Emanuel Bach's *Versuch über die wahre Art das Clavier zu Spielen* (1753), Johann Nikolaus Forkel's *Ueber Johann Sebastian Bach's Leben, Kunst und Kunstwerke* (1802), and comments written by Friederich Conrad Griepenkerl for the first published edition of Johann Sebastian Bach's *Chromatische Fantasia und Fuga* (1819). The first two texts are widely known to modern readers. Quentin Faulkner's *J. S. Bach's Keyboard Technique* remains the major modern source for information.[6] In his introduction, Faulkner argues for an intrinsic approach to the information presented by C. P. E. Bach and Forkel:

> Yet, we ask, in the more objective reporting on matters of *technique* what can we trust more? Surely not the ideas of Bach's contemporaries, most of whom never had anything to do with him. If we slight or dismiss the information on technique provided us by C. P. E. Bach and by Forkel (especially when all the relevant sources are in solid agreement about that information), what are we to substitute for it? Only our own opinions, which are likely to be far more speculative and arbitrary than their reports.[7]

And yet Faulkner's study does not explore any of the phenomena of the high-tension historical clavichord. It confines itself to "matters about which, through musical and literary evidence, it is possible to ascertain enough to remove them to some extent from the realm of speculation."[8]

The Griepenkerl text was rediscovered in 1983 by Ewald Kooiman[9] and translated into English with commentary in 1988 by Quentin Faulkner.[10] It has since formed the central work of a 1991 dissertation by Kaestner D. Robertson on weight-transference technique in piano playing[11] and has been preliminarily discussed at the 1997 Magnano Clavichord Symposium.[12] All of keyboard technique discussion has a consistent element running through it that is unbounded by time: the physiology of the human body. There are only so many ways to depress a key, and there are only so many ways to use the body at a musical instrument *efficiently*, and those ways are codified and taught as a living language. Keyboard instruments went through radical and fundamental changes in the nineteenth century, but the body, of course, changes far less. Most of us are taller than the average person in the eighteenth century, but as discussed in the introduction, we still have the tendons of our third and fourth fingers joined. The thread of this discussion of technique covers three generations in only a little more than half a century, but this small time span also coincides with the death of the four-hundred-year-old European clavichord tradition and the development of the modern piano. This brief period witnessed the single largest change in the six-hundred-year history of keyboard instruments, and as the phenomena of the keyboard instruments change, perceptions about previous published discussions of technique also necessarily change.

Johann Nikolaus Forkel (1749–1818)

Chapter 3 of Forkel's Bach biography is devoted to technique in three basic points. The original German follows the English text.

> According to Sebastian Bach's manner of placing the hand on the keys, the five fingers are bent, so that their points come into a strait [*sic*] line over the keys lying in a plane surface under them, in such a manner, that no single finger has to be drawn nearer, when it is wanted, but that every one is ready over the key which it may have to press down. From this manner of holding the hand it follows:

> Nach der Seb. Bachischen Art, die Hand auf dem Clavier zu halten, werden die fünf Finger so gebogen, daß die Spitzen derselben in eine gerade Linie kommen, die sodann auf die in einer Fläche neben einander liegenden Tasten so passen, daß kein einziger Finger bey vorkommenden Fällen erst näher herbey gezogen muß, sondern daß jeder über dem Tasten, den er etwa nieder drücken soll, schon schwebt. Mit dieser Lage der Hand ist nun verbunden:

. . . . .

1. That no finger must fall upon its key, or (as often happens) be thrown on it, but must be *placed* upon it with a certain consciousness of the internal power and command over the motion.

1) daß kein Finger auf seinen Tasten fallen, oder (wie es ebenfalls oft geschieht) geworfen, sondern nur mit einem gewissen Gefühl der innern Kraft und Herrschaft über die Bewegung getragen werden darf.

. . . . .

2. The impulse thus given to the keys, or the quantity of pressure, must be maintained in equal strength, and that in such a manner, that the finger be not raised perpendicularly from the key, but that it glide off the fore part of the key, by gradually drawing back the tip of the finger towards the palm of the hand.

2) Die so auf den Tasten getragene Kraft, oder das Maaß (sic) des Drucks muß in gleicher Stärke unterhalten werden, und zwar so, daß der Finger nicht gerade aufwärts vom Tasten gehoben wird, sondern durch ein allmähliches Zurückziehen der Fingerspitzen nach der innern Fläche der Hand, auf dem vordern Theil des Tasten abgleitet.

. . . . .

3. In the transition from one key to another, this gliding off causes the quantity of force or pressure, with which the first tone has been kept up, to be transferred, with the greatest rapidity, to the next finger, so that the two tones are neither disjoined from each other, nor blended together. The touch is, therefore, as C. Ph. Emanuel Bach says, neither too long nor too short, but just what it ought to be.

3) Beym Uebergange von einem Tasten zum andern wird durch dieses Abgleiten das Maß von Kraft oder Druck, womit der erste Ton unterhalten worden ist, in der größten Geschwindigkeit auf den nächsten Finger geworfen, so daß nun die beyden Töne weder von einander gerissen werden, noch in einander klingen können. Der Anschlag derselben ist also, wie C. Ph. Emanuel sagt, weder zu lang noch zu kurz, sondern genau so wie er seyn muß.

. . . . .

The advantages of such a position of the hand, and of such a touch, are very various, not only on the clavichord, but also on the pianoforte and the organ.[13]

Die Vortheile einer solchen Haltung der Hand und eines solchen Anschlags sind sehr mannigfaltig, nicht bloß auf dem Clavichord, sondern auch auf dem Pianoforte und auf der Orgel.[14]

Forkel's Point One

Everything that follows is dependent on beginning with a curved hand position. Point One shows that the technique does not involve the use of the finger alone. Forkel first describes two ways that a finger should not be used to attack a key at the clavichord. He uses neutral language to describe the first way, to let the finger "fall" on the key, which sounds like a natural finger technique. But when he describes the second way, he resorts to humor and a little invective when he describes "throwing the finger onto the key." Forkel uncannily describes the process I witness with many students in their first encounter with the pedal clavichord. First the student attempts to use a normal finger technique, where the individual finger falls onto the key; not enough mass or acceleration results in no sound at all. Then the student increases the speed of attack of the individual finger. This extra acceleration translates into enough extra force to make the contact between tangent and string necessary for sustained sound. But if this process of "throwing" the finger is repeated for every finger and every note, it starts to sound very quickly like C. P. E. Bach's description of "hacking, thumping and stumbling"[15] because the fingers are not equally strong at striking individually. Early twentieth-century revival clavichords often had thicker keylevers and lead weights in the backs of the keys to reduce the amount of work required of the performer, and lower string tensions to reduce the force necessary to set the strings vibrating effectively. These changes—all designed to make the initial phase of clavichord technique less challenging—radically alter many of the instrument's essential musical parameters: for example, the player's ability to produce a wide range of dynamics.

To remedy this, Forkel describes a process that leaves the work with the performer rather than the clavichord. The finger is *placed* upon the key. If neither the natural mass of the falling finger nor the artificial acceleration of the *thrown* finger is enough for Forkel's clavichord, the mass of the individual finger alone *placed* on the key certainly won't be enough. The finger is *placed* with "a quantity of pressure" that has to come from someplace other than the finger itself. The 1820 English translation reprinted above is remarkably accurate and fresh, yet there are some points that I would like to question for the purposes of this technique discussion. The translation says, for instance, that the finger is placed "with a certain consciousness of the internal power and command over the motion." This is a complicated concept but is further obscured in the English translation, that omits the term *getragen,* or "supported." From Point One:

mit einem gewissen Gefühl der innern Kraft und Herrschaft über die Bewegung getragen werden darf.
(Original German text)

with a certain consciousness of the internal power and command over the motion.
(1820 English translation)

may be supported over the [entire] movement with a certain sensitivity and mastery of the inner force.
(Author's translation)

The "consciousness of the internal power" does not *create* the movement—something that might be assumed from the 1820 English translation—because that would be a finger technique, which Forkel has just dismissed, but rather, the force or pressure is carried by the finger that has
already been placed on the key.

Forkel's Point Two

The German in Point Two confirms this sense of the internal force being
carried by the finger. Rather than giving an impulse to the keys, the German describes more accurately the interchangeability between force and
mass at the clavichord:

> Die so auf den Tasten getragene Kraft, oder das Maaß des Drucks muß in gleicher
> Stärke unterhalten werden.
> (Original German text)

> The impulse thus given to the keys, or the quantity of pressure must be main-
> tained in equal strength.
> (1820 English translation)

> The force or the mass of the downward pressure that is being borne on the key
> (by the finger) must be maintained in equal strength.
> (Author's translation)

Forkel's Point Three

Then Forkel goes on to describe how this quantity of force or pressure is
transferred from one key to the next by allowing the first finger to glide off
the front of the key until "with the greatest rapidity" the quantity of force
or pressure is automatically transferred to the next finger. Point Three contains the only information presented by Forkel that is completely absent
from C. P. E. Bach's *Versuch*. It could not be more clear to a clavichordist
that Forkel is speaking of a phenomenon particular to the clavichord, designed to promote good tone production and prolong the sounding of the
clavichord's strings. Forkel calls it a "quantity of force or pressure" that
needs to be "kept up" in order to maintain the tone. On no other keyboard
than the clavichord—at that time or since—does the mass applied to a key
need to be "kept up" as long as the note is to sound, except at the organ.
This, in my opinion, is why they are primarily related to one another as
practice and performance instrument. But the qualitative difference between
the clavichord and the organ can best be understood by experience. The
"quantity of force or pressure" maintained on a clavichord note directly
affects the sounding strings for the duration of the note, so if the amount of
pressure changes, the quality of the sound also changes. In contrast, the

pressure holding open a pallet at the organ at the bottom of a keystroke can halve or double, and the pipe sound, of course, will not change.

Forkel as Reception Historian

Forkel is also engaged in his own reception history, expressing concern about why C. P. E. Bach did not make his third point explicitly clear in the *Versuch*:

> I have often wondered that C. Ph. Emanuel Bach, in his "Essay on the True manner of Playing the Clavier," did not describe at length this highest degree of distinctness in the touch of that instrument, as he not only possessed it himself, but because in this consists one of the chief differences by which the Bachs' mode of playing on the clavier is distinguished from all others.[16]

> Ich habe mich oft gewundert, daß C. Ph. Emanuel in seinem Versuch über die wahre Art das Clavier zu spielen, diesen höchsten Grad von Deutlichkeit des Anschlags nicht ausführlich beschrieben hat, da er ihn doch nicht nur selbst hatte, sondern auch gerade hierin ein Hauptunterschied liegt, wodurch sich die Bachische Art das Clavier zu spielen, von jeder andern auszeichnet.[17]

Quentin Faulkner's reaction to this particular comment of Forkel's is enlightening but ultimately fails to consider the physical evidence of the clavichord itself:

> It is intriguing to speculate as to why the younger Bach did not transmit his father's instruction on this matter. It can hardly have been because he had forgotten it, especially considering that Forkel expressly states that Emanuel Bach practiced it. The only other possible conclusion is that C. P. E. Bach did not consider it of sufficient import or relevance to include in the *Versuch*. It is within the realm of credibility to conjecture that C. P. E. Bach's disregard of this principle arose from his almost exclusive cultivation of the clavichord and his neglect of the organ. This type of finger motion finds its greatest value in the control of the release of each note. And, Forkel's comments notwithstanding, the precise control of the release of a tone is far more crucial to organ technique than to that of stringed keyboard instruments. It is also possible, of course, that Emanuel Bach, recognizing the considerable effort necessary to master this technique, simply decided to omit mention of it for purely practical reasons, or perhaps it was even a sort of "trade secret" to be passed on to the initiated only by word of mouth. [18]

Although the final two possibilities that Faulkner offers are plausible, the concept that Forkel's third point is concerned with *releases* at the organ only seems less so. Faulkner begins with the assumption that Point Three describes the release of the *previous* note at the organ and is not concerned with the quality of the tone production of the *following* note at the clavichord. If Point Three is only about achieving slow releases, then Faulkner's argu-

ment for the organ follows logically. However the most control of the release of an organ key is achieved with a vertical movement of the finger,
which Forkel describes as something to avoid at the *Clavier.* If the finger
snaps too quickly off the front of an organ key, the pallet closes abruptly,
eliminating the subtle shadings that a musician can make at the end of a
pipe's speech when exercising full control over how it closes. So it seems we
have a real puzzle to solve. In Forkel's own words, the process described in
Point Three, where the releasing finger glides off the front of the key is *not*
meant to control the release of the previous note at all. Instead, he indicates
the releasing finger affects the way in which the *following* note is played:
the transference of the same "quantity of force or pressure" from the first
finger "with the greatest rapidity to the next finger."

The Twentieth-Century Reception of Forkel's Description

Both editions of *The Bach Reader* contain a footnote to Forkel's text that is
well worth a close look: "It should be noted that Forkel, while starting out
to give a description of keyboard technique in general, has now chiefly the
clavichord in mind."[19] A close reading of Forkel's chapter 3 in its entirety
suggests that there is no real justification for this statement. Nowhere in
this text has there been a sudden shift of gears from general to specific
keyboard instrument. The only justification for this comment seems to be
the modern orthodoxy that *Clavier* must mean general keyboard until
proven categorically otherwise, but this is as untenable as the opposite position: assuming that every historical reference to the clavier *must* mean
clavichord. The title of the chapter does not help matters. "Bach The
Clavier Player" is not Forkel's title. The titles were introduced by the
1820 English translation. Using the untranslated German term *Clavier*
suggests the English meaning of "general keyboard" rather than reflect-
ing the complexity and ambiguity of the original. Forkel for instance
demonstrably used clavier and clavichord interchangeably within a short
space in another place in the same chapter: "Zu solchen Künsten bediente
er sich zweyer Claviere und des Pedals, oder eines mit einem Pedal
versehenen Doppelflügels" ends one paragraph, and the next paragraph
begins with: "*Am liebsten spielte er auf dem Clavichord.*"[20] The first paragraph in question ends with the description of two different pedal instruments, the second of which is a pedal harpsichord, leaving no doubt that the
first description is "two [manual] clavichords and a pedal." The next paragraph uses the modern term *clavichord.* What are we to make of this? Depending on the context, Forkel does use the term *Clavier* to mean clavichord.

Sometimes, the absence of physical experience of an instrument can lead
directly to misinterpretation of texts. For instance, isn't the description at
the beginning of chapter 3 of Forkel's biography, naming specific phenom-

ena associated with this *Clavier*, proof enough that Forkel is discussing a clavichord? Let's assume for a moment that Forkel begins this chapter using the word *Clavier* in the specific sense of "clavichord" rather than the general sense of "keyboard," and re-read closely the description of phenomena in the proposition at the opening of the second paragraph:

> Wenn man von zehen gleich fertigen und geübten Spielern ein und eben dasselbe Stück spielen läßt, so wird es sich unter der Hand eines jeden anders ausnehmen. Jeder wird eine verschiedene Art des Tons aus dem Instrument ziehen. . . . Wovon kann diese verschiedene Ausnahme entstehen . . . ? Bloß von der Art des Anschlags.[21]

> If we hear the same piece played by ten equally skillful and practiced performers, it will produce, under the hand of each, a different effect. Each will draw from the instrument a different kind of tone. . . . Whence can this difference arise . . . ? Merely from the mode of touching the instrument.[22]

> If we get ten equally skillful and practiced players to perform one and the same piece, it will produce, under the hand of each, a different effect. Each will draw out of the instrument, a different kind of sound . . . where do these differences come from . . . ? Only from the art of attack.[23]

"The mode of touching the instrument" is a weak translation of the rhetorically powerful, "*Bloß von der Art des Anschlags.*" The alliteration of "Only from the art of attack" captures more of the rhetorical power of the original, although it too is problematical: "art" does not literally mean the same thing in English. But every clavichord player immediately recognizes the phenomenon described, where ten players each draw a "different kind of tone" out of the instrument. These different "kind of tones" rarely occur on the harpsichord or organ, because they are incapable of dynamic contrast in individual notes. At no other eighteenth-century keyboard instrument than the clavichord do players sound so completely different from one another, because not just the volume but the physical quality of the tone is dependent on the amount of mass applied to the key, and this mass is different for every arm. C. P. E. Bach does report that it is possible for different players to get different kinds of tone out of the same harpsichord. But Bach's example is used as an illustration of the importance of experiencing this phenomenon *first* at the clavichord, so it is not the harpsichord that produces a different color automatically for every performer, but the accomplished clavichordist who can also draw out a different color from the harpsichord:

> Those who concentrate on the harpsichord grow accustomed to playing in only one color, and the varied touch which the competent clavichordist brings to the harpsichord remains hidden from them. This may sound strange, since one would

think that all performers can express only one kind of tone on each harpsichord. To test its truth ask two people, one a good clavichordist, the other a harpsichordist, to play on the latter's instrument the same piece containing varied embellishment, and then decide whether both have produced the same effect.[24]

Spielt man beständig auf dem Flügel, so gewöhnt man sich an in einer Farbe zu spielen, und der unterschiedene Anschlag, welchen bloß ein guter Clavichord-Spieler auf dem Flügel herausbringen kan, bleibt verborgen, so wunderbahr es auch scheint, indem man glauben solte, alle Finger müsten auf einerley Flügel einerley Ton herausbringen. Man kan gar leicht die Probe machen, und zwey Persohnen, wovon dereine ein gutes Clavichord spielt, der andere aber bloß ein Flügel-Spieler ist, auf diesem letzten Instrumente ein Stück mit einerley Manieren kurtz hinter einander spielen lassen, und hernach urtheilen, ob sie beyde einerley Würckung hervorgebracht haben.[25]

Friederich Conrad Griepenkerl (1782–1849)

Griepenkerl is remembered for providing us with the first critical edition of J. S. Bach's organ works in 1844. Nearly a century after Bach's death, Griepenkerl seems very far removed in time from Bach. However, the line of transmission of information among these three generations of writers could not be clearer. Forkel's correspondence with C. P. E. Bach in the 1770s in researching material for his Bach biography is well documented, and in 1805, only a few years after Forkel published that biography, Griepenkerl began his studies at Göttingen University at the age of twenty-three. He came there to study theology, but wound up devoting himself mostly to the study of music theory, *Clavier,* and organ with Forkel.[26] Forkel's ideas about Bach's technique clearly must still have been part of his teaching method in 1805 and must have been communicated to Griepenkerl in the most direct and most practical way: at the keyboard during actual lessons. Griepenkerl's description of this teaching method, laid out in the notes attached to the published edition of Bach's *Chromatic Fantasy and Fugue,* dates from 1819, scarcely more than a decade after Griepenkerl left his studies with Forkel in Göttingen. Griepenkerl had just recently returned from a postgraduate teaching position in Switzerland and taken up a position in his home town of Braunschweig at the Catharineum. Three years after the date of publication he was promoted to a full professorship in philosophy at the Catharineum at the age of thirty-seven.[27]

This brief biographical sketch of Griepenkerl's academic career gives a context for the publishing of this gloss on Forkel's information. It is impossible to tell for sure how much this document represents an expansion of Forkel's ideas, and how much it represents an elaboration by Griepenkerl. However, its publication does not come from late in Griepenkerl's academic career. It is, in fact, published directly after Forkel's death in 1818. It comes from a time when the fundamental shift from clavichord to piano was clearly already taking place but was not yet fully accomplished, for we see the clavichord represented in this text as a living and common teaching and playing instrument. Griepenkerl's insightful comparison between the clavichord and the piano is worth noting particularly:

> It is to be noted that the clavichord [*Klavier*] is far better for training the hand in the beginning than the forte-piano, because one hears every mistake in touch more easily, and more depends on the performer than on the instrument. Transferring to the piano really presents no difficulties, since the touch remains the same and the forte-piano only allows greater carelessness without bringing about any significant alterations in execution. Anyone who is of a different opinion has probably not mastered the clavichord, just like all those who are only forte-piano players.

> Übrigens ist zur Ausbildung der Hand für den Anfang das Klavier bei weitem besser, als das Forte-Piano, weil man jeden Fehler des Anschlags leichter hört und weil mehr vom Spieler, als vom Instrument abhängt. Der Übergang zum Forte-Piano nur grössere Nachlässigkeiten zulässt, ohne bedeutende Abänderungen in der Behandlung herbeizuführen. Wer anderer Meinung ist, der hat wahrscheinlich das Klavier nicht in seiner Gewalt, wie alle blossen Forte-Piano-Spieler.[28]

According to Griepenkerl, the crucial advantage of a weight-transference method is that all of the fingers, even the weaker fourth and fifth, can apply this weight to a key with equal success, no matter what size person is playing. However, if the impulse to depress the key is coming only from the finger, the fourth and fifth fingers simply are not strong enough by themselves to accomplish the task, leaving them at a distinct disadvantage on the historically strung clavichord.

Griepenkerl gives a phenomenological description, based on his personal acquaintance with the clavichord. Technique learned at the clavichord transfers to other instruments because other instruments "only allow greater carelessness," confirming that, even in its last years, the clavichord still was regarded as a superior study instrument. The only real change is that the piano has already begun to create a new paradigm, and the two exist for a short while in parallel. There are already apparently many players in Griepenkerl's audience that exclusively play the piano, and Griepenkerl suggests, a little sarcastically, that players can best be convinced of the relevance of clavichord technique by physically coming to terms with the clavichord, essentially admitting that a written description alone is useless to convince those unwilling to be convinced. Compare this rhetorical landscape of the early nineteenth century, when the clavichord and the piano were on some kind of equal footing, with the image of the clavichord represented in Griepenkerl's introduction to the complete organ works of Bach published in 1844, five years before his death:

Actually the six Sonatas and the Passacaglia were written for a clavichord with two manuals and pedal, an instrument that, in those days, every beginning organist possessed, which they used beforehand, to practice playing with hands and feet in order to make effective use of them at the organ; and, as was the custom in those days, an organ performance had to consist of free inventions. It would be a good thing to let such instruments be made again, because actually no one who wants to study to be an organist can really do without one, and it would be unbefitting to employ the organ itself for these preparatory exercises. Now I suppose our virtuosi on the fortepiano will not rest until they get a piano with two keyboards and pedals because only then will they be able to achieve to some extent what seems to be their intended purpose, which is to reproduce the noise of the whole orchestra on the fortepiano. Yet such instruments are too expensive for our beginning organists, since they only have the prospect of finding a future position that will pay 100 to at best 300 Taler a year.

Eigentlich sind die sechs Sonaten und die Passacaille für ein Clavichord mit zwei Manualen und dem Pedal geschrieben, ein Instrument, das damals jeder angehende Organist besaß, um darauf vorher zu Hause Hände und Füße einzuüben und zu freiem Gebrauch auf der Orgel geschickt zu machen; denn im Sinne der damaligen Zeit mußte ein Vortrag vor der Orgel freie Erfindung sein. Es wäre wohlgetan, solche Instrumente wieder anfertigen zu lassen, weil sie eigentlich niemand entbehren kann, der sich zum Organisten bilden will, und es sehr unpassend wäre, auf der Orgel selbst diese Vorübungen anzustellen. Freilich werden unsere Virtuosen auf dem Fortepiano nicht ruhen, bis sie es mit diesem Instrument zu zwei Klaviaturen und Pedal gebracht haben, weil sie erst dann den beabsichtigten Zweck, den Lärm des ganzen Orchesters auf dem Fortepiano nachzuahmen, einigermaßen werden erreichen können; doch solche Instrumente sind unseren angehenden Organisten zu teuer, da sie nur die Aussicht haben, künftig eine Stelle von 100 bis höchstens 300 Talern jährlicher Einkünfte darauf zu erüben.[29]

In 1844, the clavichord was already a thing of the past, and the author was a professor in advancing years looking back on a time he himself experienced when the clavichord was a living instrument. It is unclear from this statement whether the pedal clavichord was in general use in his own lifetime, but the 1819 document makes it abundantly clear that Griepenkerl had personal knowledge of the value of the clavichord for beginning keyboard students. He recommends that the pedal clavichord be built once again, but at the same time he knows for a fact that this recommendation is going to fall on deaf ears because beginning organists who could most benefit from their use couldn't afford them anyway. The bizarre and funny aside about virtuoso pianists is a kind of inside joke. It is difficult to translate, but the sense of irony it conveys speaks volumes about how the role of the solo keyboard player in performance had changed in Griepenkerl's lifetime. In this light, the total absence of discussion of the clavier technique taught to him by Forkel is not so surprising. It may simply be due to a tacit acknowledgement that discussing a clavichord-based technique is useless in an increasingly clavichord-free environment.

The original subtitle of the 1819 publication makes it clear that the technique information is not transmitted from C. P. E. Bach to Forkel, but from his older brother, Wilhelm Friedemann: ". . . with a description of its true performance, as this [has] come from J. S. Bach to W. Friedemann Bach, from him to Forkel and from Forkel to his students."[30] This opens the possibility that Forkel was not corresponding exclusively with C. P. E. Bach and may explain Forkel's unusual public criticism of C. P. E. Bach for leaving some technique information out of his *Versuch,* particularly about Forkel's third point. Griepenkerl, however, describes Forkel's contested Point Three in a way that sheds a different light on the purpose of the technique, and these comments may explain why C. P. E. Bach didn't write about it explicitly, or to be more accurate, may clarify that C. P. E. Bach assumed it implicitly. The reader is encouraged to consult the entire Griepenkerl text in the Appendix, but the important gloss on all of Forkel's three points reads:

> Let one finger be placed upon a key and serve as the point of support for a finely adjusted weight of the arm, not stiffly or rigidly, but with the express intent of pulling it backward so that it instantly might be drawn in toward the hand, were it not for the moment prevented from doing this by the weight of the hand which has been proportionately intensified to counter this intent—or conversely, were the force directed toward the retraction of the finger not too weak to overcome the pressure of the arm. This position is impossible unless the wrist firmly supports the hand and maintains itself at the same height as the knuckles on the upper side of the hand.

> Es sey eine Finger auf eine Taste gesetzt und diene einem fein abgemessenen Gewicht des Arms zum Stützpunkte, nicht steif und starr, sondern mit fortgesetzter Absicht, ihn einzuziehen, so dass er unverzüglich in die Hand zurückschnellen würde, wenn ihn für den Augenblick das gegen diese Absicht verhältnissmässig verstärkte Gewicht der Hand und des Armes daran nicht verhinderte, oder auch umgekehrt, wenn die auf das Einziehen des Fingers verwandte Kraft gegen den Druck des Armes nicht zu schwach wäre. Diese Stellung ist unmöglich, ohne dass das Gelenk der Hand fest steht und sich in gleicher Höhe erhält mit den Knöcheln an der oberen Fläche der Hand.[31]

This description differs from Forkel's in one important aspect. For Griepenkerl, the drawing back of the finger is not physically necessary. It can be a mental trick only, to encourage the beginning student to precisely transfer the weight from the first finger to the next finger without picking the weight up off the keyboard and setting it down again.

In this light, Forkel's description also becomes clearer. They are essentially two different ways of describing the same process. The drawing back motion that Forkel describes can be the smallest possible physical movement, a mere reminder to the hand that the weight transference goes on unbroken to the next finger.

Carl Philipp Emanuel Bach (1714–88)

Finally, we turn to the information that can be gleaned about this technique description from C. P. E. Bach's *Versuch über die wahre Art das Clavier zu spielen.* Perhaps C. P. E. Bach does not make point three explicitly clear in the *Versuch* because he wanted to keep this clavichord technique a trade secret, as Faulkner has suggested, but Bach might have considered this technique to be more of a mental process than a physical one, as Griepenkerl intimates. We are essentially talking about pre-technique here, the very first description of how to approach sound production at the clavichord, upon which everything else will be based. Most of the *Versuch* deals with everything that comes afterwards: fingering, figured bass playing, ornaments, and improvisation. However, a great deal of Forkel's description of the Bach technique appears here and there at the beginning of C. P. E. Bach's keyboard treatise.

The first seventeen paragraphs of the first chapter are labeled by C. P. E. Bach as "preliminary points, all grounded in nature."[32] These first paragraphs are mostly devoted to an account of how his father introduced a new concept of fingering, including a much larger role for the thumb. Although C. P. E. Bach is not explicit in these paragraphs about Forkel's third point, neither does he describe a technique that is in any general or particular way incongruent with what is described by Forkel and Griepenkerl. The chief difference is that C. P. E. Bach discusses harpsichord and clavichord technique *simultaneously.* In §12, he describes the correct hand position with fingers curved and the thumb drawn up "always remain[ing] as close as possible to the hand."[33] His other precondition is that the muscles must remain relaxed. "The less these two conditions are satisfied, the more attention must be given to them."[34] Continuing in a phenomenological vein, he stresses that if the performer "understands the correct principles of fingering and has not acquired the habit of making unnecessary gestures, he will play the most difficult things in such a manner that the motion of his hands will be barely noticeable."[35] When talking of the difference between the harpsichord and the clavichord, C. P. E. Bach is explicit about the harpsichord's role in maintaining the strength of individual fingers while the clavichord needs a technique that sounds, upon close reading, much like what Forkel and Griepenkerl describe as a weight-transference technique. Look closely at C. P. E. Bach's original German description of the dangers of playing either the clavichord or the harpsichord exclusively. Mitchell's English translation (the top English version) is problematic in several ways. It suggests that if the clavichordist goes without playing the harpsichord too long, somehow he becomes too anemic to heave the mass of the harpsichord jacks. Perhaps a better translation might be the author's, shown below Mitchell's:

Man gewöhnt sich bey beständigem Spielen auf dem Clavicorde an, die Tasten gar zu sehr zu schmeicheln, daß folglich die Kleinigkeiten, indem man nicht den hinlänglichen Druck zu Anschlagung des Tangenten auf dem Flügel giebt, nicht allezeit ansprechen werden.
(Original German, *Versuch*, 11)

The clavichordist grows too much accustomed to caressing the keys; consequently, his wonted touch being insufficient to operate the jacks, he fails to bring out details on the harpsichord.
(Mitchell's translation, *Essay*, 38)

One becomes so accustomed through continuous playing on the clavichord to treating the keys far too gently, so that consequently the small details will not always be articulated at the harpsichord, because one does not apply sufficient thrust at the point of attack of the jacks.
(Author's translation)

In order to play *piano* and *pianissimo* at the clavichord, sometimes one depresses the key a bit to reduce the distance from tangent to string before actually making the attack motion of the finger. In this way, the amount of distance from string to tangent is reduced first, so that the amount of possible acceleration that can be converted into energy in the strings is also automatically reduced. This gentle shaping of the moment of attack happens in a vertical space smaller than the distance between the resting point of the quill and the point where it contacts the string at the harpsichord. If players focused exclusively on the clavichord, it could result in gestures at the harpsichord that did not even raise the keys far enough for the quills to pluck the strings!

But, so the reader does not assume that C. P. E. Bach's clavichord technique is always about the lightest of caresses, one must return to the description of the proper string tension for a good clavichord. C. P. E. Bach again uses *schmeicheln* to describe only one end of the spectrum of clavichord technique: "In order that the strings may be attacked as well as caressed and be capable of expressing purely and clearly all degrees of forte and piano, they must be resilient."[36] The original German uses the word *angreifen* for "attack": "Der Bezug muß vertragen können, daß man es sowol ziemlich angreifen als schmeicheln kan, und dadurch in den Stand gesetzt wird, alle Arten des forte und piano reine und deutlich heraus zu bringen."[37] Bach uses this word to delineate the absolute maximum that a clavichord can take. To understand C. P. E. Bach's technique description, and appreciate its relationship to the Forkel and Griepenkerl transmission of Bach's ideas, we have to come to grips with the word *angreifen*. *Angreifen* is related to *greifen* and *ergreifen*, meaning "to grip or grab hold of." It means to attack, but in a fundamentally different way than *schlagen*, which means "to strike." This fundamentally different quality can perhaps better be understood in idiomatic expressions like "Das hat ihn sehr angegriffen" meaning, "that affected him greatly," or literally, "that really grabbed hold of him." By introducing this other quality of *angreifen,* C. P. E. Bach's description could be retranslated.

> Der Bezug muß vertragen können, daß man es sowol ziemlich angreifen als schmeicheln kan, und dadurch in den Stand gesetzet wird, alle Arten des forte und piano reine und deutlich heraus zu bringen.
> (*Versuch,* 9)

> In order that the strings may be attacked as well as caressed and be capable of expressing purely and clearly all degrees of forte and piano, they must be resilient.
> (*Essay,* 36)

> The strings must be designed to be able to be gripped a bit as well as caressed, and through this, bring out all shades of forte and piano clearly and in tune.
> (Author's translation)

According to Griepenkerl, beginning students start with the gripping and only move on later to the caressing, beginning with the basic technique and only later applying it to all shades of dynamic variation. Friedrich Wilhelm Marpurg (1718–1795) uses the same rhetorical device to describe the spectrum of possible attacks at the keyboard, except that here *angreifen* more clearly appears as the normal mode of touch that can be modified by adjectives: the "Tasten sanft oder gewaltsam angegriffen werden."[38] The keys are *either* sweetly *or* violently "gripped," and with this example in mind, we can see the same use of the term *angreifen* as a standard mode of technique modified by adjectives also in C. P. E. Bach: *ziemlich angreifen* might be interpreted as a standard *mezzoforte.*

Albert Schweitzer

By the time Albert Schweitzer's biography of J. S. Bach appeared in German in 1930, *Klavier* with a *K* had become firmly associated with the piano in Germany. In his discussion of Forkel's keyboard technique, Schweitzer discusses clavichord technique in terms of its ability to make the instrument sustain longer. He begins by paraphrasing Forkel closely and reliably:

> His technique was very complex. He was mainly concerned with producing a singing tone. Therefore, after the depression of a key, he didn't simply let the key stay there and then rise again, but rather lifted it through a careful withdrawing of the fingertips, toward the palm of the hand, so as to allow the string time to vibrate and fade out. Through this process, not only was the tone extended, but

also embellished, and the Master made it possible, even on so tone-poor an instrument as the clavichord, to play singingly and connectedly.

Sein Anschlag war sehr kompliziert. Es kam ihm hauptsächlich auf einen singenden Ton an. Darum ließ er die Taste nach dem Niederdrücken nicht einfach liegen und aufsteigen, sondern hob sie durch ein allmähliches Zurückziehen der Fingerspitzen, nach der inneren Fläche der Hand, um so der Saite die gehörige Zeit zum Vibrieren und Ausklingen zu lassen. Dadurch wurde der Ton nicht nur verlängert, sondern auch verschönert, und der Meister sah sich instand gesetzt, selbst auf einem so tonarmen Instrument, wie das Klavichord war, sangbar und zusammenhängend zu spielen.[39]

Then Schweitzer continues by separating the concept of clavichord and clavier in a way that never appears in C. P. E. Bach:

This playing technique applies naturally only to the clavichord, where the finger and the strings are in a living relationship, not on the harpsichord. Bach's touch was therefore thoroughly modern, because all of the current and most recent experiments in "singing" on the piano are in agreement that it is not only about pressing down the key, but rather also very much about regulating the release of the key.

Also here, Bach is thoroughly modern, in that he is not referring to an attack, but rather wanted to talk about a conscious strength—or force—transmission to the key. Sébastian Érard's (1752–1831) 1823 discovery of the double escapement action, which made possible an unending variation in the gradations of repeating a note, would have been joyfully accepted by Bach, as the mechanics of the modern piano in general would have been the fulfillment of the dreams of his art.

Diese Spielart bezieht sich natürlich nur auf das Klavichord, wo Finger und Saite in lebendigem Verhältnis zueinander standen, nicht auf das Klavizimbel. Bachs Anschlag war also durch und durch modern, denn alle neueren und neuesten Untersuchungen über das "Singen" auf dem Klavier stimmen darin überein, daß sie es nicht nur vom Niederdrücken, sondern ebenso sehr von der Regulierung des Aufsteigens der Taste abhängig sein lassen.

Auch darin ist Bach ganz modern, daß er nicht von einem "Anschlag," sondern nur von einer bewußten Kraft—und Druckübertragung auf die Taste geredet haben wollte. Sebastian Erards Erfindung der doppelten Auslösung (1823), welche eine unendlich mannigfaltige Abstufung in dem Wiederanschlag eines Tones ermöglicht, wäre von Bach also mit Freuden begrüßt worden, wie überhaupt die Mechanik des modernen Klaviers nur die Erfüllung seiner kühnsten Träume ist.[40]

Schweitzer builds a picture of J. S. Bach as a *modern* musical hero during this technique discussion in much the same way as Spitta did, as we saw in chapter 2. Like Spitta, Schweitzer uses his description of J. S. Bach's keyboard technique to argue that the piano is the ideal instrument to express the cantabile spirit of Bach's keyboard music. But he goes a step further than Spitta and implies that Bach himself would have preferred the modern piano not only tonally, but also technically.

The Twentieth-Century Approach to the Bach Technique Thread

Richard Troeger, who has written extensively on harpsichord and clavichord technique in our own time, describes the phenomenology of feeling as though one is actually gripping the strings of a clavichord, in the sense that C. P. E. Bach may very well mean:

> After all, one is not merely pressing down the light load of key and tangent alone: the player is directly engaging all of the strings made to sound at a given time, for the full time of their vibration. This *is hands on* participation in the sound in the most direct (and stimulating) way a keyboard player can experience it, somewhat akin to the full grasp with which a harpist contacts the strings.[41]

The difference is that the clavichordist maintains that sensation of gripping for the full value of the notes, whereas the harpist only experiences the feeling of gripping the strings just before and during the moment of plucking them. The clavichord manages to sustain that moment of attack (or pluck), which on the piano and the harpsichord is ephemerally short.

George Stauffer presents the outlines of Bach's method of *Clavier* instruction, quoting passages from Forkel, before going on to make some speculations about Bach as an organ teacher. [42] He concludes that Bach only accepted organ students who were already thoroughly grounded in *Clavier* instruction and probably taught the organ more through improvisation than through a strict pedagogical program of written-out pieces. Stauffer analyzes what manuscripts were copied most often by students to support the theory that Bach's students of the *Clavier* followed a fairly standard regimen, through the *Two-Part Inventions* and *Sinfonias* and on to *The Well-Tempered Clavier.*

The original Forkel text puts the study of the *Two-Part Inventions* in a very specific light, related to learning to touch the *Clavier* properly: J. S. Bach's "eigene Art des Anschlags."[43] The technique description is clearly phenomenologically related to the clavichord. Bach, he says, began with small exercises for all of the fingers of both hands, and no one was excused from this practice. Forkel notes that Bach preferred ideally to have students take six to twelve months with this phase of learning to *touch* the *Clavier* properly. For those who lost patience he wrote pieces in which the exercises were connected together. Forkel states that the six *Little Preludes for Beginners* and the fifteen *Two-Part Inventions* were sketched out to meet *specific* students' needs, presumably technical needs, *during* the lessons. The emphasis in Forkel's text is not on the completion of a set of repertoire, but on the concentration of learning proper *touch,* and Bach personalizes these lessons and prolongs this phase of the student's development as much as possible by writing sketches of pieces to encourage the students' concentration. Even though Forkel himself does not present the little exercises that Bach set his students to practice for so long, Griepenkerl does; Griepenkerl also confirms that among the "little connected pieces" were the *Two-Part Inventions,* and he gives an order in which they could be used. Griepenkerl is more optimistic about how long this first phase of practicing ought take:

> All this preparatory training can and should, given the proper industry, zeal, and talent, cost even the beginner not over two months' time. After it, however, one must choose practice pieces by J. S. Bach himself, because few other composers give to the left hand a melody to execute. The most suitable pieces are Numbers 1 & 8, of the *Two-Part Inventions,* followed by Numbers 12, 11, and 5.

> Diese ganze Vorbereitung kann und darf, bei gehörigem Fleiss, Eifer und Talent, selbst den Anfänger nicht über zwei Monate kosten. Nach ihr aber müssen Übungstücke von J. S. Bach selbst gewählt werden, weil wenig andere Komponisten der linken Hand eine Melodie zu führen geben. Die passendsten sind von den zweistimmigen Inventionen Nr. 1 und 8; dann Nr. 12, 11 und 5.[44]

The following three pieces of information formed the core of the technique experiment that is discussed in Part Two:

1. the possibility that J. S. Bach began by having students play single exercises for all the fingers of both hands;
2. the fact that he wrote small pieces, less for the purpose of performing music than for the purpose of extending the period in which students could concentrate solely on playing these single exercises;
3. and, finally, the distinct possibility that these small pieces were the *Two-Part Inventions,* and that they were used in a specific order.

Part Two

Performance Practice Studies

Prelude

Tacit Knowledge and Dialectical Process

To me, [Mendelssohn's] presence was particularly beneficial, for I found my relationship to music to be still the same: I listen to it with pleasure, participation and reflection. I love the historical aspect, for who understands a phenomenon at all if he has not entered into the process of its development?
—Goethe, in a letter to Carl Friedrich Zelter

I once had the good fortune to hear Peter Brook, the well-known English theater director, discuss his autobiography at the National Theater in London.[1] Someone asked "How do you feel about being cited as the director with the most luck in realizing the famous Stanislawsky method?" Brook's answer was an epiphany for me. He said that he didn't set out to realize a theory. The *doing* had to come first, and then he read the theoretical sources and recognized his own experiences in them. Brook suggested that theory is useless for someone who is not actively practicing whatever craft that theory is trying to describe, but if you come back to the theory after practical experience, then the theory becomes a mirror of your experience and you can begin to use that theory as a guide to further development.

What Brook described so eloquently was his experience of a dialectical process between theory and practice. The human body and the phenomenology of acting change relatively little over time, but to understand those phenomena, you have to begin acting without knowing all of the answers beforehand. You learn the craft of physical acting by engaging in it. But once you take that first step, you start to learn the physical language in which the theories are engaged. Only then can there be *eureka* moments when you recognize an idea in a theoretical source from your own experience. A dialectical process has begun, going back and forth between physical practice and theoretical source, until that theory is no longer helpful for your own artistic growth.

The physical practice of acting can be described as *tacit knowledge*: a body of physical knowledge that develops through the repetition and refinement of nonverbalized practical skills. This term, originally used by Michael Polanyi, the British chemist and philosopher, who among other things researched reaction kinetics, can apply to any kind of process that the body can carry out without completely understanding consciously what it is doing.[2] David Bohm, a physics professor from the University of London likens this kind of knowing to riding a bicycle. You can't state it in words, but you know it's there.

> If a bicycle is falling, you have to turn it in the direction it's falling in order to make it come up. Mathematically, there is a formula that shows that the angle to which you turn is related in a certain way to the angle at which you're falling. This is what you'll actually do, but you don't work out the formula. Your whole body does countless movements that you can't describe, and it makes it all work. That's tacit knowledge.[3]

Because this knowledge is often difficult to verbalize, it survives best in unbroken traditions. Tacit knowledge can be lost easily when these traditions are interrupted, but skills can be recreated to some extent by reconstructing the original tools associated with them and being willing to engage with those tools physically. New tacit knowledge about acting Greek drama might be generated, for instance, by using an amphitheater with historical acoustics rather than a modern indoor stage, or about acting Shakespeare by using the newly reconstructed Globe Theater in London.

The guild systems of Europe are another good example of tacit knowledge in once-living traditions that has now disappeared. But here too, some of the tools and objects from the traditions are left, and can be used to recreate at least some of the tacit knowledge that was lost. In the first half of the book, this process led to the reconstruction of a new instrument in an old working-language.

The second half of the book explores new ways of generating knowledge about how this instrument was played, by setting it in four different dialogues.

In chapter 5, the instrument is in dialogue directly with beginning clavichord students. Through teaching experiments conducted in various forms over the five years of the study, a workable technique for the instrument emerged, by listening to how the instrument itself wanted to be played. Like Brook, we engaged in the doing and then looked at the theory. The written theories, as we have seen in Part One, are more often than not descriptions of process rather than of facts, so engaging in the process generated new insights about these historical documents. In the first year, most students of the Church Music program at the School of Music at Göteborg University (Sweden) participated, amounting to fifteen to eighteen private lessons a week. Several of these early sessions were video-documented. The historical technique material, based on Forkel and Griepenkerl and defined in chapter 4, gave us a specific point of departure but could not serve as a detailed guide of instruction and gave no direct information about pedal technique. Some beginning students at the clavichord are confronted with the initial difficulty of producing any tone at all from the instrument. Different tools for individual students were developed to help them through this initial phase, but eventually a general pattern appeared, which was then expanded in two short courses at the School of Music and intensive courses at the Göteborg International Organ Academy beginning in 1996, during which the models in chapter 5 were developed and tested.

Chapter 6 is a dialogue between the instrument and the theory of rhetorical playing from Bach's own time. Musical-rhetorical figures are used as a language for discussing technique and tone production at the clavichord. The debate about the various historical definitions and provenance of musical-rhetorical figures within the paradigm of German Baroque music notwithstanding, they have formed a valuable vocabulary for expanding and exploring the technique discussed in chapter 4.

Since 1997, the pedal clavichord has also been used in intensive courses at the International Clavichord, Organ and Improvisation Academy in Smarano, Italy, out of which grew the notational experiment documented in chapter 6. Johann Sebastian Bach's *Two-Part Inventions* provided the repertoire focus for the experiment in figural notation.

Whether there was a Bach repertoire that was intended from the beginning to be specifically for the pedal clavichord is the focus of most of the debate about the pedal clavichord's relevance throughout the twentieth century. I would rather like to argue that the instrument might have been an integral part of an organist's education and the dialogue between the pedal clavichord and the organ is what is missing from the current scene. But clearly, one can also make some personal decisions about works that are more effective than others as performance literature on the pedal clavichord. Although there is some unresolvable ambiguity about Bach's intentions for the *Trio Sonatas*, they make for convincing performance music at the pedal clavichord because they use all three instruments (both manuals and the pedal) at once; they provide ample opportunity to explore dynamics, and their texture is thin. Works written specifically to create an effective plenum on a large organ seem to be least effective at the pedal clavichord as performance literature, but may still benefit from being prepared for organ performance on the pedal clavichord. Although Bach's Passacaglia in C Minor, BWV 582, seems to fit this latter category much more than the former, there is a case to be made that it was meant to be a pedal clavichord piece based on a famous (or *infamous*) comment in Forkel's biography of Bach. Chapter 7 is therefore a dialogue between the instrument and a specific piece, using the Passacaglia to test what happens when learning a large *pedaliter* work at the pedal clavichord, both for its own sake and as preparation for performing the piece on the organ.

Finally, in chapter 8, a dialogue between the pedal clavichord and the organ explores the role of the historical pedal clavichord in preparing music for the organ in general, and specifically raises some new questions relating to the relationship of the pedal clavichord and the actions of restored historical organs.

5

Sound Production at the Pedal Clavichord

Not only does [C. P. E.] Bach play a slow, singing adagio with the most touching expression . . . he sustains, even in this tempo, a note six eighths long with all degrees of loudness.

—Johann Friedrich Reichardt

Good Sound

What constitutes good sound at the clavichord? Framed in terms of the mechanics of the instrument, the answer does not have to be subjective. Contact between the tangent and the strings that is firm and sustained enough to set the strings vibrating—for the full length of the note—creates good sound. In order to maintain this contact, the player actually has to raise the strings a little bit with the tangent. Keeping steady pressure on the strings results in a note with a steady pitch, while raising and lowering the strings changes the sounding pitch and creates the *Bebung* or vibrato effect for which the clavichord is famous. In either case, sound is sustained throughout the length of the note by the tangent's firm contact with the strings.

If sustained sound is good, its opposite, blocked sound, is bad. Blocking occurs when the tangent does not introduce enough kinetic energy into the strings to set them vibrating, or when the contact between the tangent and the strings is broken too soon. The resulting note sounds like a dull thump, or stops sounding altogether. Furthermore, if the tangent is raised only to the level of the strings, and not pushed a little above that level, the contact between tangent and string can be intermittently broken, and an unpleasant buzzing sound results as the strings vibrate against the tangent. Figure 5.1 illustrates the mechanics of good and blocked sound.

Sound Production, String Tension, and Touch

It is difficult to define completely the original touch characteristics of an historical clavichord. Many parameters that affect touch are ephemeral:

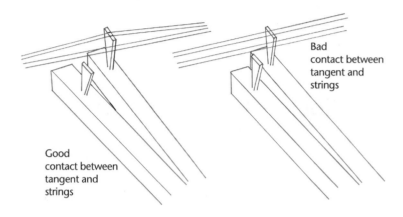

Figure 5.1. Contact between string and tangent.

we can no longer know with certainty what kind of listing cloth was used between the strings, the pattern in which it was woven, the pitch to which the instrument was tuned, or the thickness of the cloth under the backs of the keys that sets the final distance between the tops of the tangents and the strings. All of these factors affect how it feels to play the instrument. On the other hand, none of them have as much effect on the perception of touch as the string tension, and we do actually have some guidance about that. C. P. E. Bach recorded a recipe of sorts for string tension, reporting that the strings of a good clavichord had to be tight enough to withstand the full force of an attack and still stay in tune, but loose enough that the strings can be caressed and the sound will still bloom.[1]

First Experiences

During the year that it took to research and build the pedal clavichord in Edinburgh, I sat almost every evening at the copy of a five-octave Friederici clavichord that John Barnes had built,[2] and I played, or tried to. Sometimes it took me an hour to start playing without blocking the notes. At the time, I didn't know about all of the parameters that could affect the perception of touch. All I knew was my harpsichord technique wasn't working at the clavichord.

I made an assumption at this point that led to the technique research with the pedal clavichord presented in this book. I assumed that the fault lay with my own technique and not with the instrument in front of me. Changing the instrument—when one assumes it is wrong because it doesn't conform to one's preconceived notions about technique—can lead to a feedback loop in which the phenomena of the historical instrument become compromised until all that an instrument can do is confirm the player's expectations and never challenge them. In other words, instruments and techniques reinforce one another, and just as adhering to preconceived notions of technique can lead to development of nonhistorical instruments, playing on such instruments can further entrench nonhistorical ideas about technique. Just such a process played out in the harpsichord revival of the early twentieth century, led by Wanda Landowska.

Landowska's technique was based on the striking movements of individual fingers.[3] This exaggerated striking movement, where a single finger is raised high off the key, was possible on the large experimental harpsichords of the early twentieth century—essentially modern iron-framed pianos fitted with a plucking action rather than hammers. The actions on these instruments were absolutely silent. One could hammer on the key with the finger from a great height without producing any rattling at all.[4]

The historical harpsichord reacts very differently to such treatment. Marpurg comments that if one really violently attacks the harpsichord, while the actual tone production will not change as it would on the clavichord, "one will hear the wood too."[5] That is, the fronts of the wooden keys will hit the wooden touchrail. The wooden jacks will rattle in their wooden slots and fly up and strike the underside of the wooden jackrail, and the general clunking will be radiated and amplified around the whole light and resonant wooden case. Like a violin, the entire instrument is engaged in sound production, and like a violin, the historical harpsichord imposes physical limitations on technique. On a violin, a point of diminishing returns is reached when increasing the force no longer results in musical sound but in a scraping sound and an instability of pitch. Step by step, the twentieth-century revival harpsichords woud eventually shed the trappings of the modern piano until they became more like violins again, imposing a more historical set of physical limitations on the player's technique.

It was John Barnes's opinion that the Landowska harpsichord revival radically affected the way clavichords were built at the beginning of the twentieth century, perhaps because harpsichordists wanted their clavichords to work just like their harpsichords: to have a light touch, a plucking point, and be controllable with a finger technique like Landowska's. The concrete result of this impulse was the production of an instrument more like a modern piano with thick keylevers, bushed with felt so that they would be completely silent, and fitted with lead weights in the back so that the finger would not have to work so hard to lift the tangent with the strings (figure 5.2).

The balance points were also often moved much farther back along the key-lever in order to create better leverage. Now that the key-lever system was too efficient at lifting the strings, in order to keep the pitch of the

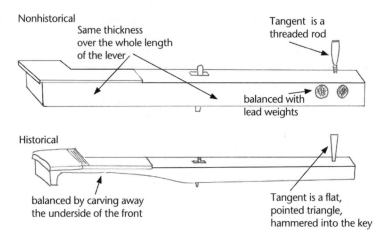

Figure 5.2. Historical and nonhistorical clavichord keylevers.

strings stable, wooden plates covered on the underside with felt were fitted over where the tangents strike the strings, limiting how high the strings could be raised. These plates stabilized the pitch of the strings but limited the amount of energy that could be introduced into the strings and greatly reduced the instrument's dynamic range.[6] A clavichord set up like this provides a performance experience that feels nothing like that which the historical treatises describe: it is no longer possible to "attack" the strings, as C. P. E. Bach says. Unfortunately, these nonhistorical clavichords made people suspect that perhaps it was the historical treatises that were wrong in their consistent praise of the clavichord as a teaching instrument.

Clavichord Dynamics and the Baroque Accents

Just as Landowska's technique is not suitable for the historical harpsichord, it does not work for the historical clavichord either. Striking with the fingers alone at the clavichord, using an exaggerated early-harpsichord-revival technique, does lift the strings of even the heaviest-strung clavichords, but an uncontrolled dynamic pattern develops in which notes are loud and soft depending on the strength of the individual fingers. The result is a dynamic pattern that sounds totally random, while the Baroque practice of *quantitas intrinseca* demands that such accents happen in an organized and repeating pattern. According to this practice, notes have an external, or notated value, but unaccented notes also have an internal or *intrinsic* length that is shorter than the notated value. Walther's *Lexicon* gives the following definition:

Quantitas Notarum extrinseca, and intrinseca is the apparent (or outward) and the inner value of the notes. According to the former, every note is performed equal to other notes of the same value, but according to the latter the notes are of unequal length: since, to be specific, the uneven-numbered parts of the beat are long and the even-numbered ones short.[7]

Quantitas Notarum extrinseca, & intrinseca [*lat.*] die äusserliche und innerliche Geltung der Noten; nach jener Art ist jede Note mit ihres gleichen in der *execution* von gleicher; nach dieser aber, von ungleicher länge: da nemlich der ungerade Tact-Theil lang, und der gerade Tach-Theil kurz ist.[8]

Walther also explains the Baroque pattern of stressed and unstressed beats by citing the Italian concept of "good" and "bad" notes: *tempo di buona* and *tempo di cattiva*. The important thing to note here is that the pattern of good and bad appears at all levels of the rhythmic structure: at the level of the measure, at the level of the half measure, in patterns of sixteenth notes, and so forth:

Tempo di buona is the good part of the beat. Under the equal *tactus,* the first of two minims, or the first half of the beat is good; also the first and third of four quarter notes, the first, third, fifth and seventh of eight eighth notes and so forth, because these *tempi,* or odd-numbered parts of the beat are suitable for the placement of a caesura, a cadence, a long syllable, a syncopated dissonance, and above all a consonance (from which comes its name—*di buona*).
    Tempo di cattiva, or *di mala* is the bad part of the beat. In the *tactu aequali* or beat with two equal strokes, the second of two minims or the second half of the beat is bad; also the second and fourth, sixth and eighth of eight eighth notes, because these *tempi* or even-numbered parts of the beat are all different from the above-mentioned parts, and are their opposites.[9]

Tempo di buona [*ital.*] der gute Tact-Theil, ist in *tactu aequali,* unter 2 Minimis die erste Minima, oder die erste Helffte des Tacts; unter 4 Vierteln, das 1ste und 3te Viertel; unter 8 Achteln, das 1ste, 3te, 5te, und 7de Achtel u.s.w. weil erwehnte *tempi* oder ungerade Tact-Theile bequehm sind, daß auf ihnen eine *Caesur,* eine *Cadenz,* eine lange Sylbe, eine *syncopirte Dissonanz,* und vor allen eine *Consonanz* (als von welcher eben die Bey-Nahme: *di buona* entstanden) angebracht werde.
    Tempo di cattiva, oder *di mala* [*ital.*] der schlimme Tact-Theil, ist in *tactu aequali,* unter 2 Minimis die zweyte Minima, oder die zweyte Helffte des Tacts; unter 4 Vierteln, das 2te und 4te Viertel; unter 8 Achteln, das 2te, 4te, 6te und 8te Achtel; weil nurbesagte *tempi* oder gerade Tact-Theile einige von ober-zehlten Stücken nicht, wohl aber deren *contrarium* leiden.[10]

Good and Bad Notes in Theory and Practice

At the harpsichord and the organ this pattern of good and bad notes can be created using articulation. If the bad note has a shorter duration, the silence before the next good note creates the illusion that the good note is a little bit louder.[11] At the clavichord one not only can but *must* create this pattern with dynamics. The instrument is too quiet for articulation alone to create it, and too touch sensitive to ignore its dynamic possibilities. If more energy is accidentally applied to a bad note in a group of two notes, then it will sound accented and the pattern is immediately lost.

Sitting at Barnes's Friederici copy, I learned by trial and error how to sustain good sound over several notes by pressing into the keys with the fingers rather than striking with them, but the more notes I tried to play in a row this way, the more tense my arm got, until I realized that I could lift my arm off the keyboard and reapply it as often as I wanted to. It was as if the weight were breath, and a singer were pressing too hard with the vocal cords, having not found the proper balance with the air pressure coming from the lungs. Or perhaps, simply, the singer needed to breathe more often.

I recognized my own experience of learning to "breathe" more often—alternately applying and removing the natural weight of the arm—reflected in the Forkel/Griepenkerl descriptions of Bach's keyboard technique. Forkel reports that Bach used *small* exercises, and Griepenkerl says the technique depends on learning to transfer weight between any two notes and between any two fingers of both hands (Appendix, §6, p. 163, 168). Next, the technique is expanded to triplets in scalar motion. What if the weight transfer described in Forkel and Griepenkerl was meant to be carried out only over the length of the two- or three-note exercise and then repeated starting with a new impulse? In between, the arm could relax completely. The relaxed motion of the whole arm toward the new good note necessitates leaving the bad note a little bit early in order to arrive at the new good note on time, and leaves the largest articulation gap always before the good note. This movement also adds some acceleration to the weight application, guaranteeing that more kinetic energy transfers to the strings of the good note than the bad, creating an automatic pattern of strong and weak notes both in duration *and* dynamics. A simple 3 4 3 4 pattern becomes a little physical dance: attack—transfer—relax—attack—transfer—relax.

The Pedal Clavichord Comes to Göteborg

During 1995, the pedal clavichord's first year at Göteborg, in about fifteen individual lessons a week with volunteers, we collaboratively explored what technique worked most efficiently to consistently produce good sound. The first experiments focused exclusively on manual technique, and in time, these experiments became more codified into the system of steps recorded here, that most people could complete within a few weeks. Those who had a piano background or extensive experience with historical North European organs tended to become more comfortable at the pedal clavichord more quickly. Those with any unconscious tension in the arms, especially in the elbows and shoulders, needed to spend some time learning to let it go before even simple exercises could be played.

Beginning Exercises

The following exercises describe some of the methods that were developed to introduce students to pedal clavichord technique. Text that directly describes a process in a lesson format is given in italics.

Writing about teaching process is made more difficult when readers do not share a physical point of reference. Our modern shared point of reference is the piano, where every keyboard player has some physical experience they can use to interpret written descriptions of technique, and indeed, the clavichord's dynamic responsiveness makes it more like the piano than other historical keyboard instruments. That shared experience may help readers of this section who do not have a clavichord nearby. But written descriptions are no substitute for experience.

Initial Experience

The most important first step for many students is simply learning to relax their arms. If the arm is being directed and held up from the elbow rather than the shoulder, the useful mass of the arm is suspended off the keyboard, leaving the performer no choice but to strike with the fingers. Often, at first, the fifth finger doesn't produce any sound at all because by itself it cannot strike hard enough. A common unconscious response, complicating the situation further, is to add a rolling wrist movement to the striking action of the fifth finger, so that the striking motion is now being accomplished by the whole hand. Unfortunately, this response produces the kind of extraneous movement that C. P. E. Bach warns us about.[12] Tension of this kind can easily go unnoticed at the organ because the sound of the pipes does not change. But at the clavichord, if a student plays a note and no sound comes out, this is a problem no one can ignore. Therefore it is often necessary to begin away from the clavichord getting students to experience, sometimes for the first time, what it is like to completely relax their arm muscles on command.

Lifting Your Arm from the Shoulder

Jacques van Oortmerssen shared an exercise at one of the first intensive clavichord courses that helps those who are holding a lot of tension in their elbows to experience what it is like to lift the arm from the shoulder.[13]

Stand with your side close to a wall and your arm at your side touching the wall from shoulder to finger tips. Press your arm against the wall

*using all the muscles of your shoulder and upper and lower arm and
your fingers. Press for five or ten seconds. Step away from the wall and
raise your arm. Notice that the movement originates entirely from the
shoulder.*

Trust Exercise

*Ask one person to sit away from the keyboard and another person to
support the arm of the person sitting so that the forearm is more or less
parallel to the floor. See if the one seated can relax enough to allow the
one standing to support the full weight of the arm. What happens if the
standing person lets go? Is the arm still hovering in the air? Does it drop
naturally into the seated person's lap? This works best away from the
keyboard where the person learning to relax can be assured the arm will
make a safe and soft landing.*

"Catching" the Weight of the Arm on the Fingers

The next step is to learn to direct this natural weight onto a key by being
able to support a certain amount of it on an individual finger.

*Building on the trust exercise, hold the arm of the seated person until
you feel the full weight of the arm in your hands. Drop the arm into the
lap and have the seated person try to "stand" the relaxed arm up on its
fingers. Notice how the wrist is involved, too. If it works, the wrist will
be suspended above the leg helping to hold the lower arm off the leg.
Only the fingers will make contact. Alternate simply letting the arm drop
onto the leg and trying to catch the weight of the arm on the fingers.*

Lifting the Arm onto the Fingers

Finding out how to balance some of the weight of the arm on a finger can
also begin with a completely relaxed arm in a resting position.

*Sit at a rather high table so that your arm is resting in contact with the
table from the elbow to the wrist. Let your fingers be in a natural curved
hand position. (If you can't find this hand position, let your arm hang
by your side, shake it out a little and relax it. Pick your arm up at the
shoulder with your hand relaxed. Look at the position your hand automatically assumes, fingers curved, the tips in a straight line with the
thumb.) Relax the muscles of your arm starting from your ear all the
way down to the tips of your fingers. Feel how heavy your arm is, how
the table feels like it is pushing up against your arm. Now stiffen your
fingers until your wrist lifts off the surface of the table and you could fit*

a golf ball in the cupped palm of your hand. Without using any other muscles in your arm, slowly lean back away from the table until your elbow comes off the surface of the table itself. The weight of your arm is now standing on your fingers.

Moving from One Finger to Another

The reason this weight-transference technique is so effective at the clavichord is because there the keystroke has no real bottom. The depth of touch depends on the tension of the strings and the amount of mass placed on those strings. This small-scale flexible depth of touch means that there is a much more yielding surface for the fingertips at the clavichord than on a tabletop or at the organ or harpsichord.

Try repeating the exercise above but with a computer mouse pad under your hand instead of the table. Feel how you can subtly control, from the large muscle groups of the upper arm, shoulder and back, how much weight gets applied to the fingers and how altering it raises and lowers the depth to which the fingertips sink into the mouse pad. Once your hand is balanced on the fingers, try to stand only on the third finger and then move to the fourth finger engaging the muscles of your arm as little as possible. Try the same technique at the keyboard. Experiment with how much weight is too much for the clavichord.

Beginning to Play

Many students independently came to the conclusion that paired fingering (playing, for instance, 3 4 3 4) is the easiest way to get a good sound out of the instrument at first. Could the use of so many paired fingerings in early keyboard music be related to tone production at the clavichord? In this simplest two-note figure, the first note, the strong one, is indicated by a downward pointing arrow in figure 5.3.

The second, weaker note is indicated by a horizontal arrow, symbolizing that the same weight transfers to the next finger. The *down* motion of the strong note includes a small amount of acceleration generated when the arm moves to that note ending in the actual attack of the note, and the *over* motion contains almost no acceleration at all. In the diagram of the keyboard in figure 5.3, the first key descends farther than the second. The difference in key depth between strong and weak beats at the clavichord is exaggerated in the figure for the sake of clarity, but it is real.

Practice this movement between every adjacent finger in both hands, first between naturals and then between naturals and sharps, and then between sharps and naturals.

Figure 5.3. Good and bad notes at the clavichord.

This may very well be the process Bach required his students to repeat for months. The 3 4 3 4 ascending scale movement is identical to the opening of the little "applicatio" fingering exercise in figure 5.4 that J. S. Bach wrote out in the *Clavierbüchlein* for W. F. Bach.

The Baroque musical-rhetorical name for this kind of movement is *transitus*.[14] Not all shapes are as easy to play as *transitus*, and learning to play *transitus* figuration does not mean that a beginning clavichord student can automatically play other shapes, because not all kinds of figuration feel the same at the clavichord. Patterns of different key-depths create different *three-dimensional shapes* for every musical motive. Because the clavichord has no defined bottom point in the key-dip, it is infinitely variable within a very small range. The three-dimensional aspect of the clavichord's depth of touch creates a different *center of gravity* in different kinds of motivic shapes. Each of them has a choreography made up of the simple steps of *down* and *over,* but each has to be learned for itself like a new word. Forkel claims that Bach wrote small pieces for those who couldn't stand simply practicing the exercises.

> The first thing he did was to teach his scholars his peculiar mode of touching the instrument, of which we have spoken before. For this purpose, he made them practise, for months together, nothing but simple passages for all the fingers of

Figure 5.4. J. S. Bach, Applicatio, right hand, first two measures.

both hands, with constant regard to their clear and clean touch. . . . But if he found, that any one, after some months of practice, began to lose patience, he was so obliging as to write little connected pieces, in which those exercises were combined together. Of this kind are the "Six little Preludes for Beginners," and still more the "Fifteen two-part Inventions." He wrote both down, during the hours of teaching, and attended only to the momentary want of the scholar.[15]

Griepenkerl also claimed that the *Two-Part Inventions* should come directly after this period of initial instruction and recommends the order in which they should be taken up (see the Appendix, §12, p. 165, 169–70). The *Two-Part Inventions* are laden with interesting musical motives. This raises an important possibility, explored in the next chapter, that these exercises and what we think of as musical-rhetorical figures are one and the same.

What if the clavichord was praised as a first teaching instrument because it encouraged students to play rhetorical "words" rather than notes?

Chapter 6 discusses how the Forkel/Griepenkerl technique was applied to an expanded repertoire of motivic shapes at the Gerstenberg clavichord.

Pedal Technique

Historical Evidence for Bach's Pedal Technique

Unfortunately, very little information about Bach's pedal technique survives. We have testimonials to his unusual level of mastery over the pedals but nothing useful pedagogically: "With his two feet he could play things on the pedals that many not unskillful clavier players would find bitter enough to have to play with five fingers."[16] Faulkner reviews the major sources about Bach's pedal technique in his study and comes to the conclusion that a reconstruction is not possible based on the surviving written evidence.[17] Could the pedal clavichord generate information that can help to fill this gap?

The first thing that the pedal instrument teaches is that playing with the heel of the foot is much more difficult to control than playing with the toe. The instrument confirms *physically* what a generation of organists have been taught intellectually: that the Baroque organists played mostly without heels.

At the manual instrument, if you play too far back on the key, the note almost always blocks, because you are playing too close to the fulcrum point of the key for the key to work efficiently (see figure 5.5). If force is exerted farther from the fulcrum point, the lever becomes more effective; closer to the fulcrum-point, more force is needed to do the same amount of work. The pedal keys work according to the same principle as the manual

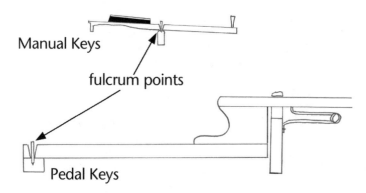

Figure 5.5. Fulcrum points on the manual and pedal keys.

keys, but, instead of being pinned in the middle, they are pinned at the end (underneath the bench) and are held up by springs at the middle.

The heel is too close to the fulcrum point of the key to control the movement of the key and avoid blocking the note. It can lift the tangent to the strings, but often the tangent bounces there and buzzes against the strings. The instrument clearly rewards toe playing with good sound, where the tangent lifts all four of the strings slightly from their resting position.

Johann Kittel

Playing without the heel is described by a student of J. S. Bach who happens to have owned and taught on a pedal clavichord. Johann Christian Leberecht Kittel (1732–1809) studied privately with Bach for the last two years of Bach's life, and Kittel's *Der Angehende Praktische Organist* (1801–1803–1808) is regarded as one of the best surviving sources for information about Bach's organ teaching method. A student of Kittel, the organist Johann Christian Heinrich Rinck (1770–1846), reports that Kittel encouraged his organ students to practice in Kittel's home on his pedal clavichord.[18] Kittel gives the use of alternating toes as the standard method of pedaling (figure 5.6) and toe and heel playing as a secondary method (figure 5.7).[19]

We know that the alternating toe method of playing was already being used as early as in the early seventeenth century. An example of pedal playing without heels appears in an early manuscript associated with the school of Johann Erasmus Kindermann (1616–55). It marks the pedaling for the left and right foot both in written-out trills and in passage playing without the use of heels.[20] It is also possible to control the sound of the pedal clavichord with the heel in some specific situations, especially moving from a sharp to a natural in slow note values, for instance in *cantus firmus* lines,

Figure 5.6. Kittel's alternating toe pedaling.

Figure 5.7. Kittel's alternating heel and toe pedaling.

where the heel is far enough forward from the pivot point to control the key's movement. Perhaps heel use might have been a secondary method reserved for certain situations. We do not know when alternating toe and heel playing began or whether this secondary method was reserved for the playing of slow note values only.

An Experimental Reconstruction

The second major lesson that the pedal clavichord teaches is that striking the key by pivoting only from the ankle does not work well. This technique increases the chances of blocking, does not provide enough control over the dynamic level of the note, and provides even less control over the note's release. An uncontrolled release results in loud action noise, since the pedal key springs back up and hits the top of the guide slot in the toeboard if it is released too quickly. Striking the pedal note from the ankle is analogous to striking the manual note using wrist motion only. In fact, thinking of the leg and foot as analogous to the arm and hand suggests a number of comparisons (see table 5.1).

The hip works like the shoulder, as it is the pivot point which moves the entire limb the greatest distance with the least effort. The knee is analogous to the elbow: if it stays as relaxed as possible, it will not cut off the use of

Table 5.1. Comparisons between arm and leg at the clavichord.

ACTION	ARM	LEG
initiates movement	shoulder	hip
stays relaxed	elbow	knee
mediates the weight application	wrist	ankle
supports the weight application	finger	toe

the mass of the larger half of the limb. The ankle, like the wrist, acts as a flexible shock absorber to mediate the amount of weight that is directed to the key. Also like the wrist, the ankle needs to stay higher than the surface of the key or it does not have enough leverage to work properly. This can easily be demonstrated at the manual instrument by lowering the level of the wrist until you find the point where balancing weight on your finger does not work anymore. The weight application on the finger is interrupted and the whole hand falls off the keyboard. The toe of the foot is analogous to the finger that supports the directed weight. It is the point of contact with the key, working like the pad of the fingertip. This approach gets a consistently good sound out of individual notes.

Thus the movement to a new position is directed by the largest muscle groups of the leg in one uninterrupted fluid motion. Upon arriving at the new position, the ankle does not flap the foot down onto the key first, followed by the weight of the leg. There is instead one continuous motion in which the toe of the foot contacts the key and immediately the ankle begins its function as a support for the weight of the leg.

Beginning Exercises

Sit backwards on the bench so that your seat is occupying about half the bench and your feet are not touching the ground. Relax the muscles of the leg so that if you were to push with your hand from behind the calf, the leg would swing freely and naturally from the knee. Note carefully the position that the foot takes naturally when your muscles are relaxed. Is it parallel to the floor or is it pointing downward? Lift the foot from the ankle several times and be aware of how many small muscles on the front and back of the lower leg it takes to accomplish this movement. Now relax the leg again, and this time lift the whole leg up and down, using the muscles of the upper leg and hip. Which movement can you do accurately in rhythm for a longer time? Which movement makes you tired first?

Stepping Down

The next step is to experience the ways in which weight from the leg can be directed onto the foot.

Sit backwards on the bench, with the bench at a slightly lower height so that with a relaxed leg the toe of the foot is just touching the floor. Lift the leg using only the upper leg muscles and set it back down. When the toe of the foot touches the floor, relax the leg muscles. Notice how the ankle suddenly engages to keep the heel from hitting the floor. Repeat the process and this time, when the toe of the foot contacts the floor, stand up on it.

Good and Bad Notes

So far, I have discussed playing only a single note on the pedal. Because a large range of dynamics is possible here, too, it becomes necessary to play with a technique that guarantees that bad notes are not accidentally accented. Like the simplest paired fingering exercise on the manual, the pedal technique needs to create a pattern of strong and weak related to the rhythmical structure of the measure. Working from the large muscle groups of the leg, it is possible to treat one leg as the strong "finger" and feel the weight applied transferring to the weak "finger." The two legs are then part of the same movement: the feeling is almost like stepping forward actively for the good note and shifting the weight sidewise over onto the other leg for the bad note. One could even go so far as to say that there is an analogy here to Baroque dance.

The initial weight impulse is always applied to the good note, generally the note which falls on the first or third beat of a measure in common time. Then the weight is allowed to transfer from one leg to the other. Be aware that the weight is transferring in the upper muscles of the leg. Imagine the moment one leg chooses to take over pedaling from the other leg on a bicycle. This transference of weight rather than an entirely new application of weight guarantees that the bad note will never sound louder than the good note.

Playing the Sharps

How are sharps prepared for and played? The original pedal sharp keys of the Gerstenberg seemed to me to be too high. They were certainly higher than I was used to on any organ that I knew. I made the mistake of allowing my own concept about technique to change the instrument model and, as mentioned earlier in this chapter, that creates a feedback loop where the instrument then confirms your expectations rather than challenging them. John Barnes trusted me to copy one of the standard historically informed sharp heights of the modern period. I had access to the Jürgen Ahrend organ at the University of Edinburgh—whose pedal dimensions are completely representative of the historical North German organ tradition—and copied the dimensions of its sharps. But if the original Gerstenberg sharps are copied instead, as we have done on the subsequent copies, the desirability of playing alternating toes in "weight groups" of two is even more obvious.

If a student plays with a modern ankle technique and then comes to a sharp in the pedal line, the original sharps of the Gerstenberg are so high that the student is forced to lift the whole leg a bit to position the foot above the sharp for the attack. Thus the student experiences the benefits of

Original Gerstenberg Sharp

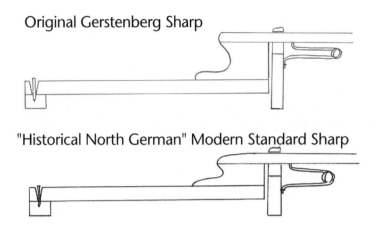

"Historical North German" Modern Standard Sharp

Figure 5.8. Original Gerstenberg and modern standard organ sharp heights.

an applied weight technique on the sharps. It is not long before this experience must be transferred to the naturals as well, because the naturals will all be noticeably quieter than the sharps until the same process is applied to all of the keys. Figure 5.8 compares the historical and nonhistorical heights of the pedal sharps.

Playing in triple meter

The sharps become even more difficult to play in a pattern of strong and weak accents when the line is in triple meter, as in the six trio sonatas discussed in chapter 2. In a passage such as the one in figure 5.9, pedaling left-right-and-right-again will automatically accent the last note because of the acceleration introduced when the same leg must move quickly to play two notes in a row. Moving the same leg from an accented natural to an unaccented sharp almost always results in the sharp sounding too loud, because of the acceleration created by the even larger movement of the leg up toward the sharp. A general rule might be:

> *Always (excluding the obvious exceptions) play the last two notes of a triple group with alternating feet. This guarantees that the weakest note in the group will never be too loud.*

Organ Articulation

Adopting this pedal technique results in high-quality articulation in organ playing. Movement necessary to change positions on the pedalboard can

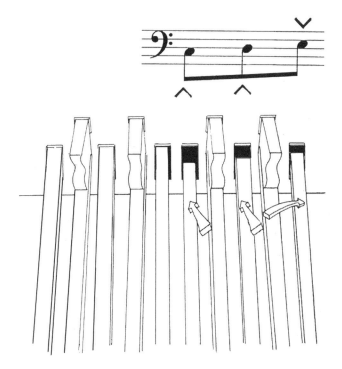

Figure 5.9. Pedaling in triple time.

then happen *between* groups of two notes, and not *within* groups of two notes. As a result, the release of the good note can be as slow and controlled as possible, and any larger articulation space happens before the next good note and *not* before the bad note. Since notes after long spaces sound stronger, the result of the pedal clavichord technique is to produce an articulation pattern on the organ that guarantees that bad notes will be less accented than good notes.

Moving through the Point of Attack

It is easier to control and repeat the amount of mass applied to a pedal key than the amount of acceleration. We use the same ability when we repeat a pattern of transferring weight from leg to leg over a constant distance every time we go up or down stairs. You have to miss a step only once to find out how completely committed the body is to guiding weight onto the foot at a pre-memorized height. This same commitment pays musical dividends at the pedal clavichord. Even after learning to produce a consistently good sound in the pedal in "weight groups" of two or three notes, it is still

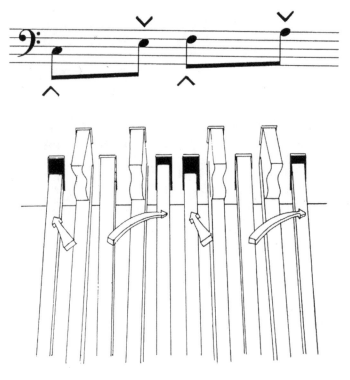

Figure 5.10. Pedaling.

tempting to move the leg until the foot is hovering over the next pedal key to be played, and then stop abruptly and depress the key from the ankle. In the same way that playing from the finger provides no control over how much mass is applied to the key, playing from the ankle also depends more on acceleration than mass and is less easily judged and exactly repeated by the body. The direct effect on the instrument's sound is apparent. The large muscles of the leg can judge and apply the same amount of mass to many pedal keys in a row, creating a good connection between tangent and string, and the same general dynamic level every time (see figure 5.10).

> At the pedal clavichord it is more efficient to make the movement of the leg to the new note an organic part of the attack. Practice moving toward notes on the pedal board at random with one leg and then the other. Concentrate on making a continuous movement toward the note, a movement that does not end early above the note but goes directly into the key and does not stop until the strings of the pedal note have been raised a few millimeters.

Position on the Bench

The original Gerstenberg bench was lost during the Second World War, but pictures of it show that it was covered with a padded leather seat. We chose to build a simple modern wooden bench that allows the player to move back and forth, but a padded leather bench forces the player to sit in the center of the bench and direct the natural weight of the leg toward the note to be played. Quick movements up and down the bench become much more difficult on a padded bench, and in time the player realizes that fewer are necessary.

In the next chapter, the simple technical process described here will be applied to the rich figural language of baroque keyboard music. I suspect that Bach encouraged his students to spend so much time on the step that is described in this chapter—simply learning to move the natural weight of your arm from one finger to another without picking your arm up off the keyboard—because when confronted with more complex figures it is so easy for the student to revert to playing only with the motion of the fingers, losing control over the all-important *tempi di buona e cattiva.*

6

Musica Poetica and Figural Notation

Musica Poëtica, or musical composition, is a mathematical science, in which one composes a lovely and pure ordering of the sounds, and commits them to the page so that afterwards they can be sung or played, and thereby in the first place to lead people into fervent prayer to God, and also to delight and amuse the Ear and the Mind.

—Johann Gottfried Walther

Musica Poetica

Originating in Martin Luther's concept that music was as powerful a tool for preaching the Gospel as the spoken word, an entire philosophy of constructing music based on the terminology of spoken rhetoric was developed in Germany in the seventeenth century known as *musica poetica*.[1] At first this discipline was most closely associated with music that had a sung text, the Cantor's music, as cantors followed Luther's admonition to preach the Gospel in song, but soon rhetoric became applied to instrumental music as well. Theorists like Johann Gottfried Walther borrowed language from rhetoric to describe musical form on every level. On a large scale, on the macro-level, for example, a piece could have an inspiring introductory *exordium,* a middle section where several themes were interwoven in *confutatio,* and resolve in a *conclusio.* At the same time, theorists also applied rhetoric to the micro-level, the level of the small musical figure that functioned like a word. Lists of these musical-rhetorical figures were published in treatises called *Figurenlehre* throughout the seventeenth and eighteenth centuries. The first *Figurenlehre* was published by Joachim Burmeister in 1606.[2]

J. G. Walther and the *Figura* from J. S. Bach's Time

The descriptions of *figura* closest in time and place to J. S. Bach are by the lexicographer Johann Gottfried Walther (1684–1748).[3] In 1708, Walther wrote a treatise on composition for Prince Johann Ernst of Weimar, the second volume of which is devoted to *musica poetica.*[4] In it, many of the *figure* discussed in his *Lexicon* already appear as compositional tools to be used in ornamenting consonances and dissonances in the melody. In his 1732 musical dictionary, Walther describes *figure* as

> the figures, consisting of several notes, which are put together in different ways, have from their specific shape [their *Gestalt*] specific names.

> . . . die aus etlichen auf verschiedene Art zusammen gesetzten Noten bestehende Figuren, haben von ihrer besondern Gestalt auch besondere Nahmen.[5]

He then gives several examples, including *figura corta,* a figure made of three notes where one note is as long as the other two, and *figura suspirans* where three notes of equal length are preceded by a rest.[6]

Both *figura corta* and *figura suspirans* are three-note figures, but neither of them demands the same physical gesture at the clavichord as the triplet of Griepenkerl's exercise described in the previous chapter. At the clavichord, *figura corta* uses the same pattern of weight application as *transitus,* but it tends to create a pattern of stronger accents on the first long note and light unaccented short notes (figure 6.1) more so than in *transitus* triplet motion. Increased acceleration toward the "good" note is generated by the increase in the speed of the notes preceding it. The fast notes literally propel the hand a little bit faster toward the next "good" note than in transitus motion, and even small differences like this are clearly audible in the dynamic response of the clavichord.

Figura suspirans, on the other hand, perfectly illustrates the way that different figures demand different physical gestures from the player. Because this figure begins with a rest, the only way to create the pattern of "good" and "bad" notes, described in the previous chapter, is to make the stron-

Figure 6.1. *Figura corta* at the clavichord.

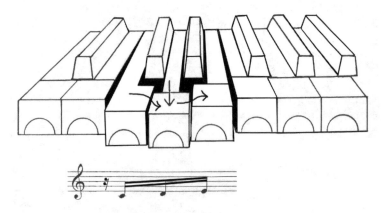

116 *Performance Practice Studies*

Figure 6.2. *Figura suspirans* at the clavichord.

gest accent in the middle. If the first note is shaped as if it is the *second* note of a *transitus* pair (one in which the first note was never played), then the good note in the middle will be more accented, because it will be prepared as if it were the beginning of a new pair. Using the fingering:—4 3 4 at first relates the figure to *transitus* playing and creates a shape in the clavichord strings like the one shown in figure 6.2.

Once the gesture is learned as a physical shape, this more awkward fingering can be replaced with:—2 3 4, and the physical gesture will still *feel* the same in the hand. This is a very important experience for the student! Once a gesture like this one is learned physically, repeating it at the keyboard no longer depends on a particular fingering. Because a pattern of work has been learned by the large muscle groups, it can be repeated using even unlikely fingerings and produce the same dynamic result. At the clavichord, the *Gestalt* of each figure—as Walther describes it—extends beyond the shape on the page and becomes a shape in the strings.

We do not know whether Walther and J. S. Bach experienced these musical-rhetorical shapes as physical gestures at the clavichord in the way suggested here, although imagining that they did so might help us understand why Walther called the clavichord the "erste Grammatica" for all the other keyboard instruments:[7] because the particular technique required to play the clavichord encouraged the shaping of notes in discrete groups, the clavichord, before all other instruments, was where you practiced your musical words.

Figures as a Tool to Create *Affekt*

Baroque teaching about the affections was built on the Renaissance idea that there were only four basic personality types: the choleric (hot-tempered), the phlegmatic (slow and impassive), the melancholic (sad, depressive), and the sanguine (calm, confident).[8] But even though everyone had a dominant personality type, the other three humors, or any combination of them, could be stimulated by music, and musical-rhetorical figures were the basic tools with which the performer could directly move people emotionally.

Later in the century, theorists wrote more explicitly about how these figures had emotional content that could be used to create these basic affects in music. For instance, in his 1788 Introduction to volume 1 of his *General History of Music,* J. N. Forkel divides figures into two categories: those of understanding and those of feeling. The figures of understanding are contrapuntal devices, while the figures of feeling are motivic shapes that can recall or create an association for the listener to a specific object, or emotion. Forkel goes on to define several of the traditional *Figuren* in terms of their emotional content, such as the difference between *dubitatio,* a musical-rhetorical figure that creates a hesitation in forward movement, and *suspensio,* one that merely creates a delay with no expression of "indecision."[9] In addition, Forkel not only describes the technique that automatically creates these word-length patterns at the clavichord (detailed in chapter 3), but also clearly sets out his theory about them:

> Syllables and words are put together from simple speech-sounds through which one can designate things and include their qualities and relationships. Likewise, for the designation of a feeling that includes its qualities and relationships, some musical syllables and words are put together from single tones that are partly of a similar and partly of a different nature. Sometimes a single tone, like all original feeling-sounds, can be sufficient for such a musical word. Sometimes, however, several are necessary, as in the common language often two, three or several syllables are necessary for a word. . . . In language, several words of different meanings are necessary for the complete designation of a thing. Through these words, the qualities and the actual relationship in which this object appears to us can be made recognizable. Just as in language, music also uses several tones of different inner meaning for the complete designation of a feeling.[10]

Like all languages, *musica poetica* functions at the level of the communal and the personal. Although Walther is closest to J. S. Bach in time and place, there were as many different lists of musical-rhetorical figures as there were theorists, indicating a diversity of opinion about the particulars of this tradition but also suggesting that it was a vital part of German Baroque music theory. Walther's names and descriptions for figures became a language with which to talk about technique and tone production at the clavichord. But modern notation makes it easier to see only endless rows of sixteenth notes and more difficult to see individual figures on the page, so an experimental notation was developed to make them more obvious for the student.

A Notation Experiment

As described in the previous chapter, the *Two-Part Inventions* seem to have served as the beginning literature for Bach's *Clavier* students, and in using them at the clavichord it became clear that we all know them entirely too well. The "little connected pieces" Bach wrote for his students were new experiences for them. But today most of us hold memorized performances of them in our fingers, or our ears. What was called for was a new notational picture that encouraged students to practice the figures as individual exercises. But reading from modern notation, it was too easy to revert to playing long lines of sixteenth notes with a finger technique only and to stop paying attention to shaping regular strong and weak beats, so that tone production at the clavichord suffered immediately.

One of the inspirations for this notation experiment was a study by Walter Heinz Bernstein of all of the *Two-Part* and *Three-Part Inventions*, in which Bernstein labels every musical-rhetorical figure in the score with a number that corresponds to a description in the introduction.[11] This publication is a helpful guide for the student who wants an introduction to the use of these figures in Bach's music. But as a performance score it still presents a normal note picture that does not address the main problem of students reverting to playing sixteenth notes without shaping each figure to produce the best possible tone at the clavichord.

What was needed was a note picture that introduced some resistance, that took a little more time and work to translate into a performance: a notation that showed motives rather than individual notes. The notation needed to be analogous somehow to the physical shaping of the musical-rhetorical figure at the clavichord. One inspiration for the notation experiment was Bach's own handwriting. The shapes of the beaming lines in the Berlin autograph manuscript of the *Two-Part Inventions*, sometimes very angular, sometimes gently rounded, seem to represent the character of the different motives visually. Even the way motives are grouped in space on the page visually clarifies structural aspects of the pieces. This kind of visual information disappears in modern notation.

The other inspiration for the notation experiment was a study of brush technique in traditional Chinese calligraphy. Chinese calligraphy and clavichord playing actually share several similar traits. Both practices create information using the simplest possible tools: in one case a stick with bristles contacting paper; in the other, a stick with a brass tangent contacting strings. Because the tools of these crafts are so simple, they demand a complex level of skill to manipulate them. The product of both processes is a language that must be readable and ought to be beautiful at the same time. Both traditions demand the manipulation of small basic finger shapes into complex gestures whose *readability* depends on their relationship in space to one another.

Even though the basic brush strokes in Chinese calligraphy take several radically different shapes, each always consists of only three separate actions. Each stroke begins with an *attack,* where the brush tip bends in order to allow ink to flow out onto the paper. It is followed by a *continuation* "sustained like a sung note, or a note played on a violin: it calls for an unflagging resolve to master the tension in the brush tip and not let it slacken for a moment." And finally there is the *release,* closing the element. It "is easier to execute. The opposite forces produced during the attack and sustained during the development are resolved; and the calligrapher relaxes his hold on the brush."[12]

The parallel to playing figures at the clavichord is astonishing. The attack at the beginning of the figure is also the moment of most active movement in the gesture, while the continuation corresponds to the transference of the same weight-application over several fingers. The gesture needs to feel like the pressure of the bow on a violin, and be carried all the way to the end of the figure. The description of the release corresponds to the total relaxation that the hand can experience between each figure as it prepares for a new gesture.

The inspiration for the notation experiment really came from the fact that the continuation of the brush stroke, like the continuation of the weight-impulse through a figure, can take so many different shapes (see figure 6.3).

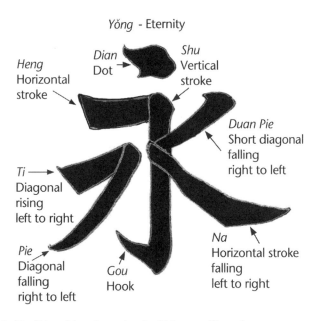

Figure 6.3. Traditional brush strokes in Chinese calligraphy.

Each one has a slightly different character and technical demand and must be mastered first for itself before it can be combined in whole characters. This family of shapes inspired the idea of creating a visual notation based on musical figures, one that gave the player only the initial note and the direction of the shape of the continuation phase of the figure. It also eliminated many notes from the page, clarifying where new weight impulses were required. The shape of the continuation line indicates the kind of figure that needs to be played, and the arrow point is meant to invoke a gentle release and relaxation at the end of the figure. Table 6.1 gives the rhetorical name and the figural notation for some of the most commonly used figures.

The *Two-Part Inventions* in Figural Notation

These figural notation ideas were combined to create versions of some of the *Two-Part Inventions*. Griepenkerl suggests that the inventions be studied in the following order: 1 and 8, followed by 12, 11, and 5. Inventions 1 and 8 are given in figural notation along with the original Bach manuscript versions in figures 6.4 through 6.7. [13]

By creating a completely new note picture for a very familiar piece, some creatively useful resistance is added to the experience of reading it at the keyboard. The note picture gives all the information necessary to practice the piece as Bach may have intended the pieces to be practiced: as connected pieces that are a series of exercises, each of which also needs to be practiced for itself. The students participating in this experiment could no longer play the *Two-Part Inventions* at sight without first taking time to learn each figure.

The result was that learning to play the figures with good tone and dynamic control, as if each figure were a small fantasia in itself, became the students' first priority, and this seems to be a necessary first step when learning new figures. The tendency at this stage in the process was for students to play each of the figures beginning equally strongly, and for the music to sound literally like a series of disconnected figures.

The final step in the process also has a close counterpart in Chinese calligraphy. Once the beginning calligrapher learns to form each of the individual strokes, then these strokes must be used to form a balanced and legible character in the same way that three or four figures must form a balanced and understandable single measure. The rules for creating balance within single characters are complex, but the most important rule is that everything can be playfully variable in proportion and placement *except* the vertical lines. Again, the parallel to baroque music is striking. Those vertical lines are like the beginnings of measures, around which musical gestures can be arranged with some variation and discretion.

Table 6.1.

1. Transitus

2. Syncopatio

3. Superjectio

4. Anticipatio

5. Subsumtio

6. Variatio

Table 6.1. *(continued)*

7. Figura corta

8. Mora

9. Messanza

10. Tirata

11. Circolo mezzo

12. Passus duriusculus

Table 6.1. *(continued)*

13. Saltus duriusculus

14. Elipsis

15. Groppo

16. Bombus

17. Suspirans

18. Tremolo

Figure 6.4. Inventio 1, C Major, BWV 772a, in J. S. Bach's hand. Statsbibliothek zu Berlin Musikabteilung mit Mendelssohn-Archiv (Mus Ms Bach P 610). Reproduced with permission.

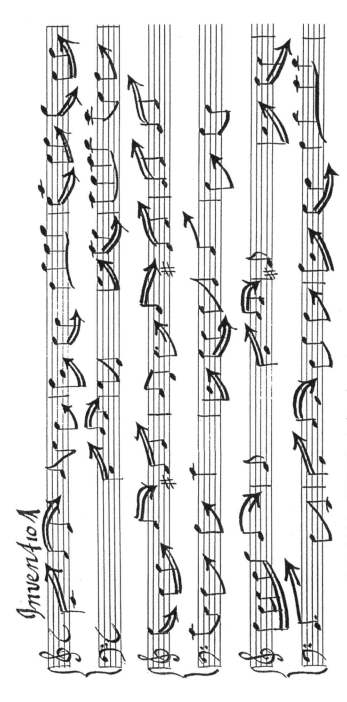

Figure 6.5. Inventio 1, C Major, BWV 772a, in figural notation.

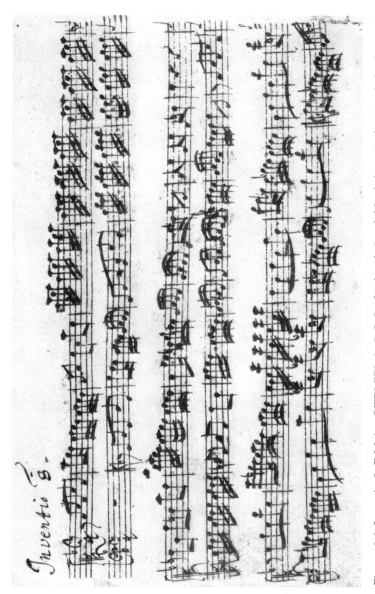

Figure 6.6. Inventio 8, F Major, BWV 779, in J. S. Bach's hand. Statsbibliothek zu Berlin Musikabteilung mit Mendelssohn-Archiv (Mus Ms Bach P 610). Reproduced with permission.

Figure 6.7. Inventio 8, F Major, BWV 779, in figural notation.

Table 6.2. The three steps in the execution of calligraphic characters and rhetorical figures at the clavichord.

CALLIGRAPHY	CLAVICHORD
Stroke	Figure
Character	Measure
Column	Stave

The complexity and creative tension in Chinese calligraphy comes from this interplay between several layers of simple organization, beginning with the three distinct steps in every stroke, continuing with the method for organizing the strokes in characters around a central axis, and concluding with how characters are written in a line along that same axis. Likewise, there are three steps in the execution of each of the rhetorical figures at the clavichord, that are organized in measures according to good and bad notes, and each measure is written on a legible horizontal axis and heard and understood on a linear time axix (see table 6.2). The final step, therefore, is to play individual figures with good tone production and dynamic control, but to also play them in a larger structure of strong and weak at the level of the measure. This creative tension between the work at the level of the figure and the work at the level of the measure often begins automatically to engage students in confident and expressive music-making.

As has been mentioned before, the clavichord is the only keyboard instrument where there is no bottom to the keydip. But there *is* a point where you know you that you have gone too far. Just as when you press too hard on a calligraphy brush and ink floods out all over your paper, if you push the key down too far on the clavichord you've made a kind of inkblot in space by bending the pitch until it becomes a completely different note. This means that the three-dimensional pattern pressed into the strings has no absolute limits, only the ones set by aesthetics and taste.

A final calligraphic thought, whose parallel to performance at the clavichord perhaps needs no further elaboration:

> The hand's main function is to hold the brush firmly and impart to it the impulses of the arm. One may speak of the "gestures of the hand," but this is a figure of speech: a calligrapher does not write with his hand, but with his whole arm. It is also a figure of speech when the Chinese refer to "wrist power" (*wan-li*), which they consider one of the main assets of the good calligrapher; actually the wrist simply transmits to the hand the force coming from higher up.[14]

Bach's Passacaglia in C Minor, BWV 582: A Case Study

To these, I add a very artfully composed Passacaglia, which is more for pedal clavichord than for the organ.
—Johann Nikolaus Forkel, as translated in *The New Bach Reader*

Early Manuscript History

Because of the lack of original manuscripts, the chronology of Johann Sebastian Bach's early works is problematic, but he probably composed the Passacaglia in C Minor, BWV 582, between 1708 and 1712 while he was living in Weimar.[1] All the surviving manuscripts of the Bach Passacaglia probably stem from two autographs, both now lost; the first was most likely in tablature, and the second, probably in score notation. The manuscript version of the Passacaglia widely regarded as closest to the first autograph of the piece appears in the *Andreas Bach Book*. The surviving manuscripts record much ambiguity about the title of this piece, including many references to *con pedale*. A 1911 catalog lists what is probably a copy of the second autograph[2] with the title *Passacaglio con Pedale pro Organo pleno.*[3] But Forkel's *Nachlaßverzeichniss* in 1819 records manuscripts with the titles *Pastorale per l'Org. F Dur* and *Passacaglia con pedale c moll* in the same line, preserving the distinction Forkel made in his Bach biography between the *Pastorale* as music for the organ and the *Passacaglia* as music "with pedal."[4]

Reactions to Forkel's Statement

Forkel's comment in his Bach biography that the Passacaglia was "more for the pedal clavichord than for the organ" has produced a long history of strong responses.[5] A very early one can be read in markings in a copy of the 1802 first edition of Forkel's Bach biography in the Library of Congress. The copy has only two penciled annotations, one of which is an addition to Forkel's repertoire list of Bach's music. On page 57, a Concerto in A for harpsichord, flute, and violin is added to the ensemble works, and the annotator cites an edition "bei Schott in Mainz 1850." The two parts of this annotation are signed "M." The second annotation, on page 60, is in the same hand, a more emotional than bibliographical note. "Passacaglia, which is more for pedal clavichord than for the organ," is crossed out twice, in pencil, and after it, written in the margin, in the same hand as the other annotation:

> ? ? Ganz unrichtig. Die Passacaglia ist eins der herrlichsten Orgelwerke. Man braucht aber eine Orgel mit 2 Clavieren oder 2 Manualen.[6]

The book was acquired by the Library of Congress in 1910, so this may represent a late-nineteenth-century reaction to Forkel, clearly after the clavichord has all but disappeared. In this personal response you can actually watch the thought-process unfold. It begins with total bafflement: "? ?," followed by denial: "Totally false," followed by defensiveness: "The Passacaglia is one of the most wonderful organ works," followed by justification: "but one needs an organ with 2 Claviers or 2 Manuals." With no active clavichord tradition left in Europe after 1850, the impulse to dismiss Forkel as "totally false" is understandable. But the justification is problematic: the piece can easily be played on an organ with a single manual and pedal, so misinterpreting the commonplace name of the pedal clavichord, "zwey Claviere und Pedal," does not prove, in and of itself, that the Passacaglia was intended for the organ.

Albert Schweitzer states that the Passacaglia is suitable for the organ because "there is no other organ piece that makes more demands on the art of registration than this."[7] Schweitzer's registration ideas become less relevant if the piece is played in a single plenum registration throughout, as some of the earliest autographs seem to suggest.

Criticism of Forkel's idea continued through the twentieth century. Two examples are the suggestion found in *The Bach Reader* that Forkel meant to imply the Passacaglia "was not a genuine organ work,"[8] and Walter Emery's conclusion that "whatever [Forkel's] opinion about the Sonatas may have been, it carries no more weight than his opinion about the Passacaglia; and the latter is absurd."[9] Forkel probably did not intend to suggest that the Trio Sonatas were more for the pedal clavichord than the organ. Chapter 2 discusses in detail the historical confusion over that rumor. But there can be no confusion about what Forkel intended to suggest about the Passacaglia, which is why the reaction of several scholars has been to claim that Forkel must have had no idea what he was talking about in general. Most recently, the 1922 catalog title, mentioned at the beginning of this chapter, has been used to lay to rest speculation about Forkel's comment once and for all,[10] and, indeed, it would be foolish to argue that Bach did not conceive of the Passacaglia as an organ piece. The fact that

Forkel chooses to list the Passacaglia among the organ works of Bach shows that he did not question that it was appropriate to the organ, but the caveat that it was also specifically appropriate to the pedal clavichord should not be dismissed as "absurd" without a careful reappraisal. In this chapter, two possibilities will be explored. First, the pedal clavichord may have played a role, for Bach and members of his circle, in preparing the piece for the organ. I practiced and taught the work on the pedal clavichord copy as a test case, and the report on the ways the pedal clavichord might be helpful to prepare the piece for organ performance concludes this chapter. The second possibility is that Forkel may have been suggesting that, of all Bach's pedaliter works, this one had a dual provenance. Maybe the passacaglia and *ciaccona* tradition in general was associated as much with domestic music making as with the organ, and Forkel's comment is meant to acknowledge this tradition while in no way removing Bach's piece from the organ canon.

The Passacaglia Genre: Its Origin and Development

The passacaglia, like the *ciaccona*, is a set of variations over a repeating ostinato bass pattern. The passacaglia is a fairly common seventeenth-century compositional form but has a different history from the other dance forms that appear in Baroque keyboard suites. Unlike the dance form of the *ciaccona*, it began as a ritornello vamp for the guitar, a bass pattern that could be ornamented upon in between verses of a song.[11] After the passacaglia and *ciaccona* were combined as a genre pair for keyboard suites by Frescobaldi in the 1630s,[12] they spread north of the Alps with the rest of the Italian music revolution. Although the passacaglia remained a guitar tradition in Spain and developed more as an orchestral and ballet genre in France, in northern Europe it became almost exclusively a keyboard tradition. (Is this because the guitar did not become popular in Germany until the late eighteenth century?) Extensive organ pedal divisions developed earlier in Germany than elsewhere, so it is not surprising that these pieces often had ostinato bass lines in the pedals, but that does not automatically make them organ music: there were also many German domestic keyboard instruments with pedals.

The single examples of passacaglia*s* from Dieterich Buxtehude (ca. 1637–1707) and Bach appear extremely late in this tradition, and so it is misleading to see them as typical examples of a living tradition at all.[13] They are, in a sense, art music about art music. They are monuments out of all proportion, in both size and complexity, to an already antique tradition of early seventeenth-century domestic keyboard playing, which in itself was an art-music interpretation of a folk guitar tradition.

Were these German ostinato-based keyboard pieces meant to capture the spirit of the original tradition? In other words, were the Passacaglias meant to sound like guitar variations even though they were for keyboard?

Passacaglias for guitar can be found throughout the eighteenth century and are still a feature of the folk music of Latin America to this day.[14] The clavichord is a logical choice to imitate the intense and intimate emotional world of the solo guitar (or any plucked stringed instrument for that matter). Although the harpsichord is plucked like the guitar, only the clavichord can imitate the guitar's intimate dynamic range and its ability to use pitch-bending as an expressive musical element. In sixteenth-century Spain, when the *ciaccona* became popular, the vihuela (a gut-stringed plucked chordophone like a lute) and the clavichord were thought of as a natural pair. Thomas de Sancta Maria, who died in 1570, wrote a teaching book intended interchangeably for the clavichord and the vihuela.[15]

There are figuration patterns found in German keyboard *ciacconas* and passacaglias which, when played on the clavichord, sound particularly guitar-like. The acoustic guitar, like the clavichord, cannot sustain a note for very long, and must frequently repeat notes for dynamic intensity. However, because it is also capable of subtle micro-dynamics, these repeated-note figures continuously change in tone color. At the end of the D-minor *Ciacona* of Johann Pachelbel (1653–1706), for instance, there are two variations, starting in m. 125 and m. 129, with a written-out overlapping legato. The bad note is often a repetition of the good note in the previous group, creating a kind of sustaining in the strings like plucking the same guitar string repeatedly (see Example 7.1).[16]

The same kind of pattern occurs in the Buxtehude Passacaglia.[17] Alternating chords, beginning in measure 80, produce a maximum sustained volume from the strings of a clavichord, akin to repeatedly strumming or plucking the same chord on a guitar, and, once again, with the dynamic sensitivity of the guitar or the clavichord, subtle crescendos and decrescendos happen almost automatically from the physical process of playing the figuration (see Example 7.2).

The same approach to figuration as a means of getting the greatest dynamic response out of the clavichord may be seen in the final two variations of the Bach Passacaglia, where a kind of pedal point is created by repeating the same *circolo mezzo* figures over and over (see Example 7.3). Unlike the Pachelbel and Buxtehude examples above, this is clearly a figure

Example 7.1. Johann Pachelbel, *Ciacona* in D Minor, mm. 144–45.

Example 7.2. Dieterich Buxtehude, Passacaglia BuxWV 161, mm. 84–85.

Example 7.3. Johann Sebastian Bach, Passacaglia BWV 582, mm. 120–21.

specifically for the keyboard, but the pattern of repetition and the dynamic response is the same. The two harmonic arpeggio variations (mm. 112–128) are also strongly reminiscent of guitar figuration.

The Passacaglia as Domestic Music?

The idea that ostinato-based pieces might also have been thought of as domestic music would remain too speculative to entertain if it were not for the fact that the earliest manuscript source of the Bach Passacaglia shows a penchant for ostinato-based pieces and an interesting tendency towards music for domestic use. It is now accepted that the *Andreas Bach Book* (ABB), which records both the Buxtehude and Bach Passacaglias as well as six other ostinato-based pieces, was compiled by Bach's eldest brother, Johann Christoph Bach (1671–1721), with whom Johann Sebastian Bach lived for five years after his father died in 1695.[18] The *Möller Manuscript* (MM) was also compiled by Johann Christoph Bach and directly preceded the ABB, giving us a record (with a few unsolved mysteries about secondary copyists) of what kind of music Johann Christoph Bach was collecting continuously between about 1703 and 1713.[19]

A survey of this music from both volumes shows a clear tendency toward domestic music-making. An extra layer of ornamentation in both manuscripts also strongly suggests that they were used not just for study, but also represented Johann Christoph Bach's personal musical taste.[20] Robert Hill's dissertation on the MM and the ABB does not make a genre study of the two manuscripts, but invites this sort of analysis of them as a logical outgrowth of his work:

> Given the breadth of styles and genres represented, the contents of the two manuscripts could be profitably studied from a variety of viewpoints. Works of the same genre, such as fugues, suites or ostinato movements could be compared with each other, for example.[21]

One logical point of departure for a survey of these two volumes is to determine first the presence or absence of independent pedal lines. The simple fact that a piece is *manualiter* doesn't exclude a performance on a large organ, but it does include the possibility of a performance on a single-manual house instrument. In the following survey it will be shown that the frequency of domestic music in the two volumes raises the possibility that they were primarily used in music study and performance outside the church.

The Möller Manuscript (MM)

The Möller Manuscript contains 54 entries, four of which are fragments, five of which are in open score notation, and two of which are ornamentation tables. Of the 43 solo keyboard works in the volume, 81 percent are *manualiter* pieces.[22] Of the remaining pieces, some make extensive use of the pedal[23] and some contain only pedal points.[24] Only six *pedaliter* pieces (14 percent of the keyboard works) in the Möller Manuscript are conceived exclusively for large organ. The two pieces with pedal points (5 percent of the keyboard works) could have been conceived for a large organ, but could just as easily have been performed on a house instrument with a simple pull-down pedal board. The pedal-point pieces also represent a South German and Italian influence as opposed to the North German tradition, which used the pedal much more extensively.

The Andreas Bach Book (ABB)

Of the 57 entries transmitted in the ABB, two are fragments and one is an ornamentation table, leaving 54 solo keyboard works, 61 percent of which are *manualiter*.[25] The pedal pieces in the ABB can be classified in three groups rather than two. As in the MM, there is a clear distinction between pieces that only have pedal points[26] and the pieces that are conceived to take full advantage of the organ pedal,[27] that both make up roughly the same percentage of the ABB as the MM (7 percent and 14 percent, respectively, for the ABB, and 5 percent and 14 percent, respectively, for the MM). In addition to these two, a new category of pedal treatment appears in the ABB: pieces that use the pedal minimally.[28] Three pieces have a single, simple bass statement in the pedal at the end. These pedal statements expand the texture of final phrases for emphasis, and could easily be performed on an instrument with a simple pull-down pedal.

Finally there are the pedal ostinato-based pieces. There are five pieces that have simple slow ostinato bass patterns throughout.[29] The Buxtehude *Ciaconna*s develop the bass-line material in sixteenth-note patterns in a way that directly foreshadows Bach's use of the pedal in his own Passacaglia. Kerala Snyder comments that the ABB is the only surviving source for these Buxtehude pieces with ostinato bass lines, and "the works of Buxtehude transmitted by these manuscripts stand in rather sharp contrast to their repertory as a whole."[30] The general trend toward house music in both volumes, combined with the repeated appearance of the *ciaccona* in *manualiter* as well as in *pedaliter* versions, must raise the question of whether the *pedaliter* ostinato-based pieces constituted another contextual genre, primarily thought of as domestic music for house instruments, not excluding the organ, but in the first place conceived for pedal harpsichord or pedal clavichord. However, the sharp contrast between the ostinato-based pieces and the rest of the volume remains. Another possibility—that several ostinato-based pieces were being collected by Johann Christoph Bach for a specific compositional study— does not exclude that they were being played at home.

Even though the ABB contains much larger *pedaliter* ostinato-based pieces, the MM and ABB each include six examples, if you count the fragment of *Overture and Chaconne*, Number 39 in the MM. The MM also has a full *ciaccona*, Number 24, and four of the dance suites (including the dance suite in open score) contain an ostinato-based piece.[31] None of these six examples is *pedaliter*.

And finally there is Number 24 in the ABB, the incomparable Bach Passacaglia, which bends rules, stretches forms, and combines traditions. It begins by using the simple pedal ostinato pattern of the other pieces and becomes a virtuoso *pedaliter* work. This brief look at the context in which the Bach Passacaglia appears in the ABB answers no questions, but it raises an important one: is the Bach Passacaglia exclusively an organ work or is it also the most advanced extant example of an eighteenth-century German house-music tradition?

Performing the Passacaglia on the Pedal Clavichord

The arguments against performing this piece on the pedal clavichord seem to be based on the idea that the pedal clavichord is not capable of competing with the organ as a performance instrument. But such a practical physical experiment wasn't possible through most of the twentieth century because of a dearth of clavichords that were close enough to the eighteenth-century instruments to make an experiment possible. Griepenkerl suggests that organists were actually paying a price for no longer using pedal clavichords to prepare performances for the organ. This case study is offered as a small down payment on that debt. There are always two levels of experience that need to be documented when discussing the pedal clavichord: a study of the Passacaglia on the pedal clavichord may benefit, rather than compete with, a performance at the organ; and that study can show the possibility of expressing musical gestures dynamically that cannot be re-created at the organ.

The Pedal

The pedal can play a critical role in ostinato-based pieces. The conscious placement of strong and weak beats in the pedal provides the steady rhythmical pulses around which the manual parts are organized. The critical role that the pedal always plays is more quickly discovered in ostinato-based pieces because the material repeats. In order for the listener to experience variations, the bass itself ought to create an impression of consistency. But to some extent, the same task applies to playing any long slow line in the pedal: a steadily recurring articulation pattern in a chorale melody, for instance, is equally important to the feeling of overarching structure and forward movement in the piece.

The organist creates a repeatably consistent pattern of articulation in the pedal. But at the pedal clavichord we must go one step further and ensure that the dynamic relationship between strong and weak beats is consistent; if a weak beat is accidentally played too loud, it is difficult for the performer to pretend that it was intentional. Their actual dynamic levels change, but the strong-weak pattern probably should not. One way to encourage consistency would be to play exactly the same pedaling for every statement of the ostinato theme. As outlined in chapter 5, one would normally play in "weight groups" of two notes starting on the strong beats of the measure (see figure 5.3). But the Passacaglia bass pattern provides an interesting exception to the rule: it presents us with a pattern of gestures that all start on beat three, the weakest beat of the measure.

There are not nearly as many kinds of figures in the pedal as in the manual, but this upbeat figure is an interesting exception. Falling naturally over the bar line, it presents a complex articulation problem, because the stronger of the two beats is still the half note on the downbeat of the measure. If we were to borrow a term from prosody, it might be called a *trochee*. In Johann Mattheson's (1681–1764) *Der vollkommene Capellmeister,* the metrical aspects of music are addressed in an individual chapter, in-

cluding the names of the basic metrical feet. Mattheson introduces a specific term for their application in music: *Klangfüsse*.[32] If we apply what was
learned in chapter 6 about the character of the *suspirans*, where the first
note of the figure is also active but weaker than the following note, this
trochee shape can create an effective articulation pattern at the organ and,
equally, a good consistent dynamic response at the clavichord. The upbeat
can be treated as a weaker note than the note that follows it. This guarantees that the articulation for the downbeats will always be consistent. Not
just the same pedaling, but the same physical gesture should be repeated in
order to achieve a consistent dynamic pattern. It is easy to slur over the bar
line toward these downbeats at the organ, and even worse, to do so incon-
sistently, so that the articulation pattern in the pedal fades in and out of
focus throughout the piece. But this pattern also physically creates a dance-
like gesture for the performer where all of the movement in the body is on
beat 3, and it is as if a dancer comes to a moment of rest at beat 1.

   Like all figures at the clavichord, the small, necessary physical movements needed to prepare to play the next group of notes are made *between*
the groups instead of in the middle of them, where the player's body can be
almost completely still. Saving all preparatory movement for the time between the figures serves a vital purpose: it provides the extra acceleration
that creates a strong beat at the beginning and contributes to the illusion
that the next figure will sound like a discreet and coherent word. This
pattern of movement is merely the basic grammar of the sentence, not the
only means of expression available to the performer. But if the basic grammar is repeated every time that the ostinato sentence is repeated, although
it naturally comes out slightly differently every time, the pattern of relative
dynamics between strong and weak notes remains consistent. If the pattern
of articulation is repeated consistently, the ostinato theme will be recognized as the same sentence, no matter how it is emoted. An actor can deliver the same Shakespearean line in many ways, with a different relationship to the iambic pentameter of the line each time, without ever actually
destroying the meter. "To be or not to be" represents a lifetime of interpre-
tive trouble (and gratifying options) without changing the sentence's grammar to: "to be or to not be."

The Passacaglia as a Dictionary of Figures

Bach provides us with many opportunities to practice playing figures gram-
matically in the variations of the Passacaglia. The *Orgelbüchlein* is often
discussed as a dictionary of musical-rhetorical figures, where each chorale
explores one or two of them often derived from the chorale melody, and
expresses a specific affect often associated with the chorale text. The
Passacaglia is also like a dictionary of musical-rhetorical figures, arranged

from simplest to most complex, and every variation exhausts the possibilities inherent in each figure before moving on to the next. One of the key differences between a clavichord and organ performance is the discovery that, at the clavichord, there is a kind of built-in dynamic crescendo. The way in which the order of the figures is arranged, when played on the clavichord, leads to a slowly increasing dynamic and rhythmical tension. The number of natural weight impulses per measure increases steadily throughout the work, from only one per measure in variation 2 to six per measure in variation 18.[33]

The following overview of the Passacaglia does not use musical-rhetorical figures to make a compositional analysis of the piece. Rather, for each variation, the essential figures and compositional elements are discussed in relation to performance, both at the pedal clavichord and the organ. Their execution on both instruments is choreographically similar but slightly different in realization.

Table 7.1 gives the dominant figure in each variation, and what that figure might look like in figural notation. Each notational sign tries to capture the very different weight-transference characteristics of the individual figures.

Variation 1, mm. 1–8: Unisono

Why does Bach choose to begin the piece with the first statement of the ostinato, unaccompanied in the pedal? It is a very rare choice among eighteenth-century ostinato-based pieces. When played on the organ, with an *organo pleno* registration (the historical organ registration indication), the piece begins simply and builds slowly to the fugue: a new level of polyphonic complexity just at the point where no greater level of figural complexity could be reached. The clavichord adds a third dimension to the experience of the Bach Passacaglia: dynamic expression. On the clavichord, unlike any other keyboard instrument, it is possible to experience the border between silence and sound. It is possible at the clavichord to play increasingly softly until the sound the performer is playing becomes indistinguishable from silence.[34] The clavichordist is familiar with this phenomenon of sound growing out of and returning to absolute silence, and, at the clavichord, the haunting *unisono* opening of the Passacaglia can come out of absolute silence. *At the organ, this experience can help students create an atmosphere from the first note of the piece.*

Variations 2 and 3, mm. 8–24: Dubitatio, *quarter note*

The second and third variations use a single suspension figure that Forkel would probably describe as *dubitatio* rather than *suspensio*. On the clavichord, it is the quietest possible figure of all, because the long slow suspensions consist of a single weight impulse for each figure, that begins

Table 7.1.

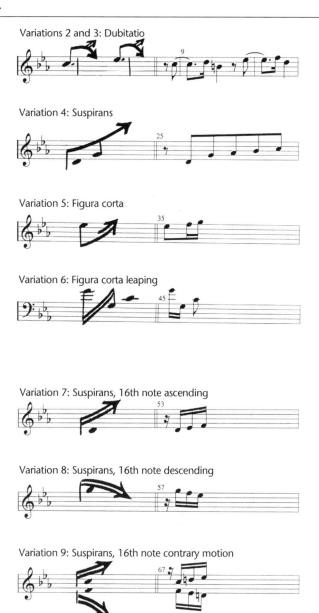

Table 7.1. *(continued)*

Variations 11 and 12: Transitus 16th note

Variation 13: Superjectio 16th note

Variation 14: Circolo mezzo 16th note

Variations 15 and 16: Harmonic variations

Variation 17: Congeries

Variation 18: Transitus 16th note

Variation 19: Figura corta

Variations 20 and 21: Circolo mezzo 16th note

on the weakest possible beat: the last eighth note of every measure. The sustained notes of the suspensions die away fairly quickly and can be prolonged effectively using *Bebung*. The articulation pattern in the pedal, discussed above, is crucially important in these two variations. *At the organ, an articulated downbeat in the pedal of each measure strengthens the effect of the suspensions in the manuals.*

Variation 4, mm. 24–32: Suspirans, *eighth note*

Variation 4 moves from quarter-note to eighth-note motion, but Bach reserves a strong weight impulse on every downbeat for later in the piece. The eighth-note figure in variation 4 consists of mostly *transitus* motion and often begins with a rest on the downbeat. At the clavichord, this *suspirans* figure helps to maintain a softer dynamic level by avoiding as many downbeats as possible: see the soprano in m. 24, the alto in m. 25, the tenor in m. 30 and the alto in m. 31. A shorter, three-note version of the *suspirans* figure also appears in the tenor in m. 24 and in the soprano in mm. 28–30. At the clavichord, a careful shaping of dynamics in the *suspirans* figure is needed, because the main weight application is organized around the second note, not the first. *At the organ, this encourages a slower release from the second good note of the figure than from the first bad note.*

Variation 5, mm. 32–40: Figura corta, *eighth and sixteenth note, transitus*

Variations 5 and 6 move to a new level of complexity using *figura corta,* the figure that combines eighth and sixteenth notes. Bach presents it first in a softer version in variation 5, where the motion is almost exclusively *transitus*. It is softer in comparison to the following variation because the weight transference in this figure in *transitus* motion does not involve the extra acceleration that leaping motion always introduces. The figure therefore tends to be strongest on the important beats and taper away toward the end. As has been pointed out before, this is just the basic grammar of the figure at the clavichord, the shape of the word only. If, however, this grammar is played with attention to the larger phrases and the Baroque hierarchy of beats in the measure, it can produce a complex and interesting result. *At the organ, playing the eighth note followed by two sixteenth notes as a figure automatically establishes a hierarchy of articulation where the sixteenth notes do not get too active, reducing the tendency to slur over the bar-line to the next important eighth-note beat.*

Variation 6, mm. 40–48: Figura corta, *eighth and sixteenth note, leaping*

The figure used in variation 6 is a leaping version of *figura corta,* naturally louder at the clavichord than the *transitus* version. The extra acceleration from the leaps translates into extra force applied to the strings. The leaping figure also appears in the pedal, in the first rhythmical statement of the ostinato theme there. It is clear from the rhythmical statement in the pedal that the motion is still a *trochee,* from beat three to beat one. Just as in the normal statement of the ostinato, discussed above, the weight goes to the strong downbeat, making sure it is dynamically stronger at the clavichord *and articulated at the organ.*

Variation 7, mm. 48–56: Suspirans, *sixteenth note, ascending*

Bach moves on logically to the next most active level of figuration: the *suspirans* at the sixteenth-note level. For the first time in the piece, there is sixteenth-note motion on every beat in the measure, but by using the *suspirans*—a figure that has no strong downbeats—Bach delays as long as possible the move to continuous sixteenth-note figuration. In variation 7 the *suspirans* is an exclusively ascending figure. The chains of *suspirans* figures in this statement almost all end in quarter notes or dotted eighth notes, which on the clavichord are softer than sixteenth-note motion. *At the organ, these new weight impulses on quarter and dotted eighth notes automatically produce clear articulation at the beginnings of measures and important beats.*

Variation 8, mm. 56–64: Suspirans, *sixteenth note, descending*

In variation 8, the *suspirans* is an exclusively descending figure. While in the previous statement the figure appeared in each voice as a three-note motive, in this statement, the figure has doubled in length, and is used in stretto with the original three note figure, in cascading descending chains. The longer version of the *suspirans* figure appears only in the soprano voice. If the player uses a single weight impulse for the whole figure, then beat two will remain completely unaccented, strengthening the feeling of the 3–1 movement over every bar. *At the organ, the soprano voice is heard sustained much more clearly on beat 2 of every measure of the variation, whereas there is always a three-part texture on beats one and three.*

Variation 9, mm. 64–72: Suspirans, *sixteenth note, contrary motion*

Bach continues the figural crescendo by next presenting the same figuration in contrary motion, using the longer version of the figure in all voices and in a consistent three part texture in the manuals. At the clavichord one of the most effective ways to strengthen a solo line is to play the line in thirds, as in the soprano and alto in m. 65 or the alto and tenor in m. 67. In order to sound at all on the clavichord, a passage like this must be practiced in groups of two notes. There is no time to play each of them with a separate impulse. *At the organ, especially one with the touch characteris-*

*tics of the North European organ, the cleanness of execution in these six-
teenth-note running-third passages can benefit technically from the performers having practiced their background grammar on the clavichord.*

Variation 10, mm. 72–80: Suspirans, *sixteenth note, leaping*

The same variation process we saw in variations 5 and 6 is followed in 8, 9,
and 10. At the end of a set of variations exploring a single figure, Bach fin-
ishes once again by restating the figure in leaping motion. And as in variation
6, it also appears in a rhythmical version of the ostinato bass in the pedal.

Variations 11 and 12, mm. 80–96: Transitus, *sixteenth note*

In the next statements, we finally reach continuous sixteenth-note motion
for the first time in the piece, and again Bach presents the figuration in its
quietest version first. Variation 11 has a solo sixteenth-note line accompanied by a quieter quarter-note version of the ostinato in the pedal. In variation 12, *transitus* motion accompanies the ostinato theme in the soprano.
The sixteenth-note figuration in this line is actually a combination of *transitus* and *circolo mezzo* figures, but the effect is of a long unbroken line of
sixteenth notes. In later variations Bach uses *circolo mezzo* figures exclusively to achieve specific effects. There is, however, a clear pattern that can
be mentioned about these two variations. The *transitus* figure always appears on beat two, and in 13 out of 16 measures, in descending motion,
continuing the weak treatment of beat 2 in the ostinato pattern. On the
clavichord, the *circolo mezzo* figures on almost every first and third beat in
both variations tend to be a little louder than the *transitus* figuration, because the sudden change of direction in the middle of the *circolo mezzo*
figure produces some extra acceleration in the attack. *At the organ, the
alternation between* circolo mezzo *and* transitus *can be used to create maximum contrast between the strong beats 1 and 3, and the weak beat 2.*

Variation 13, mm. 96–104: Superjectio, *sixteenth note*

Variation 13 is often seen as the first important moment of climax in the
piece. It is the only variation with sixteenth note motion in the pedal, and it
is flanked on either side by unusually quiet variations where the pedal is
silent. Variation 13 happens to be the golden section point of the Passacaglia:
13 of 21.[35] This might explain the sudden activity in the pedal in this variation, and it is surely one of the places where Schweitzer thought the wrong
registration changes at the organ might create a "picture of discontinuity"
in the piece. Even with the accepted *Organo pleno* registration, the contrast between variations 12 and 13 is enormous. But this is part of the
variation tradition, to create lightning-quick changes of mood and affect.[36]

And variations 12 and 13 follow the same pattern, seen twice already in the Passacaglia, of stating figuration first in a soft version and then in a louder version. However, even though variation 13 is clearly louder than the surrounding variations, the contrast between variations 12 and 13 is not so striking on the clavichord as it is on the organ. First, the presence of the ostinato theme in the soprano, the weakest range of the clavichord, necessitates that the performer play the rest of the figuration as softly as possible in order for it to be heard at all. Next, the sixteenth-note figuration appears mostly in a single voice at a time, with some overlapping, unlike the continuous sixteenth-note motion of variation 9. Finally, the eighth- and half-note passages in the other voices are much louder at the organ than at the clavichord, where the half notes especially do not sustain over their full value. At the clavichord, the paired figuration of the *superjectio* creates an underlying structure of *transitus* motion at the eighth-note level. It has to be played strictly according to the Baroque hierarchy of beats at the level of the figure and at the level of the measure: a stronger impulse for the first group of two than for the second within the figure, and a stronger impulse for the first group of four notes than the second and third groups at the level of the measure. Each note in a texture like this cannot be played with a completely new attack. If the execution of a passage like this is not planned using a larger-scale gesture, the action of the pedal is heard more than the sound of the strings. *At the organ, the extra work of shaping the pedal notes into a strict hierarchy prevents the articulation in the sixteenth-note line, especially in the pedal, from becoming too active, and creates subtle dynamic contrasts throughout the line. And at the historical organ, this approach will also control excess noise from the action.*

Variation 14, mm. 104–112: Circolo mezzo, *sixteenth note*

Bach uses the *circolo mezzo* figure exclusively for the first time in variation 14. In the 1844 Griepenkerl edition, these *circolo mezzo* figures have slurs over them that are not present in the Andreas Bach Book version of the piece. Griepenkerl's edition however, descends from a manuscript copied from a second autograph that was probably in staff notation. The ABB most likely descends from the first tablature autograph. Are these bow marks original to the second autograph or are they Griepenkerl's own addition? At the clavichord, the effect of these slurs is to make it clear that the figure has returned to a single weight impulse for every four sixteenth notes, rather than the paired figuration of the previous variation. The slur simply cancels the additional weight impulse. It appears only over *circolo mezzo* figures and is noticeably absent in m. 109 over the descending sixths in the right hand, which have to be played in groups of two in order for them to sound at all on the clavichord. The ostinato theme has moved to the middle voice, and occasionally a note of the theme is replaced by a *circolo mezzo* figure. *At the organ, the experience of training* circolo mezzo *figures at the clavichord changes the player's sense of appropriate natural rhetorical accents. For instance, in m.* 106, *the final* circolo mezzo *in the alto voice can be played convincingly, as if it were still the single weight impulse of the ostinato theme that it has replaced, and played differently from the previous* circolo mezzo *figure in the voice on beat 2, which is not as structurally important to the statement of the theme.*

Variations 15 and 16, mm. 112–128: Two part variation and unisono harmonic variation, sixteenth note

The harmonic transformation of the theme that began in variation 14 is completed in the following two variations, both of which preserve the general *trochee* movement of the ostinato theme, where beats 3 and 1 are the most important. Bach has returned to the bare bones of the theme, with only two main weight impulses for each measure.

Variation 17, mm. 128–136: Congeries, sixteenth note

Like variations 12 and 13, variations 16 and 17 also create a huge dynamic contrast, but the contrast is, once again, less great on the clavichord than on the organ. The overlapping legato of the *congeries* figure, with four weight impulses per measure, can be played on the clavichord just as effectively in a melancholy affect as in a choleric one. The performer can even choose to begin this variation softly and build to the next variation, or to suddenly add the 16 foot strings in the pedal and make the largest possible contrast between variations 16 and 17. *One effective lesson the clavichord can teach the organist about this variation is the need to shape the final eighth-note chords in each measure so that they are true after-beats, and not louder than either the previous chord, or the following downbeat chord. Having puzzled over this problem with the aid of dynamics, the organist may find it easier to discover new ways of shaping this upbeat using rhetorical accents and articulation at the organ.*

Variation 18, mm. 136–144: Transitus, sixteenth note, triplet motion

At the clavichord this variation is naturally the loudest of all. With six weight impulses and eighteen sixteenth notes per measure almost continuously in two voices, this variation produces the most sustained sound from the clavichord of any of the figurations Bach uses. In addition, there is also important movement on beat 2, a final dynamic resource that Bach has been saving up until this point. Changes of direction in the figuration in mm. 127, 138, and 139, and a change in register in m. 142 all form important new dynamic impulses for beat 2 of the measure at the clavichord.

This new importance of beat 2 creates the first feeling of continuous dynamic intensity of any of the variations. *But even when playing forte at the clavichord there is still a gradual light and shade, a natural ebb and flow of intensity in the sound that can be used as inspiration to create a more nuanced performance at the organ.*

Variation 19, mm. 144–152: Figura corta, *eighth and sixteenth note, harmonic*

Bach returns to *figura corta* for variation 19 but uses it almost exclusively harmonically, dividing the voices comfortably between the hand, and thus guaranteeing that it can be played at the fullest possible dynamic level at the clavichord. Bach continues the pattern of also accentuating beat 2 from the previous variation by placing all of the harmonic statements of the *figura corta* squarely in the middle of each measure.

Variations 20 and 21, mm. 152–168: Circolo mezzo, *sixteenth note, "pedal point"*

Bach finally returns to *circolo mezzo* figures, but uses them this time as a kind of soprano pedal point. At the clavichord, the effect is extremely idiomatic to the instrument. By repeating the same figure on the same strings again and again, alternating back and forth between left and right hands, a pattern of energy is transmitted to the soundboard at the right periodicity to create a kind of standing wave effect, so that the resulting sound is a sum larger than its individual parts. The alto voice provides the same rhythmical pattern as the pedal, so that the general character of beats 3–1 is not completely lost. The only way to increase this effect is to double the number of voices, as Bach does over the final statement of the ostinato. Bach preserves the physical effect of rhythmically alternating left and right hands by continuing the figuration in alternation between outer and inner voices. *At the organ, the intensity of this figuration can be preserved by playing the* circolo mezzo *figures rhetorically and listening for the same effect to develop in the acoustics of the church.*

The Fugue

Several aspects of performing the fugue on the pedal clavichord are also worth mentioning. The first is that the countersubject of the fugue itself can be shaped dynamically at the clavichord in order to bring more clarity to the structure of the voices. In m. 181, for instance, the countersubject and the sixteenth-note figuration can be shaped dynamically in beat 3. The choreography the hand has to memorize in order to achieve this effect translates into a similar result on the organ using slight agogic accents in the articulation.

The use of register in the piece is also unusual for Bach's organ works in general. The figuration regularly climbs up to the top of the organ keyboard, to c^3, but never in competition with heavy or strong figuration in the pedal. When the pedal is silent for between measures 197 and 220, Bach uses the top octave of the keyboard extensively, and when the pedal comes in again, the figuration sinks after the first three measures and stays out of the top octave until measure 239, where figuration begins very low in the pedal and then continues up to c^3 just when the pedal is silent in m. 240 and again in m. 242. The *tessitura* climbs to c^3 twice more in the piece, first in m. 255, where a written out trill guarantees that it will be loud enough at the clavichord, and once again in mm. 261–62, where the high manual figuration alternates with the pedal figuration. The upper octave is the weakest register of the clavichord, and Bach avoids combining it in the fugue with sixteenth-note figuration in the pedal, a texture that is very difficult to play softly enough to balance with the top octave of the manuals. The only place in the piece where sixteenth notes in the pedal accompany notes in the upper octave begins in the last statement of the theme in m. 272, and here the pedal also uses the top four or five notes, its weakest register. This careful consideration of the balance between the upper register of the manual and the pedal throughout the fugue may suggest that Bach had the inherent balance characteristics of the pedal clavichord in mind during the composition.

The long trills in both hands in mm. 269–270 sometimes create a balance problem at the organ. They are very low in the register, and can make it difficult to hear clearly the pedal line at the organ. The result is exactly the opposite at the pedal clavichord, where trills in both hands in the tenor range of the instrument are the most effective way of making *enough* sound in the manuals to balance the pedal line at a *forte*.

Finally, the figuration itself throughout the entire fugue is constant sixteenth-note motion using almost exclusively *superjectio* motion—found elsewhere only in the thirteenth variation of the Passacaglia. But Bach often extends this motion to the third above (beginning in m. 204). It means that almost continuously throughout the fugue, the performer has six weight impulses per measure to use in order to create a sustained *forte* dynamic in the fugue on the pedal clavichord. And Bach creates a final *crescendo* of intensity in the last twelve measures of the piece by stating this figuration simultaneously in arpeggios in contrary motion between manuals and pedal.

Conclusion

In the twentieth century, one of the driving engines of the historically informed performance movement was the search for the appropriate instrument for a particular piece. But this argument was most often made from the consumer's perspective rather than from the producer's. We have been conditioned as an audience to want to know that we are hearing the music performed on the "right" instrument. The eighteenth-century attitude expressed by C. P. E. Bach is more from the producer's perspective. He says that all music should be played on the harpsichord and the clavichord interchangeably.[37] His rationale is that this process creates a better performer. He very explicitly states that different aspects of the same piece can be explored by working with it on different instruments, and he also makes it clear that each keyboard instrument complements the other. The clavichord, C. P. E. Bach says, is for the study of good performance. The same attitude should also apply to the repertoire for pedal clavichord and organ: not an "either-or" choice between the two instruments, but a dialogue between them.

Although the Passacaglia will always be great organ literature, there are aspects of a pedal clavichord performance that can broaden an organist's musical concept of the piece, as well as many technical challenges that encourage the performer to deepen his or her physical understanding of the piece. Some of these are audible and can be enjoyed by consumers, but many of them are tactile and are meant for the producers. For instance, as we saw in this chapter, each variation has its own dominant figure, and each one of them has different gestural requirements at the basic level of tone production. The consumer never hears this, but the performer has to learn a different kind of gestural choreography for each variation, which results in increased security at other keyboard instruments and provides a powerful tool for musical expression at these other instruments. The kind of gestures that are created of necessity at the pedal clavichord can find direct application at any organ, but especially at the North European organs, which have touch characteristics similar to the clavichord. Also, the pedal clavichord creates a different musical landscape for the ostinato-based literature than does the organ. The dynamic response of the instrument allows the performer to create an infinite variety of ways to state the ostinato theme, creating a means for making subtle variation without changing the articulation pattern. This process can be transferred to the organ, but is not naturally found there. An exploration of how figuration is used in ostinato-based pieces to create built-in dynamic arches at the clavichord may also lead to new insights about the compositional structure of these pieces.

It is to be hoped that insights born of having to come to terms with the pedal clavichord's more difficult demands—in basic tone production, in correct hand and leg position, in the judicious use of the natural weight of the arm, in the control of attacks and releases, and in training the fingers to rest quietly just off the surface of the keys until they are needed—all can serve organists in their quest to learn to draw out even more refined sound from the organ. From the organist's perspective, some of these functional aspects of technique that are clear at the clavichord might otherwise be easily ignored. In this process, the quality of the sounding result is the ultimate goal, and that reward is worth the extra effort.

8

The Pedal Clavichord and the
Organ in Dialogue

*The keys, like those of a carillon, severally required the weight of the whole
hand, to put them down.*
—Charles Burney

The Organ in Central and Northern Europe

In the 1770s, Charles Burney visited the Cathedral in Frankfurt am Main,
and reported that the organ was "not ill-toned, but . . . the touch [was] so
heavy, that the keys, like those of a carillon, severally required the weight
of the whole hand, to put them down."[1] Burney is a notorious complainer
about some aspects of the German musical aesthetic. Occasionally, things
he said were refuted or ridiculed in his translator's footnotes, which Burney
missed because he could not read German. Perhaps unwittingly, though,
Burney describes an instrument—typical of those in the mainstream of the
Central German organ tradition of Bach's day—that simply does not function with a finger technique alone, unlike the lighter-actioned English organs to which Burney was accustomed and which he unabashedly thought
were superior. But, in fact, the English, French, Spanish, and Italian organbuilding traditions all had comparatively lighter manual actions than the
organs built in Central and Northern Europe.

Pedal clavichords were not built everywhere in Europe during the eighteenth century—as far as we know, they were built only in central and
northern Europe and Scandinavia. And, as it turns out, that is exactly where
organs with large pedal boards and where a tradition of more elaborate
pedal playing developed first. The heavier actions of these organs probably
provide a clue to the role of the historical pedal clavichord. If the clavichords were to serve as practice instruments for organists, the touch characteristics of the clavichord and the organ would need to have been closely
related. What may be considered an impossible amount of mass by a modern clavichord player (or an eighteenth-century Englishman) could have
been reasonable to an eighteenth-century German organist.

Table 8.1. Great Organ at Alkmaar (NL): Initial resistance of key measured in grams.

	C	F♯	c	f♯	c¹	f♯¹	c²	f²	c³
HW	470g	385g	310g	290g	265g	225g	250g	250g	210g
OW	495g	365g	270g	240g	275g	205g	195g	215g	265g
RP	295g	260g	210g	200g	215g	220g	210g	215g	220g

The great organ at Alkmaar, the Netherlands, is well preserved and in perfect working order. Because it is one of the few large early eighteenth-century organs with its original action, it served as an important study reference for the action of the North German Organ Research Project in Göteborg.[2] Measurements were taken of the amount of force needed to overcome the initial resistance of a key. The measurements in table 8.1 show this mass in grams for representative keys from each of the three manuals. On the Hauptwerk, the 16' plenum without reeds was drawn, and the Oberwerk and Rückpositiv were measured with 8' plenum registrations that included reeds. It takes nearly a half kilogram to open the pallet of bass C on the Hauptwerk and Oberwerk. Coupling the Hauptwerk and Oberwerk manuals results in even more force being demanded of the player, but, in a general performance situation at Alkmaar with the plenum drawn, every key stroke requires about 250 grams of force from the performer.

A Force-Measuring Experiment

What relationship did the pedal clavichord have to this kind of organ, for which it was designed as a practice instrument? A new measuring method needed to be developed to explore this question. The first step was to compare more precisely the touch characteristics of the action of the reconstructed North German Organ in Örgryte nya kyrka, Göteborg, with the Gerstenberg clavichord copy: not only the amount of mass needed to play a note on each instrument, but also the pattern created by the application of that mass to the key through time. In cooperation with Carl Johan Bergsten, the technical engineer at GOArt, an experiment was designed to compare the key-touch characteristics of the two instruments. The historically informed reconstruction of the action on the new four-manual organ has a considerable amount of mass, when compared to modern standards: the keys, the trackers, and the rollers on the rollerboards are all made of oak.

The test was designed to measure the key-touch characteristics of any keyboard instrument in real time. The force needed to press the key down was continuously measured while the key was moving from its resting position to the lowest point in its keydip. The force was measured using a

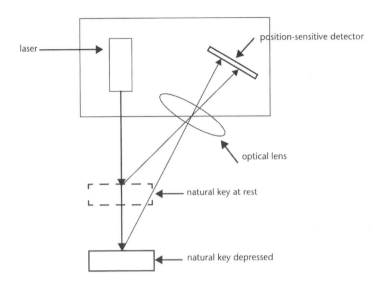

Figure 8.1. Key-position measurement by triangulation.

piezoelectric force sensor placed directly on the key (see figure 8.1). The sensor basically consists of a quartz crystal; under the action of a force, an electrical charge is set up on the crystal surfaces. The charge produced is directly proportional to the applied force. By measuring the charge that the crystal generates, the force can be calculated.

To measure the key position, a laser displacement sensor was used. The distance measurement is based on a principle called triangulation: a laser light beam sent from the sensor hits the top of the key surface. Some of the light is reflected back into the sensor through an optical lens arrangement and reaches a position-sensitive detector. The output signal from the detector depends on the position on the detector surface where the reflected light beam hits. When the key is pressed down so that the distance between the sensor and the key increases, the reflected light moves along the surface of the position-sensitive detector.

The laser displacement sensor was mounted about 40 mm above the key, and its laser beam was directed vertically down onto the key surface.[3] The test was performed on c^1 of the lower manual of the Gerstenberg copy (figure 8.2) and c^1 of the Hauptwerk of the North German Organ (figure 8.3) with 16' and 8' principals drawn.

There are two lines on each graph, the darker one measuring the force applied to the key in real time and the lighter one measuring the position of the key in real time. The line representing the position of the key on both graphs is upside down in order to show more intuitively the relationship

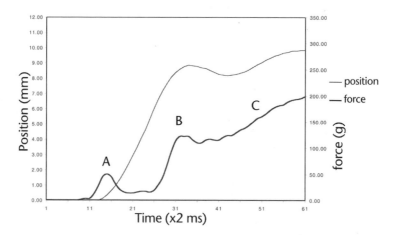

Figure 8.2. Force characteristics of Gerstenberg lower manual c¹.

between the force applied to the key and its position. Each figure can be analyzed in three sections: A) the free initial movement of the key, B) the moment of contact (when the tangent contacts the string or the pallet opens), and C) the steady state of the sound.

At A on the clavichord (figure 8.2), there is an initial spike during which the inertia of the resting key is overcome, and then the force drops again until B, when the tangent first touches the strings and the force curve spikes again to peak at 122 grams at C, where the steady state of the sound is reached. After that, the force curve follows the position curve almost exactly, showing that the steady state of the sound at the clavichord involves the continuous application of the same amount of force to the key for the length of the tone.

At A on the organ (figure 8.3), the force needed to overcome the inertia of the resting key is hidden behind the spring and pallet force. If the same experiment were done without the spring in place, and with no wind pressure on the pallet, the inertia of the organ key would be even greater than that of the clavichord key. With the pallet spring in place and the wind on, though, there is a steady increase in force as more and more resistance is produced up to B, the moment that the resistance of the wind pressure on the pallet is overcome. However, like the force exerted by the strings of the clavichord when in contact with the tangent, the force of the pallet spring remains constant. It took exactly 150 grams of force to overcome the plucking point of c¹ on the organ.[4] After that, at C, it can be seen that the application of force during the steady state of the sound at the organ is very different. The amount of force applied to the key can change radically and the key position will not change.

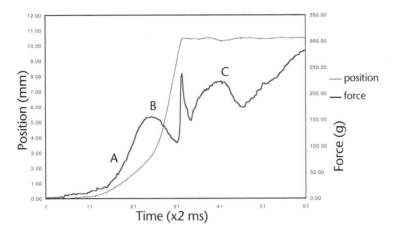

Figure 8.3. Key characteristics for North German Organ Hauptwerk c[1].

From this comparison we can see that the touch characteristics, both the amount of mass and its application through time, are comparable in both instruments if one compares the moment of opening the pallet on the organ with the moment of contacting and raising the strings with the tangent on the clavichord. On the clavichord, by playing through the moment of contact with the strings, one is practicing the moment at the organ *leading up to* the opening of the pallet. The initial touch characteristics of the two instruments are similar, but the clavichord remains more technically demanding than the organ because, unlike the organ, the same amount of force must be sustained through the length of the note. However, depending on the amount of extra resistance generated by manual couplers and larger registrations at the North European Baroque organ, this difference in technical demand may at times be even less. The experimental adoption of Edinburgh stringing on the Gerstenberg copy also creates a close similarity between clavichord touch and the touch of the historical North European Baroque organ.

The Pedal Clavichord and the North German Organist

The North German Organ Research Project in Göteborg was based on a close study of the instruments by Arp Schnitger (1648–1719), especially the extant pipework of his organ for Hamburg St. Jacobi, completed in 1693 (see figure 8.4).

Reports that two of J. S. Bach's students (Gerber and Kittel) taught organists on the pedal clavichord in their homes have already been discussed (in Chapters One and Five, respectively). How can we be sure that the

Figure 8.4. The new North German organ in Göteborg (Arvidsson, Yokota, van Eeken, 2000). Photo by Ulf Celander. Reproduced with permission from GOArt.

pedal clavichord was also relevant for organ teaching in North Germany? There are no extant pedal clavichords from Hamburg, but in 1710 the organist Friederich Erhardt Niedt published a treatise in Hamburg on the education of organists. The book has a long satirical introduction about, among other things, the organ education of a mythical Herr Tacitus.[5] Herr Tacitus had two organ teachers. The first one, Herr Orbilius of Poltersheim, was a disaster.

During the lesson, my teacher . . . played at first once or twice saying at the same time: "You have to play it thus and so, this is how I learned it." When I didn't improve, you should have seen the pleasure he took in teaching me the art through his excellent Inventions: the sixth sat on the right side behind the ear, the fourth on the left side, the seventh on the cheeks, the ninth in the hair, the diminished fifth on the nose, the second on the back, the minor third on the fingers, the major third and the fifth on the shin bone, the tenth and the eleventh were special ways of boxing the ears. Where the blow or punch fell, there I had to know what I should play, but the best of all was that my feet became fluent in pedal playing (which I started to learn at that time too) by being poked in the shin bones. . . . And one time he produced a special Invention and wanted to really kick the art of it into my body because all of his pedagogy without any foundation did not succeed in getting figured bass into my head. He dragged me by the hair off the pedal bench, on which I was sitting in front of the Clavier, threw me on the ground and dragged me into the air by my hair, so that my head in falling would strike the ground, and then stepped on my body and stomped on it for a good long while until finally . . . he dragged me out of the living room, and over to the stairs that led down to the street.[6]

Although there is a lot of pedagogy here that we probably do *not* want to reconstruct, this satire does suggest that, also in Hamburg, lessons for organists happened in the home on the *Clavier* with a pedalboard.[7] Long-suffering Herr Tacitus also finds a better teacher, Herr Prudentius from the city of Schönhall, who agrees to take Tacitus on as a student. Again, practice and probably also lessons for a beginning organ student happened in the home on the *Clavier.*

If you can afford to stay in this town for one year, I will teach you the true fundamentals both of the organist's art and the art of composition, in order that you can develop from an *Argenist* [annoyance] to an Organist. And for my trouble, I do not ask any payment, only that you promise to be industrious and to use the art for God's praise. I will teach you for free, daily, one hour between 7 and 8 in the morning, and you can also come to my house any other time, whenever you like, and practice alone in a room where there are several *Claviers.*[8]

Action and Reaction

Because so many historical North European organs have been rebuilt with lighter actions using aluminum rollerboards to make them more silent and easier to play, there were not many places that a real comparison between North European organ and pedal clavichord could be carried out. The new North German organ in Göteborg has a rollerboard with oak rollers (the ones for the Hauptwerk are almost two inches in diameter), oak trackers, and oak keyboards with an historically informed amount of damping cloth, so the entire action has both more mass and less damping than many modern copies and historical reconstructions (see figure 8.5). It is possible, if

Figure 8.5. The keyboards of the North German organ in Göteborg. Photo by Ulf Celander. Reproduced with permission from GOArt.

you strike the keys with only the fingers, to make a lot of extra rattling noise that can easily be heard over the sound of the pipes in performance. By reacting to the action and adjusting one's technique, it is possible to make the action much quieter, but it is almost impossible to make it silent.

One can either view the action noise at the Baroque organ as a problem with the instrument or as one of its most important parameters. To learn from an instrument, rather than impose modern ideas onto it, unlocks the *tacit knowledge* that historical instruments are waiting to teach. The action can be seen as one of the most important original limitations that helped to develop the literature for a specific organ type. The way the action of the instrument behaves makes some gestures more natural than others, and, especially in improvisation traditions, the direct response between player and action produces a musical language that then becomes codified in the written literature. The lighter French classical organ action, for example, invites the kind of extravagant ornamentation found codified in the music of Nicolas de Grigny. The incredibly sensitive control of speech in the Italian Renaissance organ makes playing an elevation toccata on the *voce humana* principals a profound experience for the player.

Likewise, the North German organ action affects what kind of gestures are most natural to play. It is not possible to play lightning fast on the North German organ, but that might be a help rather than a hindrance, particularly in finding appropriate tempos for the literature and for the acoustics of the room. What can be perceived as an imperfection in the action might have a real pedagogical function, because the action itself inspires the performer to play it as quietly as possible. In this respect it is similar to the experience at the pedal clavichord, because the latter instrument, too, teaches an optimal technical approach. Striking with the fingers produces uneven dynamics; actively pressing too much with each finger sends some notes out of tune. But by playing the rhetorical gestures on the page with repeated applications of weight that carry over the fingers for the entire figure, the instrument begins to breathe, forming a pattern of words with strong and weak accents. At the clavichord, one always feels more could be done; some shape could be made more elegant, some dynamic relationship could be made clearer. At the North German organ, that sense that something could be done just a little bit better comes from the noise in the action. It can be reduced, but never eliminated, so it is always there as a motivation, pointing out precisely which figures the performer has completely internalized and which still need more work. Like any description of a physical process, there is a point, perhaps already reached many pages ago, where words don't help any more and the only way to continue learning is by doing.

Some Concluding Thoughts

At the beginning of this study, I raised the question of whether the pedal clavichord was, for organists in the eighteenth century, a convenient practice instrument or a performance instrument. The question, of course, cannot be answered definitively for the eighteenth-century organists. But it can be asked of modern performers, and the answer seems to be: both. The trend throughout the twentieth century was to believe that the pedal clavichord must have been a necessary inconvenience, a contraption, an instrument on which organists were occasionally forced to practice. But this opinion was formed long after the instrument in its historical form had disappeared. Descriptions of the clavichord's use, going back to the fifteenth century, consistently called the clavichord a challenging instrument on which to perform as well as to prepare to perform music on the other keyboard instruments.

Combining the study of written sources with a physical experience of the instrument can unlock the tacit knowledge preserved in historical instrument models. This combination of information from the brain and knowledge experienced directly by the hands exists in any living instrument tradition. By reconstructing an historically informed pedal clavichord, tacit knowledge, too, can be reconstructed, putting the historical sources in a new light.

One of the clearest lessons to emerge from this work is that we can generate new perspectives on historical musical sources if we are only willing to work *with* the phenomena of historical instrument models rather than impose our will on them and change them—provided, of course, that we first establish with some degree of certainty exactly what those phenomena were. In the case of the present study, the concept of Edinburgh stringing led to the exploration of eighteenth-century sources about technique. This created a new understanding about several aspects of J. S. Bach's keyboard technique, preserved by Griepenkerl and Forkel. These texts are phenomenological descriptions and are difficult to interpret without personal physical experience of the phenomena those authors were attempting to describe.

The next step in this process was to see the historically informed pedal clavichord in the context of the North European eighteenth-century organ tradition. The work with the historically informed pedal clavichord corroborates the fact that the North European organ's key touch characteristics were significantly different from those of other parts of Europe.

In this study, the pedal clavichord directly teaches us that good tone production necessitates thinking about Baroque music in units *larger* than the single note, and *smaller* than the unbroken sixteenth-note line. The basic units that produce the best tone are three- and four-note musical motives, which can be strung together like words in a sentence. Using the Bach technique thread preserved by Forkel and Griepenkerl, we constructed and tested ways of controlling the action of the historically informed pedal clavichord and its natural application to the large eighteenth-century North European organ.

It is not possible to say definitively whether this experiment is an exact reconstruction of what Forkel was describing, but it does fit much of the evidence. It did turn out to take most people some time to come to terms with the first steps of tone production at the pedal clavichord. This suggests an intriguing explanation for why Bach's students were asked to spend months on beginning exercises. The pedal clavichord makes this kind of work not only tolerable but rewarding. The clavichord produces so much nuanced information about how you are touching the instrument that it is a source of inspiration for engaging with small-scale technical problems of the kind that are easily passed over at the organ. At the clavichord it is difficult to ignore these technical challenges when the instrument stops making any sound at all.

The bravura and self-assurance of the early historicists has now faded into memory. We have learned to be cautious about making sweeping pronouncements about historical musical practice. At the beginning of the twentieth century, instruments were called "historical" and made a great impact on our understanding of the music even though they were vastly different from the true historical tradition. The first nonhistorical Pleyel harpsichords must have been a revelatory experience for listeners who had heard Bach's music only on the modern piano, even though these harpsichords were anachronistically outfitted with piano keyboards and zinc soundboards. We now know that this was only the first step in a long process of exploring and reconstructing historical keyboard instruments.

There is, however, an expressive, even generative power, difficult to describe but easy to experience, when the patterns of a specific historical aesthetic begin to come together in the service of a study of a particular period's music. This study has been a search for some of those generative patterns through reexamining existing evidence in new ways: the role of geometry in historical instrument building, the role of sounding intervals in soundboard construction, the role of stringing in technique, the role of reception history in identifying changing concepts about the pedal clavichord over time. In addition, an attempt was made to create a new notational language that could visually realize on paper the gestural patterns that had already been experienced by the performer at the pedal clavichord when all of the other patterns, from the historical instrument and the historical sources, were brought together.

We turn finally to the question that has been implicit from the beginning: Do we need to use pedal clavichords once again in the study of Baroque organ music? Generations of excellent organists have been produced without their use. In any creative performance process nothing is ever a matter of absolute necessity. But, a similar kind of discussion and assimilation has already occurred in the not-too-distant past in the organ field. When the use of early fingerings was becoming widespread in historically informed performance in the 1970s, there was an ongoing conversation about the possibility of simply imitating the perceived effect of early fingerings while using the modern fingerings that were familiar. With artificial and conscious adjustment of articulation, modern fingerings can imitate the articulation patterns created naturally by early fingerings in Baroque music. But then articulation can never be an organic experience for the performer, or rather, it can never be the simple byproduct of a process. Ignoring early fingerings is not wrong in any extrinsic sense, but it does limit the performer from finding out where the historical fingering patterns can lead in an exploration of the music. They are, after all, part of the system of patterns that created the piece in the first place.

Perhaps the same is true of the role of the pedal clavichord for the organist. Lessons we learned at the pedal clavichord can be and are learned at the organ, and one can artificially imitate the effects of exploring the dynamic nuances of a piece. But why rob ourselves of the opportunity to experience a part of the tradition of the Baroque organist? Only shared experience has the generative power to create living languages out of the silent pieces of the past.

Appendix

Friederich Conrad Griepenkerl's Preface to J. S. Bach's *Chromatic Fantasy and Fugue* (1819)

The English translation by Quentin Faulkner begins on p. 166.

Einige Bemerkungen über den Vortrag der chromatischen Phantasie.

§1 Die Bachische Schule fordert Sauberkeit, Leichtigkeit und Freiheit des Vortrags selbst der schwersten ihr angehörigen Kunstwerke in einem Grade, der nur durch den ihr eigenen Anschlag erreicht werden kann. Diesen Anschlag hat Forkel in dem kleinen Werke: *Ueber J. S. Bachs Leben, Kunst und Kunstwerke,* so treu und deutlich beschrieben, dass ihn mehrere verständige Männer, denen es Ernst um die Sache war, und die sich durch kein beengendes Vorurtheil irre leiten liessen, darnach ohne Muster und mündliche Zurechtweisung vollkommen erlernt haben. Das Wesentliche davon ist Folgendes:

§2 Der Mechanismus der Hand ist auf das Fassen berechnet. Bei dem Fassen krümmen sich alle Finger mit dem Daumen nach dem Inneren der Hand, und äussern in dieser Bewegung alle Kraft und Sicherheit, die ihnen beiwohnen mag. Jede andere Art der Fingerbewegung ist entweder unnatürlich, oder lässt einen grossen Theil mitwürkender Muskeln unbenutzt, wie z. B. dass Niederschlagen der Finger ohne gleichzeitige Krümmung derselben. Jedes Geschäft, das die Hand in dieser Bewegung verrichten kann, muss ihr also mit Leichtigkeit, Freiheit und Sicherheit gelingen, weil es ihrer natürlichen Bestimmung angemessen ist.

§3 Zur vollständigsten Anwendung kommt der beschriebene Mechanismus der Hand bei dem Anschlagen der Tasten auf Klavierinstrumenten. Die beiden Reihen der Ober- und Untertasten liegen in zwei ebenen Flächen neben und übereinander, alle Tasten in jeder Reihe haben gleiche Länge und gleiche Breite; die Finger aber sind von ungleicher Länge. Schon dieser Umstand macht eine Krümmung der Finger bis zu dem Grade nothwendig, wo sie alle auf ebener Fläche und in gleicher Entfernung von einander mit den Spitzen in ziemlich gerader Linie stehen. Eine völlig gerade Linie unter den Fingerspitzen könnte an den meisten Händen nur erzwungen werden, und eine kleine Krümmung ist sogar nützlich, weil, den Daumen ungerechnet, die schwächeren Finger auch die kürzeren sind, und, vermöge des Mechanismus der meisten Klavierinstrumente, die Tasten vorn am äusseren Ende mit dem geringsten, weiter nach oben aber mit immer grösserem Aufwande von Kraft angeschlagen werden können. Dagegen wird es der beabsichtigten Bewegung sehr förderlich seyn, wenn die Hand in jeder Haltung so weit einwärts gedreht wird, bis alle Finger senkrecht anschlagen, auch die Gelenke, welche die Finger mit der Hand verbinden, sich nie senken, sondern stets mit der Wurzel der Hand, dem unteren Arme und dem Ellenbogen eine gerade Linie bilden.

§4 Die Ungleichheit der Finger an Kraft und Gelenkigkeit aber macht noch ein anderes künstliches Hülfsmittel nothwendig, ohne welches es niemandem, selbst bei der grössten Anstrengung und dem ausdauerndsten Fleisse, jemals gelingen wird, das natürliche Hinderniss, welches in der Schwäche des vierten und fünften Fingers liegt, zu besiegen. J.S. Bach fand dieses Mittel in der Benutzung des Gewichts der Hand und des Armes, das jeder mit Leichtigkeit und nach Willkühr entweder in gleicher Stärke unterhalten, oder vergrössern und vermindern kann. Kein Finger ist zu schwach dazu, diesem Gewicht als Stützpunkt zu dienen, der vierte und fünfte Finger kann es in gleicher Schwere tragen, wie der zweite und dritte, und es auf die Tasten in gleicher Stärke übertragen, insofern nämlich die jedem Finger inwohnende Schnellkraft dabei in Anwendung gebracht wird. Die innigste Verbindung dieser Schnellkraft mit dem Gewicht der Hand beim Anschlage ist daher das Wesentlichste am ganzen Mechanismus des Klavierspiels nach Bachs Art. Sie wird auf folgende Weise bewerkstelligt:

§5 Es sey ein Finger auf eine Taste gesetzt und diene einem fein abgemessenen Gewicht des Arms zum Stützpunkte, nicht steif und starr, sondern mit fortgesetzter Absicht, ihn einzuziehen, so dass er unverzüglich in die Hand zurückschnellen würde, wenn ihn für den Augenblick das gegen diese Absicht verhältnissmässig verstärkte Gewicht der Hand und des Armes daran nicht verhinderte, oder auch umgekehrt, wenn die auf das Einziehen des Fingers verwandte Kraft gegen den Druck des Armes nicht zu schwach wäre. Diese Stellung ist unmöglich, ohne dass das Gelenk der Hand fest steht und sich in gleicher Höhe erhält mit den Knöcheln an der oberen Fläche der Hand, die dagegen eine bedeutend höhere Lage haben, als die mittleren Knöchel der Finger. Die rechte Lage ist an der gestreckten und beinahe senkrechten Haltung des kleinen Fingers und an der schrägen des Daumes auch den Tasten zu erkennen. Aber auch kein anderes Glied ist in diese Kraftäusserung verwickelt; das Gelenk am Ellenbogen ist schlaff und die nicht anschlagenden Finger schweben ruhig und abgespannt über den nächsten Tasten etwa in der Entfernung von 1/4 Zoll. Ist die Entfernung sehr viel grösser, so fehlt die erforderliche Ruhe, und es ist eine schädliche und unnöthige Spannung an ihre Stelle getreten. Soll nun nächst dem ersten ein zweiter, gleichviel welcher, Finger anschlagen, so muss zuerst diese

Absicht mit Bewustseyn sich seiner bemächtigen und ihn in den Stand setzen, fassend stützen zu können, wie der erste. Er wird also, ehe er anschlägt, schon mit einer gewissen Spannkraft über der Taste schweben, die er nun gleich berühren soll. Alsdann muss mit der grössten Schnelligkeit die Stützkraft, welche der erste Finger vorher auf die beschriebene Weise ausübte, auf diesen zweiten übertragen werden, welches sich auf keine andere Weise bewerkstelligen lässt, als dass der erste mit Schnellkraft eingezogen wird und der zweite mit demselben Gewicht auf die Taste springt. Insofern nun der beschriebene Mechanismus mit Schnelligkeit, Sicherheit und Feinheit ausgeübt wird, klingt gewiss der so angeschlagene Ton ohne alle irdische und leibliche Noth, wie frei und geistig aus den Lüften entsprungen. Dies letztere aber ist die eigentliche Absicht und macht einen nicht geringen Theil der Virtuosität des Spielers aus. Wer nun das eben beschriebene mit allen Fingern beider Hände in jeder Verbindung, sowohl näheren als entfernteren, und in allen den verschiedenen möglichen Abwechselungen der Stärke und Schwäche, des Schnelleren und Langsameren, des Stossens und Schleifens—mit Feinheit undohne weitere körperliche Anstrengung zu leisten vermag; der hat den Anschlag J. S. Bachs, wie ihn Forkel hatte, und wie ihn viele von ihm gelernt haben.

§6 Die Anfänger, wie die schon Geübteren, können den Mechanismus auf folgende Weise am besten einüben. Damit anfänglich das Gewicht des unteren Arms ohne absichtlichen Druck und ohne absichtliche Erleichterung wirken könne, muss das Gelenk am Ellenbogen völlig schlaff und abgespannt seyn. In solcher Haltung übt man mit jeder Hand irgend zwei nächste Töne.

§7 Mit dem zweiten und dritten so lange, bis es langsam und schnell geht. Alsdann wird der Daumen mit dem zweiten, der dritte mit dem vierten und der vierte mit dem fünften Finger ohne veränderte Lage der Hand, und ohne dass sich der Daumen und kleine Finger vor den kurzen Obertasten scheue, zu denselben Uebungen gezogen. Hierauf nimmt man zu dem zweiten und dritten den vierten Finger und übt herauf und hinunter Sätze von folgender Art

§8 Zuerst langsam und allmählig schneller, sobald sich es nämlich ohne Anstrengung thun lässt. Auf dieselbe Art wird ferner der Daumen der zweite und dritte—und dritte, vierte und fünfte Finger geübt, bis kein Unterschied

im Anschlage der verschiedenen Finger mehr zu bemerken ist und alles im höchsten Grade gleichmässig und frei klingt. Nun erst folgen Figuren, zu denen vier Finger erforderlich sind

anfänglich mit dem Daumen, zweiten, dritten und vierten, dann mit dem zweiten, dritten, vierten und fünften Finger; darauf Figuren für alle fünf Finger

mit den Versetzungen, die fast in jeder Klavierschule verzeichnet sind. Der Anschlag der kürzeren Obertasten erfordert besondere Übung, zu der man sich folgender Figuren bedienen kann.

§9 Zuletzt alle Tonleitern und gebrochene Akkorde, Die linke Hand macht dieselben Übungen mit den ihr entspechenden Fingern erst klein, dann mit der rechten Hand zugleich.

§10 Ist der Daumen frei und werden bloss die vier Finger geübt, so darf er niemals herunterhangen; sondern er muss immer, wie zum Anschlagen bereit, über den Tasten schweben. Noch weniger darf der vierte und fünfte Finger, wenn der Daumen, der zweite und dritte geübt wird, weder in die Höhe gezogen, noch in die Hand geklemmt werden; auch sie müssen unter solchen Umständen in gehöriger Entfernung ruhig über den Tasten schweben.

§11 Nachdem nun die beschriebenen Übungen mit dem natürlichen Gewichte des unteren Armes und mit völlig schlaffen Gelenke am Ellenbogen durchgemacht sind, darf Verstärkung und Erleichterung dieses Gewichts durch Druck oder Hebung, vermöge des Gelenkes am Ellenbogen, hinzugezogen werden. Anfangs im höchsten Grade gleichmässig und erst zuletzt mit stufenweiser Vermehrung und Verminderung für jeden folgenden Ton, damit man das *forte* und *piano,* das Wachsen und Schwinden der Stärke, ohne alle weitere Anstrengung, und besonders das *forte* ohne Schlagen der Finger, in seine Gewalt bekomme.

§12 Diese ganze Vorbereitung kann und darf, bei gehörigem Fleiss, Eifer und Talent, selbst den Anfänger nicht über zwei Monate kosten. Nach ihr aber müssen Übungstücke von J. S. Bach selbst gewählt werden, weil wenig andere Komponisten der linken Hand eine Melodie zu führen geben. Die passendsten sind von den zweistimmigen Inventionen Nr. 1 und 8; dann Nr. 12, 11 und 5. Auch dürfen die Läufe in Zweiunddreissigsteln aus der chromatischen Phantasie, und andere der Art, eingeschoben werden. Jedes Stück aber, was man einüben will, muss man vorher mit Verstand durchsehen, die beste Fingersetzung, welches immer die bequemste ist, wohl überlegen, nichts vom Zufalle abhängig machen, und alsdann in so langsamen Tempo anfangen, dass man sicher ist, das ganze Stück gleich zum ersten Male ohne Anstoss durchführen zu können. Die grössere Schnelligkeit kommt durch fortgesetzte Übung von selbst. Auch soll man nicht früher zu einem zweiten Stücke forteilen, als bis die Schwierigkeiten des ersten ganz bezwungen sind. Wer diese Vorschriften nicht befolgt, der wird sich unfehlbar zum Stottern gewöhnen, die Zeit des Lernens verdoppeln und doch niemals mit Freiheit, Sicherheit und Selbstbewustseyn spielen lernen. Übrigens ist zur Ausbildung der Hand für den Anfang das Klavier bei weitem besser, als das Forte-Piano, weil man jeden Fehler des Anschlags leichter hört und weil mehr vom Spieler, als vom Instrument abhängt. Der Übergang zum Forte-Piano nur grössere Nachlässigkeiten zulässt, ohne bedeutende Abänderungen in der Behandlung herbeizuführen. Wer anderer Meinung ist, der hat wahrscheinlich das Klavier nicht in seiner Gewalt, wie alle blossen Forte-Piano-Spieler.

§13 Sollte es aber jemandem ein rechter Ernst seyn um seine musikalische Ausbildung und sollte er dazu die genaueste Kenntniss aller Klavier-kompositionen von J. S. Bach für unentbehrlich halten; so muss er sich entschliessen, alle Anfangsstücke dieses Meisters durchzuarbeiten, ehe er sich an dessen grössere Werke wagt. Zu den Anfangsstücken gehören vor allen die sechs kleinen Präludien für Anfänger, die fünfzehn zweistimmigen Inventionen und die fünfzehn dreistimmigen Symphonien, in der Folge wie sie hier verzeichnet sind. Wer diese sechs und dreissig Tonstücke alle zu gleicher Zeit fertig in der Hand hat, der darf sich schon für einen guten Klavierspieler halten, und es wird ihm von älterer und neuerer Klaviermusik nicht leicht etwas zu schwer seyn. Nur die vier- und fünfstimmigen Fugen von J. S. Bach bedürfen noch einer besonderen Vorbereitung, welche durch fleissiges und feines Spielen seiner vierstimmigen Choräle sehr gut geleistet werden kann.

§14 Wer sie (the fugue from the Chromatic Fantasy and Fugue accord-ing to Ewald Kooiman) mit Fertigkeit, Freiheit und Sauberkeit will spielen lernen, gewöhne sich zu der von C. Ph. E. Bach gelehrten Fingersetzung seines Vaters, nach welcher die Finger die besten sind, mit denen der Satz am bequemsten herausgebracht werden kann. Man darf den Daumen und kleinen Finger, so oft es nöthig und nützlich ist, auf die kürzeren Obertasten setzen, man darf jeden kürzeren Finger unter den längeren stecken und jeden längeren über den kürzeren setzen, trotz der einseitigen Regeln mancher neueren Theoretiker. Schrieb doch J. S. Bach Übungsstücke für solche Fingersetzung, wie denn die fünfte der zweistimmigen Inventionen ein solches ist, um den Daumen und kleinen Finger auf die Obertasten zu gewöhnen. Übrigens lassen sich nur sehr wenige von Bachs grösseren Klaviersachen ohne jene Fingersetzung gut und leicht herausbringen.

Braunschweig, den 10 April 1819
F. Griepenkerl

Some Remarks Concerning the Performance of the Chromatic Fantasy

Translation by Quentin Faulkner[1]

§1 The Bach school demands cleanness, ease and freedom in performance in even its most difficult works to a degree that can be attained only by means of its own peculiar method of touch. This touch Forkel has so accurately and clearly described in his little volume *Ueber J. S. Bachs Leben, Kunst und Kunstwerke,* that several intelligent men who were seriously concerned about the matter and have not allowed themselves to be misled by narrow prejudice have managed to master it perfectly without any example or oral instruction. That which is essential with respect to this is as follows:

§2 The mechanism of the hand is based upon its ability to grasp. In grasping, all of the fingers bend themselves together with the thumb into the palm of the hand, and by this motion reveal all of their innate force and security. Every other sort of finger motion is either unnatural or allows the majority of the collaborating muscles to go unused, as for example when a finger strikes [a key] without at the same time being curved. Every operation that the hand can accomplish by this motion it succeeds in doing with ease, freedom and security, since the operation corresponds to the hand's natural inclination.

§3 This mechanism of the hand described above is employed most completely when striking keys upon keyboard instruments. Both rows of upper and lower keys [i.e., accidentals and naturals] lie parallel to each other in two level surfaces, the one over the other, and all the keys in each row are equally long and broad. The fingers, however, are of unequal length. This circumstance already makes the bending of the fingers necessary to the degree that they all rest upon an even surface and equidistant from each other with the tips in a relatively straight line. With most hands it is possible only with force to place the fingertips in a perfectly straight line, and a slight arc is indeed advantageous, since (with the exception of the thumb) the weaker fingers are also the shorter ones and, by virtue of the mechanism of most keyboard instruments, keys may be attacked with the least expenditure of force on their forward edge, and require more and more force the further back they are struck. On the other hand, it will be very beneficial to the intended motion if the hand in every position is turned far enough inward so that every finger strikes vertically, and joints that link the fingers to the hand do not collapse, but rather always form a straight line with the palm of the hand, the lower arm and elbow.

§4 The inequality of the fingers as regards strength and flexibility however, makes yet another artistic resource necessary, one without which no one will ever succeed (even with the greatest exertion and most persistent diligence) in overcoming the natural obstacle inherent in the weakness of the fourth and fifth fingers. J. S. Bach found this resource in the use of the weight of the hand and arm that anyone may maintain with ease and at will, either at the same degree or at a greater or lesser degree of force. No finger is too weak to serve as the point of support for this weight; the fourth and fifth finger can bear it to the same degree as the second and third, and can transmit it to the keys with equal force, insofar as the elasticity inherent in each finger is brought into use. *The most intimate connection of this elasticity with the weight of the hand in the attack is therefore the most vital component in the entire technique of keyboard performance according to Bach's method.* It is achieved in the following manner:

§5 Let one finger be placed upon a key and serve as the point of support for a finely adjusted weight of the arm, not stiffly or rigidly, but with the express intent of pulling it backward so that it instantly might be drawn in toward the hand, were it not for the moment prevented from doing this by the weight of the hand which has been proportionately intensified to counter this intent—or conversely, were the force directed toward the retraction of the finger not too weak to overcome the pressure of the arm. This position is impossible unless the wrist firmly supports the hand and maintains itself at the same height as the knuckles on the upper side of the hand; the knuckles then occupy a significantly higher position than the other joints of the fingers. The correct position may be recognized by the extended and nearly vertical placement of the little finger and by the slanting of the thumb toward the keys. No other part of the body, however, is involved in this assertion of force; the elbow joint is relaxed and the fingers not involved in playing hover quietly and loosely over the nearest keys at a distance of about 1/4 inch. If this distance is very much greater, then the necessary stillness will be lacking, and a destructive and unnecessary tension will arise in its place. When a second finger (it matters not which) is ready to strike following the first one, then this intention must first consciously strengthen it, and ready it to provide continuous support, just as the first. It should then, before it strikes, already be hovering with a certain tension over the key that it is about to touch. Then the supporting force, which the first finger has previously been exerting in the way described above, must with the greatest rapidity be transferred to the second finger; this should be accomplished in no other way, than that the first [finger] be retracted with elasticity and the second spring upon the key with the same weight [as the first]. To the degree that the mechanism described above is carried out with rapidity, security and finesse, so will each note (when it is struck) sound without any difficulty whatsoever, as if it has sprung free and unfettered out of thin air. This quality is of course exactly what is intended; it constitutes no small part of the performer's virtuosity. Whoever now is able to accomplish what I have just been describing with all the fingers of both hands in every situation, with the fingers either in normal or extended positions, and in all possible varieties of loudness and softness, speed or slowness, staccato and slurring—all these with finesse and security and without additional bodily exertion—whoever can do this possesses the method of performance taught by J. S. Bach as Forkel possessed it, and as many have learned it from him.

§6 Beginners, as well as those already more accomplished, may best accustom themselves to this action in the following way. At first, so that the weight of the lower arm may operate without either any intentional pressure or lightening, the joint at the elbow must be completely relaxed and loose. In this posture, one should practice with the second and third fingers each type of adjoining notes.

§7 First with one hand [second and third fingers] and then with the other, until one can play them both slowly and rapidly. Then should be added to this practice the thumb with the second, the third with the fourth and the fourth with the fifth finger, without altering the position of the hand, and without trying to avoid placing the thumb and little finger on an upper key. Next, one should add the fourth finger to the second and third, and practice passages such as these following, both ascending and descending,

§8 Slowly at first and then gradually faster and faster, as soon as this can be accomplished without exertion. In the same fashion one should exercise the thumb, second and third fingers, as well as the third, fourth and fifth fingers, until there is no longer any difference to be noticed in the attack of the various fingers and everything sounds to the highest degree equal and free. Only then should patterns be undertaken in which four fingers are necessary,

at first with the thumb, second, third and fourth finger, and then with the second, third, fourth and fifth fingers;

finally patterns of all five fingers using transposing exercises that are to be found in almost every keyboard method book. Playing the shorter upper keys demands special practice, for which one may use the following patterns:

§9 Finally one must practice all scales and arpeggios. The left hand should do the same exercises with its corresponding fingers, first alone, and then together with the right hand.

§10 Should the thumb be omitted and only the other four fingers used, it must certainly never be allowed to hang down from the keyboard; rather it must always hover over the keys, as if prepared to play. Even less should the fourth and fifth fingers (if the thumb, second and third fingers are being used alone) be either drawn up high or clenched into the hand; in such circumstances they must also hover quietly over the keys at the proper distance.

§11 After all of the exercises described above have been completed using the natural weight of the lower arm and with completely relaxed elbow joints, then one may begin to increase and decrease this weight by using either more or less pressure, controlled by the elbow joint. At first this must be uniform to the highest degree, and only then with gradual crescendos or diminuendos for every successive tone, in order to master "forte" and "piano," the ebb and flow of dynamics, without any further exertion, and especially the "forte" without striking with the fingers.

§12 All this preparatory training can and should, given the proper industry, zeal and talent, cost even the beginner not over two months' time.

After it, however, one must choose practice pieces by J. S. Bach himself, because few other composers give to the left hand a melody to execute. The most suitable pieces are Numbers 1 & 8 of the Two Part Inventions, followed by Numbers 12, 11 and 5. The 32nd note runs from the Chromatic Fantasy may also be undertaken, and other passages of this sort. However, one must first thoughtfully examine each piece that is to be practiced, carefully considering the best fingering (which is always the most comfortable), and leaving nothing dependent on chance; then one should begin with a tempo slow enough that one can be sure of being able to perform the entire piece, even the first time through, without stumbling. Greater speed will come automatically through continued practice. One also ought not to hurry on too early to a second piece, until the difficulties of the first are entirely conquered. Those who do not follow these directions will assuredly accustom themselves to "stuttering" [in performance]; it will take them twice as long to learn a piece, and even then they will never learn to play with freedom, confidence and self assurance. It is to be noted that the clavichord (Klavier) is far better for training the hand in the beginning than the forte-piano, because one hears every mistake in touch more easily, and more depends on the performer than on the instrument. Transferring to the piano really presents no difficulties, since the touch remains the same and the forte-piano only allows greater carelessness without bringing about any significant alterations in execution. Anyone who is of a different opinion has probably not mastered the clavichord, just like all those who are only forte-piano players.

§13 If anyone is genuinely serious about his musical training and if he considers the most precise knowledge of all J. S. Bach's keyboard compositions to be indispensable for this purpose, then he must resolve to work through all the beginners' pieces written by this master before he ventures to undertake any of his larger works. To these beginners' pieces belong above all the Six Little Preludes for Beginners, the fifteen Two Part Inventions and the fifteen Three-Part Inventions (Symphonien), in the order they are listed here. Whoever has all 36 of these pieces under his fingers at the same time may already consider himself a good keyboard performer, and there is little keyboard music, either new or old, that will give him much trouble. Only the four- and five-voice fugues of J. S. Bach require any special further preparation, which may be very well accomplished by the industrious and refined performance of his four-voice chorales...

§14 Anyone who wishes to learn this piece [i.e., the fugue of the Chromatic Fantasy] with finesse, freedom and cleanness ought to accustom himself to J. S. Bach's method of fingering as taught by his son C. P. E. Bach, according to which the fingers are best ordered to perform the music with the greatest ease. One may use the thumb and the little finger on the shorter upper keys as often as is useful and necessary: one may pass any shorter finger under a longer one, and any longer one over a shorter one, in spite of the narrow minded, limiting rules of many a recent theoretician. J. S. Bach indeed wrote practice pieces for this sort of fingering, of which the fifth two-part invention is an example, to accustom the thumb and the little finger to the accidentals. Furthermore, there are very few of Bach's larger keyboard works that can be performed easily and well without this sort of fingering.

Braunschweig, April 10, 1819
F. Griepenkerl

Notes

Introduction

1. Carl Philipp Emanuel Bach, *Essay on the True Art of Playing Keyboard Instruments*, 1753, trans. William J. Mitchell (New York: Norton, 1949), 37.
2. Ibid., 38.
3. More about this study can be read in *The North German Organ Research Project*, ed. Joel Speerstra (Göteborg: GOArt, 2003).
4. Charles Rosen, *The Frontiers of Meaning: Three Informal Lectures on Music* (New York: Hill and Wang, 1994), 72.
5. Ibid.
6. Ibid., 78.
7. Leo Treitler, *Music and the Historical Imagination* (Cambridge, Mass.: Harvard University Press, 1989), 89.
8. Ibid., 89.
9. Lawrence LeShan and Henry Margenau, *Einstein's Space and Van Gogh's Sky: Physical Reality and Beyond* (New York: Macmillan, 1982), 108.

Prelude 1

1. For instance, the Valentinus Zeis Claviorganum, Salzburg: Museum Carolino Augusteum, catalog number B 13/6, which combines a harpsichord and an organ.
2. There are, for example, references to independent "pedal-board" harpsichords from 1684 and 1701 in the Archives Nationales in Paris. Frank Hubbard, *Three Centuries of Harpsichord Making* (Cambridge, Mass.: Harvard University Press, 1965), 111.
3. Ibid., 37.
4. "Every keyboardist should own a good harpsichord and a good clavichord to enable him to play all things interchangeably." Carl Philipp Emanuel Bach, *Essay on the True Art of Playing Keyboard Instruments, 1753*, trans. William J. Mitchell (New York: Norton, 1949), 37.
5. Russell Stinson, *The Bach Manuscripts of Johann Peter Kellner and his Circle: A Case Study in Reception History* (Durham, N.C., and London: Duke University Press, 1989), 3.

Chapter 1

1. Leipzig, Musikinstrumenten-Museum der Universität Leipzig, Catalog Number 23.
2. Nürnberg, Germanisches Nationalmuseum, Catalog Number 270.
3. Jochen Rácz Mizushima, "Das Pedalclavichord: Entwicklung, Geschichte und Bedeutung eines vergessenen Instruments" (A-level thesis, Hochschule für Musik Köln, 1996), 85.

4. Eisenach, Bachhaus Museum, Catalog Number 82.

5. The Hague, Gemeentemuseum, Catalog Number Ec.495–1933.

6. Rácz Mizushima, "Das Pedalclavichord," 75.

7. Munich, Deutsches Museum, Catalog Number 34072.

8. Rácz Mizushima, "Das Pedalclavichord," 84.

9. Eva Helenius-Öberg, *Svenskt Klavikordbygge 1720–1820* (Stockholm: Almqvist & Wiksell, 1986), 262–77.

10. Skara, Skaraborgs länsmuseum, Catalog Number S 16 VM 67049.

11. Östersund, Jämtlands länsmuseum, Catalog Number S 23 JLM 17656.

12. Skellefteå, Skellefteå museum, Catalog Number S 24 SM 838.

13. Stockholm: Musikmuseet, Catalog Number *S 01 SMS/MM 2912.

14. Göteborg: Göteborgs Stadsmuseum, Catalog Number S 14 GM 4772.

15. For more on the Wolthersson clavichord, see Joel Speerstra, "Two Mid-Eighteenth-Century Swedish Clavichords: A Professional Instrument by an Amateur Builder and an Amateur Instrument by a Professional One" in *De Clavicordio* 5 (2002), 173–84.

16. Eva Helenius-Öberg, "Connections between Organ Building and Keyboard Instrument Building in Sweden before 1820," in *GOArt Research Reports 1* (1999), 170.

17. Bernard Brauchli, *The Clavichord* (Cambridge: Cambridge University Press, 1998), 40.

18. The original Latin refers to *suo calcatorio*: "to tread upon it with the feet." Ibid., 304.

19. Ibid., 41. The original manuscript is at the Würtembergische Landesbibliothek, Stuttgart.

20. Beth Bullard, *Musica getutscht: A Treatise on Musical Instruments by Sebastian Virdung* (Cambridge: Cambridge University Press, 1993), 127.

21. Bohuslav Cizek, "Clavichords in the Czech Lands," *De Clavicordio* 2 (1995): 34.

22. Michael Praetorius, *Syntagma Musicum II: De organographia, parts I and II,* trans. David Z. Crookes (Oxford: Clarendon Press, 1986), 65.

23. Claas Douwes, *Grondig Ondersoek van de Toonen der Musijk (Franeker, 1699),* facsimile edition by Peter Williams (Amsterdam: Frits Knuf, 1970), 104.

24. John Barnes, "The Anatomy of a Clavichord" (unpublished manuscript), 12.

25. "Beydes ist zwar sehr gemein und bekannt: jedoch damit in der Musica mechanica organœdi nichts wegbleibe, was dazu gehört; so will ich von beyden etwas beybringen." Jakob Adlung, *Musica mechanica organœdi (Berlin: F. W. Birnstiel, 1768),* facsimile edition by Christhard Mahrenholz (Kassel: Bärenreiter, 1961), Chapter 26, §571.

26. K. A. Bierdimpffl, *Die Sammlung der Musik-Instrumente im Baierischen Nationalmuseum* (Munich: no pub., 1883), 54–56.

27. A private communication to the editor in Donald H. Boalch, ed., *Makers of the Harpsichord and Clavichord 1440–1840,* 3rd ed. (Oxford: Clarendon Press, 1995), 71.

28. Stephen L. Clark, *The Letters of C. P. E. Bach* (Oxford: Clarendon Press, 1997), 70.

29. "Am liebsten spielte er auf dem Clavichord." Johann Nikolaus Forkel, *Ueber Johann Sebastian Bachs Leben, Kunst und Kunstwerke* (Leipzig: Hoffmeister und Kühnel, 1802), 17. English translation from Forkel, *Life of John Sebastian Bach*

with a Critical View of His Compositions (London: T. Boosey and Co, 1820), 28. This translation was made in 1808 and first published in 1820. English translations of Forkel are taken directly from the original, without any changes in orthography. The reader can compare these with the translations that appear in *The New Bach Reader*, ed. H. T. David and A. Mendel, rev. and enlarged Christopf Wolff (New York and London: Norton, 1998).

30. Forkel, *Life of John Bach*, 28.

31. Forkel, *Ueber Bachs Leben*, 60. Forkel, *Life of John Bach*, 101. Here the 1820 translation of "kunstreich gearbeitete" is dated.

32. Philipp Spitta, *Johann Sebastian Bach*, trans. Clara Bell and J. A. Fuller-Maitland, (New York: Dover Publications, 1951), 3:358.

33. W. Neumann and H.-J. Schulze, ed., *Bach Dokumente* (Basel, Kassel: Bärenreiter, 1969), 2:504.

34. Raymond Russell, *The Harpsichord and Clavichord*, ed. Howard Schott (London: Faber, 1973), 183.

35. Robert Marshall, "Organ or "Klavier"? Instrumental Prescriptions in the Sources of Bach's Keyboard Works," in *J. S. Bach as Organist: His Instruments, Music, and Performance Practices*, ed. George Stauffer and Ernest May (Bloomington: Indiana University Press, 1986), 224.

36. Forkel, *Ueber Bachs Leben*, 17.

37. Charles Sanford Terry, *Johann Christian Bach*, ed. H. C. Robbins Landon (Oxford: Oxford University Press, 1967), 3.

38. Forkel, *Life of John Bach*, 28.

39. Denise Restout, *Landowska on Music* (New York: Stein and Day, 1964), 142.

40. Some surviving historical clavichords have register stop knobs. The Gerstenberg apparently had a stop knob for damping the 16-foot strings. The M. Christiansen clavichord at Fredriksborg Castle in Denmark has a moderator stop of leather and a "pantaleon" stop that turns that clavichord into a kind of hammer dulcimer. What all of the registers controlled on the pyramid clavichord, Gerber does not report.

41. Ernst Ludwig Gerber, *Historisch-biographisches Lexicon der Tonkünstler* (Leipzig: J. G. I. Breitkopf, 1790–92), §495.

42. Boalch, ed., *Makers*, 69.

43. Neumann and Schulze, *Bach Dokumente*, 3:477.

44. H. T. David and A. Mendel, eds., *The Bach Reader* (New York and London: Norton, 1966), 265.

45. Ibid., 85, note 26.

46. Restout, *Landowska*, 145, note.

47. Ibid., 149.

48. Georg Kinsky, *Musik-historisches Museum von Wilhelm Heyer in Cöln* (Cologne: no pub., 1912), 655.

Chapter 2

1. Wolfgang Schmieder, *Thematisch-Systematisches Verzeichnis der Werke Joh. Seb. Bachs*, (Wiesbaden: Breitkopf & Härtel, 1966), 410. This citation also appeared in the 1950 edition.

2. Johann Nikolaus Forkel, *Life of John Sebastian Bach with a Critical View of His Compositions* (London: T. Boosey and Co., 1820), 28.

3. Johann Nikolaus Forkel, *Ueber Johann Sebastian Bachs Leben, Kunst und Kunstwerk* (Leipzig: Hoffmeister und Kühnel, 1802), 17.

4. Forkel, *Life of John Bach*, 27–28.

5. Forkel, *Ueber Bachs Leben*, 16–17.

6. Stephen L. Clark, *The Letters of C. P. E. Bach* (Oxford: Clarendon Press, 1997), 70.

7. Ibid.

8. Ibid., 71.

9. Forkel, *Life of John Bach*, 101–2.

10. Forkel, *Ueber Bachs Leben*, 60.

11. Forkel, *Life of John Bach*, 101.

12. Forkel, *Ueber Bachs Leben*, 60.

13. Philipp Spitta, *Johann Sebastian Bach*, 3 vols., trans. Clara Bell and J. A. Fuller-Maitland (New York: Dover Publications, 1951). Spitta published his chronological study of Johann Sebastian Bach between 1873 and 1880.

14. Spitta, *Bach*, trans. Bell, 2:44.

15. Philipp Spitta, *Johann Sebastian Bach*, 2 vols. (Wiesbaden: Breitkopf & Härtel, 1979), 1:655.

16. Spitta, *Bach*, trans. Bell, 2:44.

17. Spitta, *Bach*, 1:655.

18. Spitta, *Bach*, trans. Bell, 2:44.

19. Ibid., 2:44.

20. Spitta, *Bach*, 1:655.

21. Spitta, *Bach*, trans. Bell, 2:44.

22. Spitta, *Bach*, 1:655.

23. Spitta, *Bach*, trans. Bell, 3:211.

24. Spitta, *Bach*, 2:691–92.

25. Dietrich Kilian, *Sechs Sonaten und verschiedene Einzelwerke: Kritische Bericht*, Johann Sebastian Bach: Neue Ausgabe Sämtlicher Werke 4th ser., vol. 7 (Basel, London, New York, Kassel: Bärenreiter, 1988), 17–27.

26. Ibid., 22.

27. Albert Schweitzer, *J. S. Bach* (Leipzig: Breitkopf und Härtel, 1930), 256.

28. Albert Schweitzer, *J. S. Bach le musicien-poète* (Leipzig: Breitkopf & Härtel, 1905), 177.

29. Ibid.

30. Schweitzer, *Bach*, 257.

31. Forkel, *Life of John Bach*, 101.

32. Georg Kinsky, "Pedalklavier oder Orgel bei Bach?" *Acta Musicologica* 8 (1936): 161.

33. Kinsky, "Pedalklavier," 160.

34. There were restorations of the Gerstenberg pedal clavichord in 1950 and 1968, neither of which brought the instrument back to a playable state. Only the pedal is playable now, and it is hard to imagine that the instrument functioned like a new instrument fourteen years before its first restoration in the twentieth century.

35. Max Reinhardt and Dan H. Laurence, eds., *The Bodley Bernard Shaw: The Complete Musical Criticism in Three Volumes* (London: The Bodley Head, 1981), 1:320.

36. Hipkins "had been apprenticed as a piano tuner at Broadwood's at the age of fourteen . . . purchased some of Engel's early instruments in 1881, and began lecturing in London, Oxford and Cambridge on Carl Philipp Emanuel Bach and the clavichord." Bernard Brauchli, *The Clavichord* (Cambridge: Cambridge University Press, 1998), 279.

37. Reinhardt and Laurence, eds., *The Bodley Bernard Shaw,* 1:780.

38. Walter Emery, *Notes on Bach's Organ Works: A Companion to the Revised Novello Edition Books IV-V, the Six Sonatas for Two Manuals and Pedal* (London: Novello, 1957), 196–200. GOArt's library owns Dr. Wolfgang Schmieder's copy of this work. It is personally autographed to "Dr. Wolfgang Schmieder from Walter Emery 17 July 1957"; Schmieder would therefore have received the book before publishing the 1966 edition of his catalog of Bach's works.

39. Ibid., 198.

40. Ibid., 200.

41. Susi Jeans, "The Pedal Clavichord and Other Practice Instruments of Organists," in *Proceedings of the Royal Musical Association* (London: The Royal Musical Association, 1950–52), 13.

42. Ibid.

43. Peter Williams, *The Organ Music of J. S. Bach,* ed. Peter le Hurray John Stevens, Cambridge Studies in Music, 3 vols. (Cambridge: Cambridge University Press, 1980), 1:9.

44. H. T. David and A. Mendel, eds., revised and enlarged by Christoph Wolff, *The Bach Reader* (New York and London: Norton, 1998), 304.

45. Williams, *Organ Music,* 1:9.

46. Robert Marshall, "Organ or 'Klavier'? Instrumental Prescriptions in the Sources of Bach's Keyboard Works," in *J. S. Bach as Organist: His Instruments, Music, and Performance Practices,* ed. George Stauffer and Ernest May (Bloomington: Indiana University Press, 1986), 214.

47. Ibid., 221.

48. Ibid., 224.

49. H. T. David and A. Mendel, eds., *The Bach Reader* (New York and London: Norton, 1966), 346 note 54.

50. Clark, *Letters of C. P. E. Bach.*

51. Ibid., 66.

52. Carl Philipp Emanuel Bach, *Verzeichniß des musikalischen Nachlasses (Hamburg: Gottlieb Friedrich Schniebes, 1790),* facsimile edition by William S. Newmann (Buren: Frits Knuf, 1991), 67.

53. Spitta, *Bach,* trans. Bell, 3:44.

54. Forkel, *Life of John Bach,* 102.

55. Ibid.

56. Clark, *Letters,* 61.

57. Ernst Suchalla, *Carl Philipp Emanuel Bach Briefe und Dokumente: Kritische Gesamtausgabe,* 2 vols. (Göttingen, Vandenhoeck and Ruprecht, 1994), 1:432.

58. Clark, *Letters,* 66.

Chapter 3

1. Leipzig, Musikinstrumenten-Museum der Universität Leipzig, Catalog Number 23.

2. A re-dating of 1766 based on a photograph of the date on the nameboard can be argued for. The nameboard itself is now missing. See Hubert Henkel, *Clavichorde: Musikinstrumenten-Museum der Karl-Marx-Universität, Leipzig, Katalog 4* (Leipzig: VEB Deutscher Verlag für Musik, 1981), Table 61.

3. Leipzig, Musikinstrumenten-Museum der Universität Leipzig, Catalog Number 30.

4. "Ein fünf Octäviges Clavier vom alten Friederici, von Eichenholz, der Deckel von Feuernholz, schön von Ton. An diesem Claviere sind fast alle in Hamburg verfertigte Compositionen componirt worden." Carl Philipp Emanuel Bach, *Verzeichniß des Musikalischen Nachlasses (Hamburg: Gottlieb Friedrich Schniebes, 1790), facsimile edition by William S. Newman (Buren: Frits Knuf, 1991)*, 92.

5. "Die Friedericischen Clavicorde haben bey mir einen großen Vorzug vor den Fritzischen u. Haßischen wegen des Tractaments u. wegen des Baßes ohne Octave, welche ich nicht leiden kan." Ernst Suchalla, *Carl Philipp Emanuel Bach Briefe und Dokumente: Kritische Gesamtausgabe* (Göttingen: Vandenhoeck & Ruprecht, 1994), 1:343.

6. For instance the unfretted clavichord, FF–d^3 by Johan Christoph Fleischer [Fe: Hamburg Anno 1723], at Drottningholm, Drottningholm Theater Museum (no catalog number).

7. Henkel, *Clavichorde*, 52–55.

8. Ibid., 53.

9. A study of the possible foot measurements was carried out and the closest match was discovered to be the Leipzig foot found in F. B. de Felice, *"Pied"* in *Encyclopedie, ou, Dictionnaire universel raisonné des connoissances humaine* (Yverdon, 1774), 513.

10. Stephen Birkett and William Jurgenson, *Geometrical Methods in Stringed Keyboard Instrument Design and Construction*, 2, *http://www.aps.uoguelph.ca/~birketts/* [accessed 11/99].

11. For a complete description of the geometrical design of the Gerstenberg, see Joel Speerstra, "Measuring the Gerstenberg Pedal Clavichord: A Detective Story," *GOArt Research Reports 3* (2003), 75–93. Plans of the instrument are also available from GOArt at http://www.goart.gu.se.

12. Carl Philipp Emanuel Bach, *Essay on the True Art of Playing Keyboard Instruments, 1753*, trans. William J. Mitchell (New York: Norton, 1949), 36.

13. Ibid.

14. Carl Philipp Emanuel Bach, *Versuch über die wahre Art das Clavier zu spielen, (Berlin: Henning, 1753 und 1762)*, facsimile edition by Lothar Hoffmann-Erbrecht (Leipzig: VEB Breitkopf und Härtel, 1957), 9.

15. Adlung, *Musica*, chapter 26, §571.

16. Peter Bavington, "Keylever, Tangent and String—A Preliminary Analysis of Clavichord Touch and Action," *De Clavicordio 3* (1997): 70.

17. John Koster, "The Stringing and Pitches of Historical Clavichords," *De Clavicordio 1* (1993): 232.

18. ". . . Am jetzigen Platz auf den Windladen war ursprünglich Schnitgers Gedackt 8' im Kammerton plaziert." Jürgen Ahrend, "Die Restaurierung der Arp Schnitger-Orgel von St. Jacobi in Hamburg" in *Die Arp Schnitger-Orgel der Hauptkirche St. Jacobi in Hamburg* (Hamburg, 1995), 189. For references to central German instruments with *Kammerton* registers, see Paul Smets, *Orgeldispositionen: Eine Handschrift aus dem XVIII. Jahrhundert, im Besitz der Sächsischen*

Landesbibliothek (Dresden, 1931), 227 (Forsta); 237–39 (Hohenstiftskirche in Halberstadt); 255–56 (Merseburg); 257–58 (Merseburg); 259–60 (Mühlhausen); 282 (Schlosse zu Weimar).

See also George Stauffer and Ernest May, _J. S. Bach as Organist: His Instruments, Music, and Performance Practices_ (Bloomington: Indiana University Press, 1986), 15: "Like most Dresden organs of the eighteenth century, it was tuned to chamber pitch (approximately 415.5 Hz); the organs in Leipzig during Bach's time were tuned to choir pitch."

19. "Ich will soviel sagen, die Tangenten sollen nicht so hoch liegen, daß die Blätter fast an die Seyten reichen: den solchergestalt darf man nur an die Palmulen rühren, so schlagen sie gleich an. Es spielt sich zwar fein; mir aber gefällt es nicht, weil 1) dadurch der Stärke viel abgehet. . . . 2) Sie heulen mehr als andere. 3) Wenn man die Scholaren bey der Information daran gewöhnet, und sie kommen hernach auf die Orgel, allwo die Palmulen ungleich tiefer fallen; so müssen sie von vorn anheben zu lernen: da hingegen, wenn sie auf tieffallenden Clavichordien gewohnt sind, es ihnen auf der Orgel gar nicht spanisch vorkommen wird." Adlung, _Musica_, chapter 26, §

20. The factors that contribute to what Peter Bavington has described as "the hardness of touch," a term encompassing how a player perceives the action of a clavichord, have been covered in Bavington, "Keylever," 61–100. John Koster, in "The Stringing and Pitches of Historical Clavichords," _De Clavicordio_ 1 (1993): 225–44, analyzes the role that the three parts of the clavichord string play in the perception of the clavichord's touch. Koster defines them as the speaking length, which defines the pitch; the after length, from the tangent to the hitchpin, which if too short increases the perception of hardness of touch; and the extra length from the bridge to the tuning pin, which if very long can decrease the perception of hardness of touch.

21. Henkel, _Clavichorde_, 53.

22. Grant O'Brien gives a fuller description of this research in "Stringing Materials and Gauges from Clavichords by I. C. Gerlach and H. A. Hass," _De Clavicordio_ 1 (1993): 125. The conclusion of the article defines the advantages of what has come to be known as Edinburgh stringing.

23. Henkel, _Clavichorde_, 61.

24. O'Brien, "Stringing Materials," 133.

25. Bach, _Essay_, 36.

26. Adlung, _Musica_, chapter 22, §523: "Auch pflegt man die Decke im Basse etwas dicker zu machen, der Gravität wegen." English translations of Adlung in this chapter are by Quentin Faulkner (unpublished manuscript).

27. "Hierzu kommt auch der Stand des Steges unter der Decke, da es nur auf ein Punkt ankömmt, so wird der Klang nicht, wie er seyn könnte, wie man solches aus der Stimme bey der Violine gar deutlich siehet." Ibid., chapter 26, §582.

28. "Wenn die Decke nicht in der Sonnenstunde gelegt würde, nämlich wenn sie aufgeht; so klängen sie nicht so gut, als andere. Aber solche astrologische Anmerkungen gelten bey mir nicht viel." Ibid.

29. Oscar Hedlund, _Georg Bolins gitarrbok_ (Stockholm: Reuter & Reuter, 1982), 90–91, documents the guitar builder, Georg Bolin's process of "tuning" the soundboard of a guitar after it is assembled, as Bolin says "to correct the sound balance after the same tonal principles that organ builders use when they file the tongues of (reed) pipes."

30. For instance, the bells of seventeenth-century bellmaker H. H. Rausch show a tendency to pythagorean minor thirds or even wide whole steps while the bells of the eighteenth-century Erfurt bellmaker, N. J. Sorber, show a tendency from 1712 to 1757 toward wider minor thirds, or even thirds that alternate between minor and major. Von Veit Heller, "Musikalische Strukturen in den Geläuten von N. J. Sorber and H. H. Rausch," *Glocken und Glockenspiele: Michaelsteiner Konferenzberichte* 56 (Michaelstein: Stiftung Kloster Michaelstein, 1998), 106–21. A mid-eighteenth-century description of the 1696 great bell in the Peter and Paul Church in Görlitz says that it rang D at the 32', 16', and 8' pitch "und spielet zugleich in der Tertia das H." (and plays at the same time the third H.). Ibid., 121.

31. See also Joel Speerstra, "Some Questions about Clavichord Soundboards," GOArt Research Reports 1 (1999), 173–92.

Chapter 4

1. Ludger Lohmann and Richard Troeger, among others.

2. Treatises by Couperin, Kittel, Knecht, Marpurg, Mattheson, Quantz, Rameau, Türk, Wolff, and others.

3. Carl Philipp Emanuel Bach, *Essay on the True Art of Playing Keyboard Instruments, 1753,* trans. William J. Mitchell (New York: Norton, 1949), 38 note 18.

4. Although Mitchell gives no footnote for this citation, it comes from Johann Friedrich Reichardt, "Briefe eines aufmerksamen Reisenden" (Frankfurt and Breslau, 1776), 2:19.

5. "The Italians have never used the clavichord, but rather use only the harpsichord." Ibid.

6. Quentin Faulkner, *J. S. Bach's Keyboard Technique: A Historical Introduction* (St. Louis: Concordia Publishing House, 1984).

7. Ibid., 12 note 3.

8. Ibid., 12.

9. Ewald Kooiman, "Bachs Klaviertechniek," *Het Orgel* 79, no. 1 (January 1983): 2–15.

10. Quentin Faulkner, "Griepenkerl on J. S. Bach's Keyboard Technique: A Translation and Commentary," *The American Organist* 22 (January 1988): 63–65.

11. Kaestner D. Robertson, "Arm-Weight and Weight-Transference Technique: Its Systematic Use as a Technical and Artistic Vehicle in Piano Playing" (D.M.A. diss., Boston University, 1991).

12. Joel Speerstra, "The Pedal Clavichord as a Pedagogical Tool for Organists," *De Clavicordio* 3 (1997): 112.

13. Johann Nikolaus Forkel, *Life of John Sebastian Bach with a Critical View of His Compositions* (London: T. Boosey and Co., 1820), 21–22.

14. Johann Nikolaus Forkel, *Ueber Johann Sebastian Bachs Leben, Kunst und Kunstwerke* (Leipzig: Hoffmeister und Kühnel, 1802), 12–13.

15. C. P. E. Bach, *Essay,* 30.

16. Forkel, *Life of John Bach,* 20.

17. Forkel, *Ueber Bachs Leben,* 12.

18. Faulkner, *Keyboard Technique,* 19–20.

19. H. T. David and A. Mendel, eds., revised and enlarged by Christoph Wolff, *New Bach Reader* (New York and London: Norton, 1998), 308 n. 10.

20. Forkel, *Ueber Bachs Leben,* 17.

21. Ibid., 11.

22. Forkel, *Life of John Bach,* 19.

23. Author's translation.

24. Bach, *Essay,* 38.

25. Carl Philipp Emanuel Bach, *Versuch über die wahre Art das Clavier zu spielen (Berlin: Henning, 1753 und 1762),* facsimile edition by Lothar Hoffmann-Erbrecht (Leipzig: VEB Breitkopf & Härtel, 1957), 11.

26. "Griepenkerl," *Die Musik in Geschichte und Gegenwart,* 17 vols. (Kassel: Bärenreiter, 1949–86):5 (1956):907–8: "1805 nahm er in Göttingen das Theologiestudium auf, beschäftigte sich ausgiebig mit Philosophie und Pädagogik auf Grund der Vorlesungen J. F. Herbarts, widmete sich aber unter J. N. Forkel vorwiegend der M[usik]Th[eorie] und dem Kl[avier]- bzw. Orgelspiel."

27. Ibid.

28. Preface to Friederich Konrad Griepenkerl, *Chromatische Fantasia und Fugue* (1819). Translation by Quentin Faulkner. See the Appendix, p. 000.

29. Friederich Konrad Griepenkerl, preface to his edition of *Bach Orgelwerke* (London, Leipzig, New York: C. F. Peters, 1844), 1:iii-iv. (Author's English translation.)

30. Griepenkerl, Preface. See the Appendix, p. 000.

31. Ibid., §5.

32. Bach, *Essay,* 41.

33. Ibid., 43.

34. Ibid., 42.

35. Ibid., 43.

36. Bach, *Essay,* 36.

37. Bach, *Versuch,* 9.

38. Wilhelm Marpurg, *Anleitumg zum Clavierspiel* (1755), in Max F. Schneider, *Beiträge zu einer Anleitung Clavichord und Cembalo zu spielen,* Sammlung Musik-Wissenschaftlicher Abhandlungen, 16 (Strassburg: Heitz & Co, 1934), 53.

39. Albert Schweitzer, *J. S. Bach*. Leipzig: Breitkopf und Härtel, 1930, 181.

40. Ibid.

41. Richard Troeger, "The Clavichord and Keyboard Technique," *The American Organist* 30, no. 3 (March 1996): 61.

42. George Stauffer, "J. S. Bach as Organ Pedagogue," in *The Organist as Scholar: Essays in Memory of Russell Saunders,* ed. Kerala J. Snyder, 25–44 (Stuyvesant, N.Y.: Pendragon Press, 1994).

43. C. P. E. Bach, *Essay,* 38.

44. Griepenkerl, Preface. See the Appendix, p. 000.

Prelude 2

1. Peter Brook, *Threads of Time: Recollections* (London: Methuen, 1998).

2. The term was coined by Michael Polanyi in *Personal Knowledge: Towards a Post-Critical Philosophy* (Chicago: University of Chicago Press, 1958).

3. David Bohm, *On Dialogue* (London and New York, 1996), 52.

Chapter 5

1. Carl Philipp Emanuel Bach, *Essay on the True Art of Playing Keyboard Instruments, 1753*, trans. William J. Mitchell (New York: Norton, 1949), 36.
2. The Friederici clavichord built by John Barnes and Darryl Martin in 1993 is now at the Open University in Milton Keynes, England. This instrument was strung quite heavily according to the principles outlined in chapter 3.
3. Denise Restout, *Landowska on Music* (New York: Stein and Day, 1964), plates 17 and 18.
4. Harald Vogel, in a lecture given at the International Clavichord Symposium at Göteborg University, February 22 and 23, 1995.
5. "Man das Holtz zugleich dabey höret." Wilhelm Marpurg, *Anleitung zum Clavierspiel* (Berlin : A. Haude und J. C. Spener, 1755). Quoted from Max F. Schneider, *Beiträge zu einer Anleitung Clavichord und Cembalo zu spielen,* Sammlung Musik-Wissenschaftlicher Abhandlungen, 16 (Strassbourg: Heitz & Co, 1934), 53.
6. There are some historical clavichord traditions with these kinds of plates, called damper rails. But the historical damper rails, like those found on Christian Gottlob Hubert (1714–93) clavichords, are very thin and flexible and do not limit the dynamic range of the instrument. See, for instance Nürnberg, Germanisches National Museum, MIR 1054, in Koen Vermeij, *The Hubert Clavichord Data Book: A Description of All Extant Clavichords by Christian Gottlob Hubert* (Bennebroek: Clavichord International Press, 2000), 53.
7. English translation from George Houle, *Meter in Music, 1600–1800: Performance, Perception, and Notation* (Bloomington and Indianapolis: Indiana University Press, 1987), 82. Language indications in brackets in the German were removed from the English translation.
8. Johann Gottfried Walther, *Musikalisches Lexicon* (Leipzig: Wolffgang Deer, 1732), 507.
9. Houle, *Meter in Music,* 83.
10. Walther, *Lexicon,* 598.
11. Ludger Lohmann, *Studien zu Artikulationsproblemen bei den Tasteninstrumenten des 16.–18. Jahrhunderts,* Kölner Beiträge zur Musikforschung (Regensburg: Gustav Bosse Verlag, 1982), 51–56.
12. "If he understands the correct principles of fingering and has not acquired the habit of making unnecessary gestures, he will play the most difficult things in such a manner that the motion of his hands will be barely noticeable." Bach, *Essay,* 43.
13. For more about Oortmerssen's analysis of good posture at the organ, see Jacques von Oortmerssen, *Organ Technique* (Göteborg: GOArt, 2002) 13–17.
14. See Dietrich Bartel, *Musica Poetica: Musical-Rhetorical Figures in German Baroque Music* (Lincoln and London: University of Nebraska Press, 1997), 413–27. *Commisura, symblema,* and *celeritas* were also used to describe a passing note or passing dissonance—see Athanasius Kircher, *Musurgia Universalis Rom 1650,* reprint ed. by Ulf Scharlau (Hildesheim and New York: G. Olms, 1970), 366—but they were less intuitively helpful for students at the keyboard than the transiting of *transitus.*

15. Johan Nikolaus Forkel, *Life of John Sebastian Bach with a Critical View of His Compositions* (London: T. Boosey and Co., 1820), 64–65.

16. Quentin Faulkner, J. S. *Bach's Keyboard Technique: A Historical Introduction* (St. Louis: Concordia Publishing House, 1984), 45. "Mit seinen zweenen Füssen konnte er auf dem Pedale solche Sätze ausführen, die manchem nicht ungeschikten Clavieristen mit fünf Fingern zu machen sauer genug werden würden." From the "Nekrolog" of 1754, cited in W. Neumann and H.-J. Schulze, eds., *Bach Dokumente,* (Kassel, Basel: Bärenreiter, 1972), 3:88.

17. Faulkner, J. S. *Bach's Keyboard Technique,* 45.

18. "Beim praktischen Orgelunterricht legte Kittel Wert auf das häusliche Ueben am Pedalklavier. Bei ihm zuhause waren "zwei Klaviere übereinander" gestellt, ein Pedal darunter. Dieses Instrument stand den Schülern zur Verfügung." Friedrich Wilhelm Donat, *Christian Heinrich Rinck und die Orgelmusik seiner Zeit: Ein Beitrag zur Geschichte der deutschen protestantischen Kirchenmusik um 1800* (Bad Oehnhausen: Theine & Peitsch, 1933), 34. Rinck describes Kittel's "Pedalklavier" in his autobiography as "zwei Klaviere übereinander" with a pedal underneath. Christian Heinrich Rinck, *Selbstbiographie Johann Christian Heinrich Rinck's: aus der Musikzeitschrift Eutonia besonders abgedruckt* (Breslau: G.P. Aderholz, 1833), 9.

19. Johann Christian Leberecht Kittel, *Der angehende Praktische Organist, 1801,* (Buren: Frits Knuf, 1981), 17.

20. Michael Belotti, commentary in Johann Pachelbel, *Complete Works for Keyboard Instruments,* vol. 1, *Baroque Organ Repertoire* (Colfax, N.C.: Wayne Leupold Editions, 1999), xv. The pedaling example comes from a Toccata in G from the Yale University Music Library, New Haven, Conn., manuscript LM 5005.

Chapter 6

1. For an overview, see Dietrich Bartel, *Musica Poetica: Musical-Rhetorical Figures in German Baroque Music* (Lincoln and London: University of Nebraska Press, 1997).

2. Joachim Burmeister, *Musica poetica (Rostock: S. Myliander, 1606),* facsimile edition by Martin Ruhnke (Kassel: Bärenreiter, 1955).

3. Walther was a contemporary, a relative, and a friend of J. S. Bach. During the years that they both lived in Weimar, Walther wrote the treatise for Prince Johann Ernst. and Bach probably composed the Passacaglia that will be discussed in the following chapter. Walter Emery and Christoph Wolff, "Bach, §III: (7) Johann Sebastian Bach, 5. Weimar," *The New Grove Dictionary of Music Online,* ed. L. Macy, http://www.grovemusic.com (accessed 1/30/03).

4. *Johann Gottfried Walther, Praecepta der Musicalischen Composition (MS, 1708),* ed. by Peter Benary (Leipzig: Breitkopf und Härtel, 1955), 75–208.

5. Johann Gottfried Walther, *Musikalisches Lexicon* (Leipzig: Wolffgang Deer, 1732), 244.

6. Ibid.

7. Ibid., 169.

8. Bartel, *Musica Poetica,* 37.

9. Johann Nikolaus Forkel, "Einleitung" in his *Allgemeine Geschichte der Musik* (Leipzig: Schwickert, 1788–1801), §98. English translation by Doris Bosworth Pow-

ers in "Johann Nikolaus Forkel's Philosophy of Music in the *Einleitung* to volume 1 of his 'Allgemeine Geschichte der Musik' (1788): A Translation" (Ph.D. diss., University of North Carolina, 1995), 136.

10. Forkel, "Einleitung" §15. Powers, "Johann Nokolaus Forkel's Philosophy," 58–59.

11. Walter Heinz Bernstein, *Die musikalischen Figuren als Artikulationsträger der Musik von etwa 1600 bis nach 1750* (Leipzig: Ebert Musik Verlag, 1994).

12. Both quotations in this paragraph are from Jean François Billeter, *The Chinese Art of Writing* (New York: Skira/Rizzoli, 1990), 64.

13. *Two- and Three-Part Inventions: Facsimile of the Autograph Manuscript* (New York: Dover Publications, 1968), 2–3, 16–17.

14. Billeter, *The Chinese Art of Writing,* 62.

Chapter 7

1. Christoph Wolff, "Johann Sebastian Bach," *The New Grove Dictionary of Music Online* ed. L. Macy, http://www.grovemusic.com (accessed 1/28/03).

2. The original German text as it appeared in the catalog of the antiquarian bookshop of Liepmannssohn in 1911: "Bach (Joh. Seb.) Alte Abschrift: Passacaglio con Pedale pro Organo pleno. 10 Seiten. folio.—Aus dem Besitz Franz Hausers, mit Dedication an Moscheles. Das Manuscript, obwohl kein Autograph, ist doch wichtig zur Textkritik." Dietrich Kilian, *Sechs Sonaten und Verschiedene Einzelwerke: Kritische Bericht, Johann Sebastian Bach: Neue Ausgabe Sämtlicher Werke,* 4th ser., vol. 7 (Kassel, New York: Bärenreiter, 1988), 124.

3. See also Yoshitaka Kobayashi, "Franz Hauser und seine Bach-Handschriftensammlung" (Ph.D. diss., Georg-August-Universität zu Göttingen, 1973), 72.

4. Kilian, *Kritische Bericht,* 125.

5. "Zu diesen setze ich noch eine sehr kunstreich gearbeitete Passacaglia, die aber mehr für zwey Claviere und Pedal als für die Orgel ist." Johann Nikolaus Forkel, *Ueber Johann Sebastian Bachs Leben, Kunst und Kunstwerk* (Leipzig: Hoffmeister und Kühnel, 1802), 60.

6. With thanks for the assistance of Susan Claremont, Music Division of the Library of Congress, Washington, D.C.

7. "Andrerseits gibt es kein Orgelstück, das an die Registrierkunst solche Anforderungen stellt wie dieses." Albert Schweitzer, *J. S. Bach* (Leipzig: Breitkopf und Härtel, 1930), 257.

8. H. T. David and A. Mendel, eds., *The Bach Reader* (New York and London: Norton, 1966), 345 note 10.

9. Walter Emery, *Notes on Bach's Organ Works, A Companion to the Revised Novello Edition Books IV-V, The Six Sonatas for two Manuals and Pedal* (London: Novello, 1957), 200.

10. See George Stauffer, "Bach's Organ Registrations Reconsidered," in *J. S. Bach as Organist,* ed. George Stauffer and Ernest May (Bloomington: Indiana University Press, 1986), 197.

11. Alexander Silbiger, "Passacaglia," *The New Grove Dictionary of Music Online* ed. L. Macy (Accessed 2/12/03), <http://www.grovemusic.com>.

12. Alexander Silbiger, "Passacaglia and Ciaccona: Genre Pairing and Ambiguity from Frescobaldi to Couperin," *Journal of Seventeenth-Century Music* 2, no. 1 (1996), http://www.sscm-iscm/v2/no1/Silbiger.html, §2, 4, and 5.

13. Ibid., §3.

14. Richard Hudson, *Passacaglio and Ciaccona: From Guitar Music to Italian Keyboard Variations in the 17th Century* (Ann Arbor, Mich.: UMI Research Press, 1981), 280.

15. Thomas de Sancta Maria, *Libro llamado arte de tañer fantasia: assi para tecla como para vihuela y todo instruméto* (Valladolid, 1565).

16. *Ciacona. ex D?. di Joh. Pachelbel*. Andreas Bach Book, 67v–69 (MB Lpz III.8.4).

17. *Passacalia. Pedaliter di Diet: Buxtehude*. Andreas Bach Book, 107v–109 (MB Lpz III.8.4).

18. Robert Hill, *Keyboard Music from the Andreas Bach Book and the Möller Manuscript* (Cambridge, Mass.: Harvard University Press, 1991), xxi.

19. Ibid.

20. Ibid., xxvii.

21. Robert Hill, "The Möller Manuscript and the Andreas Bach Book: Two Keyboard Anthologies from the Circle of the Young Johann Sebastian Bach" (Ph.D. diss., Harvard University, 1987), 166.

22. 20 Dance Suites (1, 6, 8, 9, 10, 11, 14, 15, 20, 26, 31, 36, 38, 44, 45, 46, 47, 48, 49, and 50); 2 Preludes (12, 16); 2 Capriccios (13 and 35); 3 Fugues (17, 18 and 19); 1 Variation set (21); 1 Ciaconne (24); 1 Sonata (33); 1 Prelude and Fugue (34); 1 Gigue (37); 1 Fatasia [*sic*] (52); 2 Toccatas (28 and 29).

23. 4 Preludia (25, 30, 32, and 53); 1 Prelude and Fugue (23), 1 Chorale Prelude (43).

24. 1 Toccata (41); 1 Preludium and Fantasia (42).

25. 11 Dance Suites (7, 8, 11, 12, 13, 16, 17, 18, 38, 39, and 43); 5 Kuhnau Biblical Sonatas (1, 2, 3, 4, and 5); 3 Variation Sets (14, 36, and 46); 3 Manualiter Fugues (19, 26, and 48); 3 Manualiter Toccatas (20, 25, and 27); 3 Manualiter Fantasias (45, 52, and 56); 2 Manualiter Cappricios (34 and 44); 1 Sonatina (35); 1 Chanberceau (49); 1 Manualiter Chorale (41).

26. 3 Toccatas with Pedal Points (21, 22 and 31); 1 Cappricio with Pedal Point (10).

27. 3 Preludia (6, 23 and 55); 2 Fugues (28 and 50), 1 Toccata (15); 1 Organ Chorale in Tablature (30); 1 Fantasia in Tablature (33).

28. 2 Praeludia (32 and 54); 1 Fuga (40).

29. Numbers 9, 29, 42, 47, and 51.

30. Kerala Snyder, *Dieterich Buxtehude: Organist in Lübeck* (New York: Schirmer, 1987), 317.

31. Ciaconna in suite Number 4; Ciaconna in Suite Number 7; Chaconne grave in Suite Number 47; Chaconne in Suite Number 49; Overture and Chaconne, Number 39; Ciaconne, Number 24.

32. Johann Mattheson, *Der vollkommene Capellmeister* (Hamburg: C. Herold, 1739), facsimile edition, ed. Margarete Reimann (Kassel and Basel: Bärenreiter, 1987), 164–66.

33. Many analyses see the passacaglia as a theme with 20 variations. I chose to label the opening ostinato statement in mm. 1–8 "Variation One" because this

analysis sees it as an integral part of the structure of the piece, not a separate statement of a theme.

34. Harald Vogel shared this impression in an interview conducted by the author for *Clavichord International* 2, no. 2 (1998): 34–36.

35. Piet Kee makes this observation in: "Zahl und Symbolik in Passacaglia und Ciacona," *Musik und Kirche* 58, no. 5 (1988): 247, but gives it as one of several possible, sometimes competing symbolic systems.

36. Natalie Jenne and Meredith Little, in *Dance and the Music of J. S. Bach* (Bloomington: Indiana University Press, 1991), 201, give a reference to a 1754 pantomime performed to the Passacaille of *L'Europe galante* (a ballet suite for voices and orchestra by André Campra first presented in 1697), where "one read in her expression a succession of feelings" and at a certain dramatic moment in the story, "all her carriage rapidly assumed a new form; she tore herself from the stage with a despair. . . ."

37. Carl Philipp Emanuel Bach, *Essay on the True Art of Playing Keyboard Instruments* (1753), trans. William J. Mitchell (New York: Norton, 1949), 37. "Jeder Clavierist soll von Rechtswegen einen guten Flügel und auch ein gutes Clavichord haben, damit er auf beyden allerley Sachen abwechselnd spielen könne." C. P. E. Bach, *Versuch*, 10–11.

Chapter 8

1. Charles Burney, *The Present State of Music in Germany, the Netherlands, and United Provinces, 1773: Dr. Burney's Musical Tours in Europe* (London: T. Becket, 1775), trans. P. Scholes (London: Oxford University Press, 1959), 2:27. See also Marc Schaefer, *Das Silbermann-Archiv: Der handschriftliche Nachlaß des Orgelmachers Johann Andreas Silbermann (1712–1783)* (Winterthur: Amadeus Verlag Bernhard Päuler, 1994), 241. In his handwritten comments, Silbermann recorded Burney's comments about organs.

2. Documentation carried out by the organbuilders Henk van Eeken and Munetaka Yokota, GOArt Archives.

3. Thanks to Carl Johan Bergsten, GOArt's research engineer, for helping to design the protocol and analyze the results. The equipment used for the force measurement included a force sensor, Kistler 9131A21; a charge amplifier, Kistler 5038A1; and a laser displacement sensor, Omron Z4M-S40 and Z4M-W40. The force and the key position signals were recorded and stored using a laptop computer and Microsoft Excel software.

4. "Plucking point" refers to the place in the keydip where the finger opens the pallet.

5. With thanks to Ibo Ortgies, who both pointed out and translated the quotations in the Niedt introduction.

6. "Bey der *Information* . . . mein Lehr-Herr . . . spielte es erstlich mir ein oder zweymahl vor, dabey sagend: Du mußt es so und so spielen, so hab ichs gelernet, wann es nun nicht mit mir fort wolte, so hätte einer seine Lust sehen sollen, wie mein Lehr-Meister so trefliche *Inventiones* hatte, mir die Kunst *quasi* bey zubringen. Die *Sexta* saß mir auf der rechten Seiten hinter dem Ohr, die *Quarta* auf der lincken Seiten, die *Septima* auf den Backen, die *Nona* in den Haaren, die falsche *Quinta* auf

der Nasen, die *Secunda* aufm Rücken, *Tertia minor* auf den Fingern, die *Tertia major* und *Quint* auf den Schienbeinen, *Decima* und *Undecima* waren sonderliche Sorten von Ohrfeigen. Wo nun der Schlag oder Stoß hintraf, darnach muste ich auch wissen, wie ich greiffen solte, doch war das beste dabey, daß meine Füsse, durch das stossen an die Schienbeine auf dem *Pedall* (welches ich damahls auch zu lernen anfieng) fein läuffig gemacht wurden. . . . Einsmahls aber suchte er eine sonderliche *Invention* hervor, und wolte mir die Kunst gar in dem Leib treten, weil ja alle *Tractamenten* ohne *Fundament* den *General-Bass* nicht in den Kopff bringen kunten. Er zog mich bey den Haaren von der *Pedall-Banck*, darauf ich vor dem *Clavier* saß, herunter, warff mich auf die Erde, und schleiffete mich bey den Haaren in die Höhe, daß der Kopf im Niederfallen an die Erde prallen muste, tratt mir endlich auf den Leib, und stampfte den eine gute weile, biß endlich…er mich zur Stuben hinaus nahe an eine daselbst nach der Strassen niedergehende Treppe hinschlepte." Friederich Erhardt Niedt, *Musikalische Handleitung* (Hamburg; Benjamin Schillern, 1710, facsimile ed. (Hildesheim: Georg Olms Verlag, 2003), §XI.

7. See also Friederich Erhardt Niedt, *The Musical Guide,* trans. Pamela L. Poulin and Irmgard C. Taylor (Oxford: Clarendon Press, 1989), 15. The otherwise excellent translation chooses to translate "Pedall-Banck" as "organ bench" and "Clavier" as "keyboard."

8. Ich will euch dennoch, wann ihr nur in dieser Stadt euch vor euer Geld ein Jahrlang auffhalten könnet, innerhalb solcher Zeit die rechten *Fundamenta* so wol in der Organisten-Kunst, als in der *Composition* lehren, daß ihr aus einem Argenisten ein Organiste werden sollet und für meine Mühe begehr ich keinen Heller, sondern wann ihr mir versprechet nur fleissig zu seyn, und die Kunst zu GOttes Ehr anzuwenden, so wil ich euch umsonst täglich eine Stunde vormittags von 7. biß 8. Uhr *informiren,* und könnet ihr sonsten in mein Hauß kommen, wenn ihr wollet, und euch alleine in einer Cammer, da etliche *Clavier* stehen, vor euch selbst *exerci*ren. Wer war frölicher als ich? Niedt, *Musikalische Handleitung,* §XX.

Appendix

1. Faulkner's translation, originally published in his "Griepenkerl on J. S. Bach's Keyboard Technique: A Translation and Commentary," *The American Organist* (January 1988): 63–65, is used by permission of the American Guild of Organists.

Bibliography

Aanstad, Odd. "Two Unusual Clavichords." *Galpin Society Journal* 43 (1990): 147–50.

Adlung, Jakob. *Musica Mechanica Organœdi.* Berlin: F. W. Birnstiel, 1768. Facsimile edition edited by Christhard Mahrenholz. Kassel: Bärenreiter, 1961.

———. *Musical Mechanics for the Organist 1768.* Translated by Quentin Faulkner. Unpublished manuscript.

Agay, Denes. "The Search for Authenticity." *Clavier* 14, no. 8 (1975): 19–31.

Ahrend, Jürgen. "Die Restaurierung der Arp Schnitger-Orgel von St. Jacobi in Hamburg." In *Die Arp Schnitger-Orgel der Hauptkirche St. Jacobi in Hamburg* (Hamburg, 1995), 189.

Ahrens, Christian. "Zum Bau und zur Nutzung von 16'-Registern und von Pedalen bei Cembali und Clavichorden. In *Cöthener Bach-Hefte 8: Beiträge zum Kolloquium "Kammermusik und Orgel im höfischen Umkreis—Das Pedalcembalo am 19. September 1997 im Johanngeorgsbau des Schlosses Köthen,* 57–72. Köthen: Dr. Siethen Verlag, 1998.

Alexander, Christopher. *The Timeless Way of Building.* New York: Oxford University Press, 1979.

Altmann, Wilhelm. "Karl Philipp Emanuel Bach als Kunstfreund: Ein Autograph des Komponisten." *Der Kunstwanderer* 1 (1919): 36–37.

André, C. A. *Der Clavierbau in seiner Geschichte, seiner technischen und musikalischen Bedeutung.* Offenbach am Main: J. André, 1855.

Auerbach, Cornelia. *Die Deutsche Clavichordkunst des 18. Jahrhundert.* 3rd ed. Kassel: Bärenreiter, 1959.

Bach, Carl Philipp Emanuel. *Essay on the True Art of Playing Keyboard Instruments, 1753.* Translated by William J. Mitchell. New York: Norton, 1949.

———. *Selbstbiographie.* In *Tagebuch seiner Musikalischen Reisen 3. Charles Burney.* Hamburg: Bey Bode, 1773. Facsimile edition by William S. Newman. Buren: Frits Knuf Publishers, 1991.

———. *Versuch über die wahre Art das Clavier zu spielen.* Berlin: Henning, 1753 und 1762. Facsimile edition by Lothar Hoffmann-Erbrecht. Leipzig: VEB Breitkopf und Härtel, 1957.

———. *Verzeichniss des musikalischen Nachlasses des verstorbenen Capellmeisters Carl Philipp Emanuel Bach.* Hamburg: Schniebes, 1790. Facsimile edition by William S. Newman. Buren: Frits Knuf, 1991.

Bach, Johann Sebastian. *Chromatishe Fantasie fur das Pianoforte von Johann Sebastian Bach: Neue Ausgabe mit einer Bezeichnung ihres wahren Vortrags, wie derselbe von J. S. Bach auf W. Friedemann Bach, wo diesem auf Forkel und von Forkel auf seine Schüler gekommen.* Leipzig, im Bureau de Musique von C. F. Peters [1819?].

———. *Two- and Three-Part Inventions: Facsimile of the Autograph Manuscript.* New York: Dover Publications, 1968.

Badura-Skoda, Eva. "Vom Pedalcembalo zum Fortepiano pedale." In *Cöthener Bach-Hefte 8: Beiträge zum Kolloquium "Kammermusik und Orgel im höfischen*

Umkreis—Das Pedalcembalo am 19. September 1997 im Johanngeorgsbau des Schlosses Köthen, 73–82. Köthen: Dr. Siethen Verlag, 1998.

Bakeman, Kenneth. "Stringing Techniques of Harpsichord Builders." *Galpin Society Journal* 27 (1974): 95–112.

Barford, Philip. "C. P. E. Bach: Master of the Clavichord." *Musica Antiqua* 76 (1953): 601–3.

———. "Some Afterthoughts by C. P. E. Bach." *Monthly Musical Record* 90 (1960): 94–98.

Barnes, John. "The Anatomy of a Clavichord." Unpublished manuscript.

*———. "Covered Strings for Clavichords and Square Pianos." *Quarterly of the Fellowship of Makers and Researchers of Historical Instruments*, no. 22 (1981).

———. "Italian Stringing Scales." *Galpin Society Journal* 21 (1968): 179–83.

———. *Making a Spinet by Traditional Methods*. Welwyn: Mac and Me, 1985.

———. "A Method for Making Traditional Harpsichord Tuning Pins." *Quarterly of the Fellowship of Makers and Researchers of Historical Instruments*, no. 15 (1979).

———. *The Stringing of Italian Harpsichords*. Graz, 1971.

———. "A Theory of Soundboard Barring." In *De Clavicordio 1, Proceedings of the International Clavichord Symposium*, edited by Bernard Brauchli, Susan Brauchli, and Alberto Galazzo. Magnano: Musica Antica a Magnano, 1995.

Bartel, Dietrich. *Musica Poetica: Musical-Rhetorical Figures in German Baroque Music*. Lincoln and London: University of Nebraska Press, 1997.

Bavington, Peter. "Keylever, Tangent and String—A Preliminary Analysis of Clavichord Touch and Action." In *De Clavicordio 3, Proceedings of the International Clavichord Symposium*, edited by Bernard Brauchli, Susan Brauchli, and Alberto Galazzo. Magnano: Musica Antica a Magnano, 1997.

Belotti, Michael. Commentary in Johann Pachelbel: *Complete Works for Keyboard Instruments*, Volume 1, *Baroque Organ Repertoire*. Colfax, N. C.: Wayne Leupold Editions, 1999.

Bellerman, H. "Nachtrag zu Kirnberger's Briefen." *Leipzig Allgemeine musikalischer Zeitung* 7 (1872): 441–44.

Benson, Joan. "Bach and the Clavier." *Clavier* 29, no. 2 (1990): 25–29.

Berg, Darrell. "C. P. E. Bach's 'Variations' and 'Embellishments' for His Keyboard Sonatas." *Journal of Musicology* 2 (1983): 151–73.

———. "The Keyboard Sonatas of C. P. E. Bach: An Expression of the Mannerist Principle." Ph.D. diss., State University of New York, 1975.

———. "C. Ph. E. Bachs Umarbeitungen seiner Claviersonaten." *Bach-Jahrbuch*, 74 (1988): 123–61.

———. "Towards a Catalogue of the Sonatas of C. P. E. Bach." *Journal of the American Musicological Society* 32 (1979): 276–303.

———, ed. *The Collected Works for Solo Keyboard by Carl Phillip Emanuel Bach, 1714–1788*. 6 vols. New York: Garland, 1985.

———, ed. *Klaviersonaten Auswahl*. Munich: G Henle Verlag, 1986.

Bernstein, Walter Heinz. *Die musikalischen Figuren als Artikulationsträger der Musik von etwa 1600 bis nach 1750*. Leipzig: Ebert Musik Verlag, 1994.

Beurmann, E. "Die Klaviersonaten Carl Philipp Emanuel Bachs." Ph.D. diss., Georg-August-Universität, 1952.

———. "Die Reprisensonaten Carl Philipp Emanuel Bachs." *Archiv für Musikwissenschaft* 13 (1956): 168–79.

Bierdimpffl, K. A. *Die Sammlung der Musik-Instrumente im Baierischen Nationalmuseum.* Munich, 1883.

Billeter, Jean François. *The Chinese Art of Writing.* New York: Skira/Rizzoli, 1990.

Birkett, Stephen, and William Jurgenson. "Geometrical Methods in Stringed Keyboard Instrument Design and Construction." *http://www.aps.uoguelph.ca/~birketts/*, accessed November 1999.

Bitter, Karl Hermann. *Carl Philipp Emanuel und Wilhelm Friedemann Bach und deren Brüder (1868).* Kassel: Bärenreiter, 1973.

Boalch, Donald H., ed. *Makers of the Harpsichord and Clavichord 1440–1840.* 3rd ed. Oxford: Clarendon Press, 1995.

Brauchli, Bernard. *The Clavichord.* Cambridge: Cambridge University Press, 1998.

Brothier, Jean Jacques. "Carl Philipp Emanuel, le Bach de Berlin." *Revue international de musique* 8 (1950): 123–32.

Brown, Peter A. "The Earliest English Biography of Haydn." *Musical Quarterly* 59 (1973): 339–54.

———. *Joseph Haydn and C. P. E. Bach: The Question of Influence.* New York: Norton, 1975.

Bullard, Beth. *Musica getutscht: A Treatise on Musical Instruments by Sebastian Virdung.* Cambridge: Cambridge University Press, 1993.

Burmeister, Joachim. *Musical Poetics.* Translated by Benito V. Rivera. New Haven, Conn., London: Yale University Press, 1993.

Burney, Charles. *The Present State of Music in Germany, the Netherlands, and United Provinces, 1773, Dr. Burney's Musical Tours in Europe.* Translated by P. Scholes. London: Oxford University Press, 1959.

Carlsson, Albert. *Med Mått Mätt: Svenska och utländska mått genom tiderna.* Stockholm: LTS Förlag, 1989.

Cherbuliez, A. E. *Carl Philipp Emanuel Bach, 1714–1788.* Zurich: Hug, 1940.

Chrysander, F. "Briefe von Karl Philipp Emanuel Bach an G. M. Telemann." *Leipzig Allgemeine musikalischer Zeitung* 4 (1869): 177–192.

Cizek, Bohuslav. "Clavichords in the Czech Lands." In *De Clavicordio 2, Proceedings of the International Clavichord Symposium,* edited by Bernard Brauchli, Susan Brauchli, and Alberto Galazzo, 36–42. Magnano: Musica Antica a Magnano, 1995.

Clark, Stephen. *The Letters of C. P. E. Bach.* Oxford: Clarendon Press, 1997.

———. "The Letters of Carl Philipp Emanuel Bach to Georg Michael Telemann." *Journal of the American Musicological Society* 3 (1984): 177–95.

———., ed. *C. P. E. Bach Studies.* Oxford: Clarendon Press, 1988.

Clercx, Suzanne. "Le Forme du rondo chez Carl Philipp Emanuel Bach." *Revue de musicologie* 16 (1935): 148–67.

Cooper, Kenneth. "The Clavichord in the Eighteenth Century." Ph.D. diss., Columbia University, 1971.

Cramer, Hermann. "Two Sons of Music." *Music and Musicians* 13 (1964): 14–15.

David, H. T., and A. Mendel, eds. *The Bach Reader.* New York and London: Norton, 1966.

———. *The New Bach Reader.* Revised and enlarged by Christoph Wolff. New York and London: Norton, 1998.

Daymond, E. R. *Carl Philipp Emanuel Bach.* London: 1907.

Dietrich, F. "Matthias Claudius und C. Ph. E. Bach." *Zeitschrift für Hausmusik* 9 (1940): 73–75.

Doflein, Erich. "Carl Philipp Emanuel Bach." *Der Musikerzieher* 35, no. 1 (1938): 62–63.

———. "Neues von und über Ph. E. Bach." *Zeitschrift für Hausmusik* 9 (1940): 109–14.

Donat, Friedrich Wilhelm. *Christian Heinrich Rinck und die Orgelmusik seiner Zeit: Ein Beitrag zur Geschichte der deutschen protestantischen Kirchenmusik um 1800.* Bad Oehnhausen: Theine & Peitsch, 1933.

Douwes, Claas. *Grondig Ondersoek van de Toonen der Musijk, (Franeker, 1699, 1722, 1773).* Facsimile edition by Peter Williams. Amsterdam: Frits Knuf, 1970.

Edler, A. "C. P. E. Bach within the Life of His Epoch." *Studia Musicologica Norvegica* 15 (1989): 9–29.

Eitner, Robert. *Biographisch-Bibliographisches Quellen-Lexikon,* 2nd ed. Graz: Akademische Druck- und Verlagsanstalt, 1959.

———. "Quantz und Emanuel Bach." *Monatshefte für Musik-Geschichte* 34 (1902): 39–46, 55–63.

Emery, Walter. *Notes on Bach's Organ Works: A Companion to the Revised Novello Edition Books IV-V, The Six Sonatas for Two Manuals and Pedal.* London: Novello, 1957.

Engel, Hans. "Gerstenberg und die Musik seiner Zeit." *Zeitschrift der Gesellschaft für Schleswig-Holsteinische Geschichte* 56 (1927): 417–48.

Faulkner, Quentin. "Griepenkerl on J. S. Bach's Keyboard Technique: A Translation and Commentary" *The American Organist* (January 1988): 63–65.

———. *J. S. Bach's Keyboard Technique: A Historical Introduction.* St. Louis, Mo.: Concordia Publishing House, 1984.

Felice, F. B. de. "*Pied.*" In *Encyclopedie, ou, Dictionnaire universel raisonné des connoissances humaine.* Yverdon: 1774.

Ferrara, Lawrence. *Philosophy and the Analysis of Music.* New York, London: Greenwood Press, 1991.

Ford, Karrin. "The Pedal Clavichord and the Pedal Harpsichord." *The Galpin Society Journal* 1 (1997): 161–79.

Forkel, Johann Nikolaus. *Allgemeine Geschichte der Musik.* 2 vols. Leipzig: Schwickert, 1788/1801. English translation by Dorothy Bosworth Powers in her "Johann Nikolaus Forkel's Philosophy of Music in the *Einleitung* to volume 1 of his "Allgemeine Geschichte der Musik (1988): A Translation." Ph.D. diss., University of North Carolina, 1995.

———. *Life of John Sebastian Bach with a Critical View of His Compositions.* London: T. Boosey and Co., 1820.

———. *Ueber Johann Sebastian Bachs Leben, Kunst und Kunstwerk.* Leipzig: Hoffmeister und Kühnel, 1802.

Freyse, Conrad. *Unbekannte Jugendbildnisse Friedemann und Emanuel Bachs.* Leipzig: Peters, 1950.

Friedrich, Felix. "Orgel- oder Klavierbauer? Historische und soziologische Annotationen." In *Cöthener Bach-Hefte 8: Beiträge zum Kolloquium "Kammermusik und Orgel im höfischen Umkreis-Das Pedalcembalo am 19. September 1997 im Johanngeorgsbau des Schlosses Köthen,"* 105–10. Köthen: Dr Siethen Verlag, 1998.

Geiringer, Karl. "Artistic Interrelations of the Bachs." *Musical Quarterly* 36 (1950): 363–75.

———. *The Bach Family: Seven Generations of Creative Genius.* London: Oxford University Press, 1954.

Gerber, Ernst Ludwig. *Historisch-biographisches Lexicon der Tonkünstler.* Leipzig: J. G. I. Breitkopf, 1790–92.

Godt, I. "C. P. E. Bach and his Mark." *College Music Symposium* 19 (1979): 154–62.

Griepenkerl, Friederich Konrad. Preface to Johann Sebastian Bach, *Chromatische Fantasia und Fugue.* Leipzig: C. F. Peters, 1819.

———, ed. *Bach Orgelwerk.*, vol. 1. London, Leipzig, New York: C. F. Peters, 1844.

Grosses vollständiges Universal Lexicon Aller Wissenschafften und Künste. Halle and Leipzig: 1735.

Hedlund, Oscar. *Georg Bolins gitarrbok.* Stockholm: Reuter and Reuter, 1982.

Helenius-Öberg, Eva. "Connections between Organ Building and Keyboard Instrument Building in Sweden before 1820." In *Research Reports of the Göteborg Organ Art Center 1,* edited by Sverker Jullander, 127–72. Göteborg: GOArt, 1999.

———. *Svenskt Klavikordbygge 1720–1820.* Stockholm: Almqvist and Wiksell, 1986.

Heller, Von Veit. "Musikalische Strukturen in den Geläuten von N. J. Sorber and H. H. Rausch." In *Glocken und Glockenspiele: Michaelsteiner Konferenzberichte 56.* Michaelstein: Stiftung Kloster Michaelstein, 1998.

Helm, Eugene E. *Carl Philipp Emanuel Bach.* New Haven, Conn.: Yale University Press, 1989.

———. *The Catalog of the Works of C. P. E. Bach.* New Haven, Conn., and London: Yale University Press, 1989.

———. "Six Random Measures of C. P. E. Bach." *Journal of Music Theory* 10 (1966): 19–51.

Henkel, Hubert. *Clavichorde: Musikinstrumenten-Museum der Karl-Marx-Universität, Leipzig, Katalog 4.* Leipzig: VEB Deutscher Verlag für Musik, 1981.

Heyde, Herbert. *Musikinstrumentenbau, 15.–19. Jahrhundert. Kunst Handwerk Entwurf.* Leipzig: VEB Deutscher Verlag für Musik, 1986.

Hill, Robert. *Keyboard Music from the Andreas Bach Book and the Möller Manuscript.* Cambridge, Mass.: Harvard University Press, 1991.

———. "The Möller Manuscript and the Andreas Bach Book: Two Keyboard Anthologies from the Circle of the Young Johann Sebastian Bach." Ph.D. diss., Harvard University, 1987.

Hoffman-Erbrecht, Lothar. "Johann Sebastian und Carl Philipp Emanuel Bachs Nürnberger Verleger." In *Die Nürnberger Musikverleger und die Familie Bach,* edited by Willi Wörthmüller, 5–10. Nürnberg: Bollman, 1973.

Hogwood, Christopher. "A Repertoire for the Clavichord Including a Brief History of *Bebung.*" In *De Clavicordio 3, Proceedings of the International Clavichord Symposium,* edited by Bernard Brauchli, Susan Brauchli, and Alberto Galazzo. Magnano: Musica Antica a Magnano, 1996.

Houle, George. *Meter in Music, 1600–1800: Performance, Perception, and Notation.* Bloomington and Indianapolis: Indiana University Press, 1987.

Hubbard, Frank. *Three Centuries of Harpsichord Making.* Cambridge, Mass.: Harvard University Press, 1965.

Huber, Alfons. "Konstruktionsprinzipien im Clavichordbau: Überlegungen zu Mensurierung, Stimmtonhöhe und Besaitung bei Clavichorden des 15.–18. Jahrhunderts." In *"Musik muß man machen": Eine Festgabe für Josef Mertin zum neunzigsten Geburtstag am 21. März 1994,* edited by Michael Nagy, 241–316. Wien: Vom Pasqualatihaus, 1994.

Hudson, Richard. *Passacaglio and Ciaccona: From Guitar Music to Italian Keyboard Variations in the 17ᵗʰ Century.* Ann Arbor, Mich.: UMI Research Press, 1981.

Jacobi, E. R. "Five Hitherto Unknown Letters from C. P. E. Bach to J. J. H. Westphal." *Journal of the American Musicological Society* 23 (1970): 227–38.

———. "Three Additional Letters from C. P. E. Bach to J. J. H. Westphal." *Journal of the American Musicological Society* 27 (1974): 119–32.

Jeans, Susi. "The Pedal Clavichord and Other Practice Instruments of Organists." In *Proceedings of the Royal Musical Association.* London: The Royal Musical Association, 1950–1952, 1–15.

Jung, Hans Grosse, and Hans Rudolf, eds. *Georg Philipp Telemann, Briefwechsel.* Leipzig: VEB, 1972.

Kee, Piet. "Mass und Zahl in Passacaglia und Ciacona: Astronomie in Buxtehudes Passacaglia." *Ars organi* 32, no. 4 (1984): 232–41.

———. "Zahl und Symbolik in Passacaglia und Ciacona." *Musik und Kirche* 58, no. 5 (1988): 231–55.

Kilian, Dietrich. *Sechs Sonaten und Verschiedene Einzelwerke: Kritische Bericht. Johann Sebastian Bach: Neue Ausgabe Sämtlicher Werke,* 4th ser., vol. 7. Kassel: Bärenreiter, 1988.

Kinsky, Georg. *Musik-historisches Museum von Wilhelm Heyer in Cöln.*Leipzig: Kommissionsverlag von Breitkopf und Härtel, 1912.

———. "Pedalklavier oder Orgel bei Bach?" *Acta Musicologica* 8 (1936): 160–164.

Kirkpatrick, Robert. "C. P. E. Bach's Versuch Reconsidered." *Early Music* 4 (1976): 384–92.

Kobayashi, Yoshitaka. "Franz Hauser und seine Bach-Handschriftensammlung." Ph.D. diss., Georg-August-Universität zu Göttingen, 1973.

Kittel, Johann Christian Leberecht. *Der angehende praktische Organist* (1801). With an introduction by Gerard Bal. Buren: Frits Knuf, 1981.

Kivy, Peter. *Authenticities: Philosophical Reflections on Musical Performance.* Ithaca, N.Y., and London: Cornell University Press, 1995.

Kochevitsky, George. "Letters." *Musical Quarterly* 113 (1981): 2.

Köhler, Karl-Heinz. *Carl Philipp Emanuel Bach.* Frankfurt an der Oder: Meesedruck, 1974.

Kooiman, Ewald. "Bachs Klaviertechniek." *Het Orgel* 79, no. 1 (1983): 2–15.

———. "Eine Quelle zu Bachs Klaviertechnik." *Ars Organi* 31, no. 1 (1983): 21–25.

Koster, John. "The Harpsichord Culture in Bach's Environs." In *Bach Perspectives,* edited by David Schulenberg, 57–77. Lincoln and London: University of Nebraska Press, 1999.

———. "The Stringing and Pitches of Historical Clavichords." In *De Clavicordio 1, Proceedings of the International Clavichord Symposium,* edited by Bernard Brauchli, Susan Brauchli, and Alberto Galazzo. Magnano: Musica Antica a Magnano, 1993.

Kurzwelly, Albrecht. "Neues über das Bachbildnis der Thomasschule und andere Bildnisse Johann Sebastian Bachs." *Bach Jahrbuch* 2 (1914): 1–37.

Laaff, Ernst. "Carl Philipp Emanuel Bach: Der Klavierspieler und Komponist." *Musica* 51 (1960): 1–6.

———. "Carl Philipp Emanuel Bach: Lebenslauf und Künstlerpersönlichkeit." *Musica* 50 (1959): 364–68.

Lang, Paul Henry. *Musicology and Performance.* Edited by Alfred Mann and George J. Buelow. New Haven, Conn., and London: Yale University Press, 1997.

Lawlor, Robert. *Sacred Geometry: Philosophy and Practice.* London: Thames and Hudson, 1982.

LeShan, Lawrence, and Henry Margenau. *Einstein's Space and Van Gogh's Sky: Physical Reality and Beyond.* New York: Macmillan, 1982.

Little, Meredith, and Natalie Jenne. *Dance and the Music of J. S. Bach.* Bloomington and Indianapolis: Indiana University Press, 1991.

Lohmann, Ludger. *Studien zu Artikulationsproblemen bei den Tasteninstrumenten des 16.–18. Jahrhunderts.* Kölner Beiträge zur Musikforschung. Regensburg: Gustav Bosse Verlag, 1982.

Marpurg, Friedrich Wilhelm. *Anleitung zum Clavierspielen: Der schönern Ausübung der heutigen Zeit gemäss.* Berlin: A. Haude und J. C. Spener, 1755.

Marshall, Robert. "Organ or 'Klavier'? Instrumental Prescriptions in the Sources of Bach's Keyboard Works." In *J. S. Bach as Organist: His Instruments, Music, and Performance Practices,* edited by George Stauffer and Ernest May, 212–39. Bloomington: Indiana University Press, 1986.

Martine Engberg, Eilen. "The Sons of Johann Sebastian Bach." SMM Thesis, Union Theological Seminary, 1945.

Mattheson, Johann. *Der Volkommene Capellmeister* (Hamburg: C. Herold, 1739). Facsimile edition by Margarete Reimann. Kassel: Bärenreiter, 1987.

Miesner, Heinrich. "Aus der Umwelt Philipp Emanuel Bachs." *Bach Jahrbuch* 34 (1937): 132–43.

———. "Beziehungen zwischen den Familien Stahl und Bach." *Bach Jahrbuch* 30 (1933): 71–76.

———. "Die Grabstätte Bachs." *Bach Jahrbuch* 29 (1932): 164–65.

———. "Graf von Keiserlingk und Minister Von Happe, Zwei Gönner der Familie Bach." *Bach Jahrbuch* 31 (1934): 101–15.

———. *Philipp Emanuel Bach in Hamburg.* Wiesbaden: Breitkopf und Härtel, 1969.

———. "Philipp Emanuel Bachs musikalischer Nachlaß Vollständiger, dem Original entsprechender Neudruck des Nachlaßverzeichnisses von 1790." *Bach Jahrbuch* 36 (1939): 81–112.

———. *Porträts aus dem Kreise Philipp Emanuel und Wilhelm Friedemann Bachs.* Kassel: Bärenreiter, 1938.

———. "Ungedruckte Briefe von Philipp Emanuel Bach." *Zeitschrift für Hausmusik* 14 (1931–32): 224–50.

———. "Urkundliche Nachrichten über die Familie Bach in Berlin." *Bach Jahrbuch* 29 (1932): 157–62.

Niedt, Friederich Erhardt. *The Musical Guide.* Translated by Pamela L. Poulin and Irmgard C. Taylor. Oxford: Clarendon Press,, 1989. (Translation of his *Musikalische Handleitung.*)

———. *Musikalische Handleitung* (Hamburg: Benjamin Schillern, 1710). Facsimile edition. Hildesheim: Georg Olms Verlag, 2003.

Neumann, Werner, and Hans Joachim Schulze, eds. *Bach Dokumente.* 3 vols. Kassel: Bärenreiter, 1963, 1969, 1972.

Neupert, Hanns. *Das Klavichord: Geschichte und technische Betrachtung des "Eigentlichen Claviers."* Kassel: Bärenreiter, 1956.

Newman, William. "Emanuel Bach's Autobiography." *Musical Quarterly* 51 (1965): 363–72.

Nohl, Ludwig. *Letters of Distinguished Musicians: Gluck, Haydn, P. E. Bach, Weber, Mendelssohn.* London: Longmanns Green, 1867.

Norman, Gertrude, and Miriam Schrifte, eds. *Letters of Composers: An Anthology 1603–1945.* New York: Knopf, 1946.

O'Brien, Grant. "The Clavichord by G. C. Rackwitz Stockholm, 1796." In *De Clavicordio 2, Proceedings of the International Clavichord Symposium,* edited by Bernard Brauchli, Susan Brauchli, and Alberto Galazzo. Magnano: Musica Antica a Magnano, 1995.

———. "Stringing Materials and Gauges from Clavichords by I. C. Gerlach and H. A. Hass." In *De Clavicordio 1, Proceedings of the International Clavichord Symposium,* edited by Bernard Brauchli, Susan Brauchli, and Alberto Galazzo. Magnano: Musica Antica a Magnano, 1993.

Ottenburg, Hans Günther. *C. P. E. Bach.* Oxford: Oxford University Press, 1991.

———, ed. *Briefe der Musikerfamilie.* Frankfurt: Fischer, 1985.

Paap, Wouter. "Carl Philipp Emanuel Bach, de Meester van het Clavichord." *Mens en Melodie* 19, no. 4 (1964): 98–103.

Petzsch, Christoph. "Ein unbekannter Brief von Carl Philipp Emanuel Bach and Ch. G. von Nürnberg." *Archiv für Musikwissenschaft* 22 (1965): 208–13.

Plamenac, Dragan. "New Light on the Last Years of Carl Philipp Emanuel Bach." *Musical Quarterly* 35 (1949): 565–87.

Potvlieghe, Joris. "Het pedaalklavichord." *Orgelkunst viermaandelijks tijdschrift,* 11 (1988): 113.

Powers, Doris Bosworth. "Johann Nikolaus Forkel's Philosophy of Music in the 'Einleitung' to Volume One of his *Allgemeine Geschichte der Musik* (1788): A Translation." Ph.D. diss., University of North Carolina, 1995.

Praetorius, Michael. *Syntagma Musicum II: De organographia parts I and II.* Translated by David Z. Crookes. Oxford: Clarendon Press, 1986.

Quantz, Johann Joachim. *Versuch einer Anweisung die Flöte traversiere zu spielen: Reprint der Ausgabe Berlin (1752).* Leipzig: VEB Deutscher Verlag für Musik, 1983.

Rácz Mizushima, Jochen. "Das Pedalclavichord: Entwicklung, Geschichte und Bedeutung eines vergessenen Instruments." A-Level Thesis, Hochschule für Musik Köln, 1996.

Rampe, Siegbert. *Interpretation of 16th-Century Iberian Music on the Clavichord, Keyboard Studies.* Buren: Frits Knuf Publishers, 1989.

———. "Kompositionen für Saitenclaviere mit obligatem Pedal unter JSBs Clavier- und Orgelwerken." In *Cöthener Bach-Hefte 8: Beiträge zum Kolloquium "Kammermusik und Orgel im höfischen Umkreis-Das Pedalcembalo am 19. September 1997 im Johanngeorgsbau des Schlosses Köthen,* 143–86. Köthen: Dr Siethen Verlag, 1998.

Reeser, Edouard. *The Sons of Bach.* Stockholm: Continental Book Company, 1949.

Reichardt, Johann Friedrich. *Briefe eines aufmerksamen Reisenden die Musik betreffend.* Frankfurt and Breslau: 1776.

Reinhardt, Max, and Dan H. Laurence, eds. *The Bodley Bernard Shaw: The Complete Musical Criticism in Three Volumes.* London: The Bodley Head, 1981.

Restout, Denise. *Landowska on Music.* New York: Stein and Day, 1964.

Riefling, Reimar. "Om Johan Sebastian Bachs aetlinger." *Norsk Musiktidskrift* 12, no. 4 (1975): 137–46.

Riemann, Hugo. "Die Söhne Bachs." *Blätter für Haus- und Kirchenmusik* 1 (1987): 28–30.

Riemer, Otto. "Johann Sebastian II: Ein Gedenkblatt für den jüngsten Sohn Philipp Emanuel Bach." *Baseler Jahrbuch für Historische Musikpraxis* 9 (1985): 157–72.

Rinck, Christian Heinrich. *Selbstbiographie Johann Christian Heinrich Rinck's: Aus der Musikzeitschrift Eutonia besonders abgedruckt.* Breslau: G. P. Aderholz, 1833.

Robertson, Kastner D. "Arm-Weight and Weight-Transference Technique: Its Systematic Use as a Technical and Artistic Vehicle in Piano Playing." D. M. A. diss., Boston University, 1991.

Rochlitz, Friedrich. "Karl Philipp Emanuel Bach." *Für Freunde der Tonkunst* 5 (1832): 157–72.

Rosen, Charles. *The Frontiers of Meaning: Three Informal Lectures on Music.* New York: Hill and Wang, 1994.

Russell, Raymond. *The Harpsichord and Clavichord.* Edited by Howard Schott. London: Faber, 1973.

Sachs, Arjeh. "C. P. E. Bach and his Book 250th Anniversary of his Birth." *Tatzlil: Forum for Music Research and Bibliography* 5 (1965): 93–95, 157.

Schaefer, Marc. *Das Silbermann-Archiv: Der handschriftliche Nachlaß des Orgelmachers Johann Andreas Silbermann (1712–1783).* Winterthur: Amadeus Verlag Bernhard Päuler, 1994.

Schmid, Ernst Fritz. "Carl Philipp Emanuel Bach." In *Die Musik in Geschichte und Gegenwart,* edited by Friedrich Blume, § 914–42. Kassel: Bärenreiter, 1949–1951.

Schmidt, Christopher. "Philipp Emanuel Bach und das Clavichord." *Schweizerische Musikzeitung* 92 (1952): 441–46.

Schmidt, Martin-Christian. "Das pedalcembalo-ein fast vergessenes Tasteninstrument." In *Cöthener Bach-Hefte 8: Beiträge zum Kolloquium "Kammermusik und Orgel im höfischen Umkreis-Das Pedalcembalo am 19. September 1997 im Johanngeorgsbau des Schlosses Köthen,* 83–104. Köthen: Dr Siethen Verlag, 1998.

Schmieder, Wolfgang. *Thematisch–Systematisches Verzeichnis der Werke Joh. Seb. Bachs.* Wiesbaden: Breitkopf und Härtel, 1950 and 1966.

Schmitz, Arnold. *Die Bildlichkeit der wortgebundenen Musik Johann Sebastian Bachs.* Mainz: B. Schotts Söhne, 1950.

———. "Figuren, musikalisch-rhetorische." In *Musik in Geschichte und Gegenwart.* Kassel: Bärenreiter (1955) 4:176–83.

Schneider, Max F. *Beiträge zu einer Anleitung Clavichord und Cembalo zu spielen.* Sammlung Musik-Wissenschaftlicher Abhandlungen, 16. Strassbourg: Heitz and Co., 1934.

Scholes, Percy A., ed. *Dr. Burney's Musical Tours in Europe.* Vol. 2: *An Eighteenth-Century Musical Tour in Central Europe and the Netherlands.* London: Oxford University Press, 1959.

Schulenberg, David. "Versions of Bach: Performing Practices in the Keyboard Works." In *Bach Perspectives,* edited by David Schulenberg, 111–35. Lincoln and London: University of Nebraska Press, 1999.

Schünemann, Georg. "Friederich Bachs Briefwechsel mit Gerstenberg und Breitkopf." *Bach Jahrbuch* 1 (1916): 20–35.

Schweitzer, Albert. *J. S. Bach.* Leipzig: Breitkopf und Härtel, 1930.

———. *J. S. Bach le musicien-poète.* Leipzig: Breitkopf und Härtel, 1905.

———. *Out of My Life and Thought: An Autobiography.* Translated by C. T. Campion. New York: Henry Holt and Company, 1933.

Sherman, Bernard. *Inside Early Music: Conversations with Performers.* New York, Oxford: Oxford University Press, 1997.

Silbiger, Alexander. "Passacaglia," *The New Grove Dictionary of Music.* Online edition, edited by L. Macy. Accessed February 2003. http://www.grovemusic.com.

———. "Passacaglia and Ciaccona: Genre Pairing and Ambiguity from Frescobaldi to Couperin." *Journal of Seventeenth-Century Music* 2, no. 1 (1996).

Sittard, Josef. *Geschichte des Musik- und Konzertwesens in Hamburg.* Altona und Leipzig: A. C. Reher, 1890, 1971.

Smets, Paul. *Orgeldispositionen: Eine Handschrift aus dem XVIII. Jahrhundert, im Besitz der Sächsischen Landesbibliothek.* Dresden: no pub., 1931.

Snyder, Kerala. *Dieterich Buxtehude: Organist in Lübeck.* New York: Schirmer, 1987.

Speerstra, Joel. "Bach, the Pedal Clavichord and the Organ," Ph.D. diss. in Musicology, Göteborg University, 2000.

———. "Documenting a Clavichord by Lindholm and Söderström, and a Brief History of Swedish Measurements." In *De Clavicordio 4, Proceedings of the International Clavichord Symposium,* edited by Bernard Brauchli, Susan Brauchli, and Alberto Galazzo. Magnano: Musica Antica a Magnano, 1999.

———. "An Interview with Harald Vogel." *Clavichord International* 2, no. 2 (1998): 34–36.

———. "Measuring the Gerstenberg Pedal Clavichord: A Detective Story." In *Research Reports of the Göteborg Organ Art Center.* Vol. 3, edited by Sverker Jullander, 75–93. Göteborg: GOArt, 2003.

———. "The Pedal Clavichord as a Pedagogical Tool for Organists" In *De Clavicordio 3, Proceedings of the International Clavichord Symposium,* edited by Bernard Brauchli, Susan Brauchli, and Alberto Galazzo, 109–18. Magnano: Musica Antica a Magnano, 1997.

———. "Some Questions about Clavichord Soundboards." In *Research Reports of the Göteborg Organ Art Center.* Vol. 1, edited by Sverker Jullander, 173–92. Göteborg: GOArt, 1999.

———. "Towards an Identification of the Clavichord Repertoire among C. P. E. Bach's Solo Keyboard Music: Some Preliminary Conclusions." In *De Clavicordio 2, Proceedings of the International Clavichord Symposium,* edited by Bernard Brauchli, Susan Brauchli, and Alberto Galazzo. Magnano: Musica Antica a Magnano, 1995.

———. "Two Mid-18th-Century Swedish Clavichords: A Professional Instrument by an Amateur Builder and an Amateur Instrument by a Professional One." In *De Clavicordio 5, Proceedings of the International Clavichord Symposium,* edited by Bernard Brauchli, Alberto Galazzo, and Ivan Moody. Magnano: Musica Antica a Magnano, 2002.

Speerstra, Joel, ed. *The North German Organ Research Project.* Göteborg: GOArt, 2003.

Spitta, Philipp. *Johann Sebastian Bach,* 2 vols. Wiesbaden: Breitkopf und Härtel, 1979.

———. *Johann Sebastian Bach,* 3 vols. Translated by Clara Bell and J. A. Fuller-Maitland. New York: Dover Publications, 1951.

Stauffer, George. "J. S. Bach as Organ Pedagogue." In *The Organist as Scholar: Essays in Memory of Russell Saunders,* ed. Kerala J. Snyder, 25–44. Stuyvesant, N.Y.: Pendragon Press, 1994.

Stauffer, George, and Ernest May. *J. S. Bach as Organist: His Instruments, Music, and Performance Practices.* Bloomington: Indiana University Press, 1986.

Stinson, Russell. *The Bach Manuscripts of Johann Peter Kellner and His Circle: A Case Study in Reception History.* Durham, N.C., and London: Duke University Press, 1989.

Suchalla, Ernst, ed. *Briefe von Carl Philipp Emanuel Bach an Johann Gottlob Breitkopf und Nikolaus Forkel.* Tutzing: Hans Schneider, 1985.

———. *Carl Philipp Emanuel Bach Briefe und Dokumente: Kritische Gesamtausgabe.* 2 vols. Göttingen: Vandenhoeck and Ruprecht, 1994.

Taruskin, Richard. *Text and Act: Essays on Music and Performance.* New York, Oxford: Oxford University Press, 1995.

Tegtmeier, Konrad. "Carl Philipp Emanuel Bachs letzte Ruhestätte." *Deutsche Rundschau* 249 (1936): 45–48.

Terry, Charles Sanford. *Johann Christian Bach.* Edited by H. C. Robbins Landon. Oxford: Oxford University Press, 1967.

Terry, Miriam. "C. P. E. Bach and J. J. H. Westphal—A Clarification." *Journal of the American Musicological Society* 22 (1969): 106–15.

Treitler, Leo. *Music and the Historical Imagination.* Cambridge, Mass.: Harvard University Press, 1989.

Troeger, Richard. "The Clavichord and Keyboard Technique." *The American Organist* 30, no. 3 (March 1996): 59–63.

———. *Technique and Interpretation on the Harpsichord and Clavichord.* Bloomington and Indianapolis: Indiana University Press, 1987.

van Ree Bernard, Nelly. *Seven Steps in Clavichord Development between 1400 and 1800: An Annotated Audio-Visual Review.* Buren: Frits Knuf Publishers, 1987.

Vermeij, Koe. *The Hubert Clavichord Data Book: A Description of All Extant Clavichords by Christian Gottlob Hubert.* Bennebroek: Clavichord International Press, 2000.

von Fischer, Kurt. "C. Ph. E. Bach's Variationenwerke." *Revue Belge de Musicologie* 6 (1952): 190–95.

von Hase, Hermann. "Carl Philipp Emanuel Bach und Joh. Gottl. Im Breitkopf." *Bach Jahrbuch* 8 (1911): 86–92.

Wade, Rachel. *The Catalogue of Carl Philipp Emanuel Bach's Estate: A Facsimile Edition of Schniebes, Hamburg, (1790).* New York: Garland, 1981.

Wagner, Günther. "Der gravitätische Klang. Pedalcembali und 16–Fuß-Register." In *Cöthener Bach-Hefte 8: Beiträge zum Kolloquium "Kammermusik und Orgel im höfischen Umkreis-Das Pedalcembalo am 19. September 1997 im Johanngeorgsbau des Schlosses Köthen,* 111–20. Köthen: Dr Siethen Verlag, 1998.

Waldersee, P., ed. *Karl Hermann Bitter: Carl Philipp Emanuel und Wilhelm Friedemann Bach und deren Brüder, (1868).* Sammlung Musikalischer Vorträge, 5. Wiesbaden: Breitkopf und Härtel, 1976.

Walther, Johann Gottfried. *Musikalisches Lexicon*. Leipzig: Wolffgang Deer, 1732. Facsimile edition by Richard Schaal. Kassel: Bärenreiter, 1953.

Weiss, Piero, ed. *Letters of Composers through Six Centuries*. Philadelphia: Chilton, 1967.

Werner, Richard Maria. "Gerstenbergs Briefe an Nicolai nebst einer Antwort Nicolais." *Zeitschrift für deutsche Philologie* 23 (1891): 43–67.

Williams, Peter. *The Organ Music of J. S. Bach*. Edited by Peter le Hurray and John Stevens. 3 vols. Cambridge Studies in Music. Cambridge: Cambridge University Press, 1980.

Wotquenne, Alfred. *Thematisches Verzeichniss der Werke von Carl Philipp Emanuel Bach 1714–1788*. Wiesbaden: Breitkopf und Härtel, 1964.

Wurm, Karl. "Christus Kosmokrator: Ein hermeneutischer Versuch zu D. Buxtehudes Passacaglia in d BuxWV 161 und zu J. S. Bachs Präludium und Fuge C-dur BWV 547." *Musik und Kirche* 54 (1984): 263–71.

Index

Adlung, Jakob, 17, 23, 27, 45, 52, 62–63, 67
Musica mechanica organœdi, 17, 23, 24
Affekt, 116
Agricola, Johann Friedrich, 45
Ahrend, Jürgen, 109
Alkmaar, the Netherlands, 150
angreifen, 83–84
anschlag, 72, 75, 77–79, 83, 85–86
articulation, 159
    organ, harpsichord, 99
    organ, 110–11, 135–37, 141–42, 144–46
Arvidsson, Mats, 154
attack
    calligraphy brush, 119
    clavichord, 62, 65, 72–73, 77, 83–86, 96, 98, 100, 103, 143–44, 148
    harpsichord, 2, 83
    harpsichord, clavichord, organ, 86, 97
    pedal, 109, 111–12
authenticity, 4

Bach, Anna Magdalena, 39
Bach, Carl Philipp Emanuel, 25, 27, 41, 46–47, 77
    Cantabile, 48
    letters to Forkel, 33–35, 49–50, 52, 78
    Nachlassverzeichniss, 48
    on clavichord technique, 69–70, 81–85, 98, 101
    on preparing for performance, 1–2, 148
    on stringing, 61–62, 65, 96
    Versuch über die wahre Art das Clavier zu Spielen, 61, 70, 74, 75–96, 81–84
Bach, Johann Christoph, 133–35
    Andreas Bach Book, 129, 133–35, 144

Möller Manuscript, 133–35
Bach, Johann Sebastian, 8, 15, 25, 44, 52, 114, 116–17, 133
    À 2 Clav et pedale, 44—46
    and house instruments, 15, 24, 27, 29, 53, 153
    and pedal clavichord, 46
    Applicatio, 104
    Chromatische Fantasia und Fuga, 70, 78
    clavichord technique, 13, 69–71, 81, 86
    improvising trio sonatas, 25, 27, 34
    Inventions, 37
    Inventio 1, C Major, 124–25
    Inventio 8, F Major, 126–27
    Last Will and Testament, 25–27
    Orgelbüchlein, 137
    Passacaglia in C Minor, 25, 35, 36, 40–42, 44, 46, 80, 93, 129–48, 184n33
    pedal technique, 105
    Sinfonias, 37
    Six Keyboard and Violin Sonatas, 48
    Six Trio Sonatas, 32, 35, 38–39, 41, 43, 47, 50, 93
        as organ music, 44–45
    Sonata à 2 Clav: et Pedal, 39
    Sonatas for Violine and Klavier, 50
    Two-Part Inventions, 86–87, 93, 105, 118, 120
    Well-Tempered Clavier, 5, 29, 30, 34, 53, 86
Bach, Wilhelm Friedemann, 25, 35, 39, 41, 44, 46–47, 81
    Clavierbüchlein, 104
Bachhaus, 18
Barnes, John, 1–2, 4, 9, 13, 16, 23, 53, 54, 64–66, 96–97, 100, 109
Bebung, 30, 95, 141
Bergen, Norway, 18–19
Bergsten, Carl Johan, 150, 185n3
Bernstein, Walter Heinz, 118

Birkett, Stephen, 59
Blaise, Gary, 9
blocking, 95–96, 106–7
Boalch, 28, 31
Bohm, David, 91
Brauchli, Bernard, 20, 24
Brook, Peter, 91–92
Bukofzer, Manfred, 6
Bullard, Beth, 173n20
Buolach, Egidius de, 20
Burmeister, Joachim, 114
Burney, Charles, 149
Buxtehude, Dieterich, 131–33, 135
    Passacaglia BuxWV 161, 133

cantabile, 36, 48, 50, 51, 85
chekker, 1
Chinese calligraphy, 118–20, 128
    attack, continuation and release, 119
    comparison to clavichord strokes, 128
    traditional brush strokes, 119
Chorton, 63
ciaccona, 131–32, 135
Cizek, Bohuslav, 22
Clark, Stephen, 47, 48, 50
clavichord, 36
    by organbuilders:
        Gerber, 28–29
        Gerstenberg, 52
        Friederici, C. E., 52
        Schiörlin, 19
        Silbermann, 51
        Wolthersson, 19
    keylevers, 18, 64, 73, 97–98
    non-historical, 32, 97–98, 110
    pedal, 3, 15, 17–31, 23, 55, 136–37
    soundboards, 52, 54, 56–57, 67–68, 146, 159
    stringing, 16, 61, 63–66, 68, 153, 158–59
    technique, manual
        exercises, 101–5
    technique, pedal
        exercises, 108–13
        historical information on, 106–7
Clavier
    as clavichord, 15, 25–26, 29–30.

34–36, 38–39, 44–46, 51, 69, 75, 78, 86, 118, 155
    as general keyboard, 15, 29–30, 35–37, 39–40, 42–43, 46, 48, 50, 71, 76, 86, 105, 132
    and J. S. Bach's technique, 13, 52–53, 70, 80, 86
Cologne, Germany: Heyer Collection in, 30, 54
craft process, 9, 34, 91, 118

Davidsson, Hans, 2
De Grigny, Nicolas, 157
de Sancta Maria, Thomas, 132
Dolmetsch, Arnold, 43
Doppelflügel, 26, 34, 76
Douwes, Claas, 22–24, 29
    Grondig ondersoek van de Toonen der Musijk, 22–23

Eastman School of Music, 9
Edinburgh, Scotland, 3–4, 53, 96
    University of Edinburgh, 109
Eisenach, Germany, 18
Emery, Walter, 32, 43, 45, 130
Empfindsamkeit, 33, 70
ephemera, 64, 95
Érard, Sébastian, 43, 85
essentialist, 6

Faulkner, Quentin, 70–71
    on J. S. Bach's keyboard technique, 70
    on pedal technique, 105
    on *Versuch über die wahre Art das Clavier zu Spielen,* 75–76, 82
    translation of Friederich Conrad Griepenkerl's Preface to J. S. Bach's *Chomatic Fantasy and Fugue* (1819), 166–71
Ferrara, Lawrence, 8
figural notation, 93, 114, 120–27, 138–40
Figurenlehre, 114
fingering, 82, 103–4, 109, 116, 159
finger pressure, 65, 72, 75–76, 95
finger technique, 72–74, 97, 118, 149
Fleischer, Johan Christoph, 177n6

Flentrop organ, 2
Flores Musicae, 21
Flügel, 26, 33, 37, 69–70, 78, 83
Forkel, Johann Nikolaus, 24–27, 30–
    33, 36, 39–40, 44–47, 70, 86
    as reception historian, 75
    correspondence with C.P.E. Bach,
        34–35, 47, 49–52
    General History of Music, 117, 138
    Nachlaßverzeichniss, 129
    on C. P. E. Bach's *Clavier* technique,
        75
    on J. S. Bach and the clavichord, 46–
        47, 70
    on J. S. Bach's *Clavier* technique,
        71–76, 81–84, 86–87, 92, 100,
        104, 158
    on J. S. Bach's *Organ Pieces,* 35
    on J. S. Bach's *Trio–Sonatas,* 34, 45,
        48, 130
    on J. S. Bach's *Passacaglia,* 41, 44,
        93, 129–31
    Twentieth Century reception of, 76–
        78
    *Ueber Johann Sebastian Bachs
        Leben, Kunst und Kunstwerke,*
        24, 70–71
        Library of Congress copy, 129–30
fortepiano, 33
Frankfurt am Main, Germany, 149
Friederici, Christian Ernst, 52–53
Friederici, Christian Gottfried, 52–53,
    64
    John Barnes's copy, 96, 100
    single manual clavichord, 52, 54
    stringing scale, 64–65
Fritz, Barthold, 52

Galpin Society Journal, 1
Gerlach clavichord, 64, 66
German idealism, 7
Gerber, Ernst Ludwig, 27–29, 46
    *Historisch-biographische Lexicon
        der Tonkünstler,* 27
Gerber, Heinrich Nikolaus, 27–29, 46,
    153
Gerstenberg, Johann David, 52
    as builder, 58–59

Gerstenberg pedal clavichord, 6, 9, 24,
    18, 28–30, 41–42, 55–57
    bench, 56, 113
    case construction, 54, 177n11
    history of, 52, 59–61, 175n34,
        177n2
    hole in, 54, 58
    illustration of, 6, 55–57
    in Leipzig Collection, 52
    John Barnes and Joel Speerstra copy,
        3–4, 16, 52, 54, 58–59, 105,
        150–51, 153
    other copies, 9
    keydip, 128
    keylevers, 106,
    parts of, 53–57
    sharp keys, 109–10
    stringing, 61, 63–69
    soundboards, 67
Glonner, Joseph, 24
Göteborg, Sweden, 19–20
Göteborg University, 92
    Göteborg Organ Art Center
        (GOArt) 3–5, 14
    North German Organ Research
        Project, 150, 153–156
    Göteborg International Organ
        Academy, 93
    School of Music, 53, 92–93, 100
Griepenkerl, Friederich Conrad, 78, 80
    Preface to J. S. Bach's *Chromatic
        Fantasy and Fugue* (1819), 70–
        71, 79, 81–84, 161–71
    Preface to J. S. Bach's *Organ Works,*
        Vol. 1 (1844), 46, 78–80
    on J. S. Bach's clavier technique, 83–
        84, 100, 115, 120, 158
    on J. S. Bach's *Passacaglia,* 144
    on J. S. Bach's *Two-Part Inventions,*
        87, 105, 120
    on the pedal clavichord, 136
guild system in Europe, 9, 67, 92

harpsichord, 1–2, 24, 26, 32–34, 37–
    38, 69–70, 77–78, 130, 132, 148
    non-historical, 30, 45, 97, 169
    pedal, 14, 25–27, 34–35, 40, 45–46,
        76, 135, 172n2

harpsichord *(continued)*
   stringing, 64
   technique, 82–83, 85–86, 96–97, 99,
      103
Hamburg, Germany
   C. P. E. Bach in, 52
   clavichords in, 53, 64, 68, 154–55
   St. Jacobi organ in, 63, 153
Hass, Johann Adolph, 43, 52
   clavichords, stringing of, 64–66
   family, 64
   Hamburg Hass tradition, 64–65
Helenius-Öberg, 173n16
Henkel, Hubert, 54, 64
Heringen, Germany, 28
Heyer Collection
   Cologne, 30, 54
   Leipzig, 41
Hill, Robert, 134
Hipkins, Alfred James, 43, 176n36
Horn, Gottfried Joseph, 64
   instruments, 64–68
human physiology, 71, 107–8
   humours, 116–17
      choleric, 116
      melancholic, 117
      phlegmatic, 117
      sanguine, 117
Hume, David, 7

interdisciplinary, 3, 14

Jeans, Lady Susi, 44–45
Johann Ernst, Prince of Weimar, 114
Jurgenson, William, 59
Kalmus Publishing, 30
Kammermusik, 37, 39, 49–50
Kammerton, 63
Kant, Immanuel, 7
key action, 150–53
Kindermann, Johann Erasmus, 106
Kinsky, Georg, 30, 41–42, 45, 47
Kinström, Lars, 19–20
Kittel, Johann, 106, 153
   Der Angehende Praktische Organist,
      106
   pedaling technique, 107
Klangfüsse, 137

Klavizimbel, 39–40, 85
Kooiman, Ewald, 71
Koster, John, 24, 63
Krämer, Johann Paul & Söhne, 18

Landowska, Wanda, 27, 30, 41, 45,
   97–98
Lang, Paul Henry, 6–7
Leipzig, Germany, 28–29, 53
   Heyer Collection in, 41
Leipzig foot, 59
Leipzig inches, 59
Leipzig University Musical Instrument
   Museum, 10, 52–53, 64–65, 68
Ling, Jan, 3
London, England
   Globe Theater in, 92
   J. S. Bach in, 26
   London Great Exhibition, 42–43
   National Theater in, 91
   University of London, 91
Luther, Martin, 114

Magnano Clavichord Symposium, 71
Mattheson, Johann, 136–37
   Der volkommene Capellmeister, 136
Marckert, Georg, 18
Marpurg, Friedrich Wilhelm, 84, 97
Marshall, Robert, 26, 46
Mitchell, William J., 82–83
Mueller, John, 6
musica poetica, 114, 115, 117
musical-rhetorical figures. *See under*
   rhetoric.
Müthel, Johann Gottfried, 27

Niedt, Friederich Erhardt, 154
nominalist, 6–7

Oberlin College and Conservatory of
   Music, 1–2
O'Brien, Grant, 64–66
O'Brien, Michael, 9
Oehme, Adam Gottfried, 19
organ, 4–5, 14–15, 17–20, 22, 24–25,
   30, 32, 36–43, 45–47, 50–51,
   72, 74, 77
   and Bach, C. P. E., 75

and Bach, J. S., 86, 106
    and *Passacaglia in C Minor,* 129–
        31, 135–48
and Bach, W. F., 35, 41
and Burney, 149
and Eastman School of Music, 9,
    28–29, 134
and Forkel, 33
and Griepenkerl, 78, 136
and pedal clavichord, 14, 93, 129–
    31, 135–60
and Schweitzer, 40, 143
and Silbermann, 41–42, 149
and Spitta, 37–39
by Ahrend in Edinburgh, 109
by Flentrop in Oberlin, 2
by Gerber, 28–29
by Schnitger, A. in Hamburg, 63,
    153
by Schnitger, F. C. in Alkmaar, 150
central German, 149
English, 149
French classical, 157
house instrument, 2
Italian Renaissance, 157
North European, historical, 2, 3, 6,
    7, 9, 19, 100, 109, 131, 143,
    148, 155–58
North German Organ Research
    Project in Göteborg 3, 4, 150–57
technique, 75–76, 80, 99, 101, 103,
    109–11
Thuringian, 63
Ortgies, Ibo, 185n5
Östersund, Sweden, 19
overtone production, 67

Pachelbel, Johnann, 132
    Ciacona in D Minor, 132
passacaglia, 131–32
Paulirinus, Paulus, 20
Pedalklavier, 41
pedalboards, 2–3, 14, 17–18, 20, 26–
    28, 53, 110, 112, 149, 155
Peters, Jack, 9
phenomenology, 7–8, 41, 45, 47, 51,
    62, 71, 74, 76–77, 78, 82, 86,
    91, 97, 138, 158

pitch, 9, 20, 53, 61, 96
    bending, 128, 132
    Chorton, 63
    Kammerton, 63
    of Gerstenberg copy, 65
    relationships in soundboards, 67
    stability, 65, 95, 97–98
plucking point, 97, 185n4
Polany, Michael, 91–92
Praetorius, Michael, 22
    De Organographia, 22

Rácz Mizushima, Jochen, 172n3,
    173n6
reception history, 13–15, 32, 41, 44,
    46, 69, 75, 159
realist, 6–7
registers
    organ stops, 27, 42, 45, 54, 63,
        174n40
    range, 145–47
Reichardt, Johann Friedrich, 46, 69–
    70, 95
release
    in calligraphy, 119
    on harpsichord, 1
    on organ, 75–76, 111, 141, 148
    on pedal clavichord, 107, 120
    on piano, 85
Reutlingen, Hugo von, 20
rhetoric, 114
    musical-rhetorical figures, 114, 117,
        137–38
    anticipatio, 121
    bombus, 123
    circolo mezzo, 122, 132, 140,
        143–46
    congeries, 140, 145
    dubitatio, 117, 138, 139
    ellipsis, 123
    figura corta, 115, 122, 139, 140–
        41, 146
    groppo, 123
    messanza, 121
    mora, 122
    passus duriusculus, 122
    saltus duriusculus, 122
    subsumtio, 121

rhetoric, musical-rhetorical figures
(*continued*)
   superjectio, 121, 140, 143–44,
    147
   suspensio, 117, 138
   suspirans, 115–116, 123, 137,
    139, 141–43
   syncopatio, 121
   tirata, 122
   transitus, 104, 115–16, 121, 140–
    41, 143–45, 181n27
   tremelo, 123
   variatio, 121
Rinck, Johann Christian, 106
Robertson, Kaestner D., 71, 179n11
Rosen, Charles, 1, 5
Russell Collection of Historical
   Keyboard Instruments, University of Edinburgh, 2, 13, 53
Russell, Raymond, 26

scaling, 58, 63–65
schlagen, 83–84
Schnitger, Arp, 63, 153
   Hamburg, Germany, St. Jacobi
   organ, 63, 153
Schweitzer, Albert, 32, 39, 40–44, 46
   on Bach and the piano, 85
   on J. S. Bach's *Passacaglia,* 130, 143
   on J. S. Bach's technique, 84–85
Schiörlin, Pehr, 19
schmeicheln, 83–84
Schmieder, Wolfgang, 32, 46, 49,
   176n38
   Thematisch-Systematisches
   Verzeichnis der Werke Joh. Seb.
   Bachs, 32, 46, 49, 174n1
Shaw, George Bernard, 42, 47
Sherman, Bernard, 4
Skara, Sweden, 19
Skellefteå, Sweden, 19
Smarano, Italy, International
   Clavichord, Organ and
   Improvisation Academy, 93
Snyder, Kerala, 135
Sondershausen, Germany, 28
Spitta, Philipp, 32–34, 36–39, 41, 43–
   44, 46, 48, 85

   on J. S. Bach and the piano, 37,
    86
Stauffer, George, 86
Stinson, Russell, 15
Strasbourg University, 40
strings, 18, 23–24, 53–54, 61, 83, 118
   4-foot, 52, 64
   8-foot, 53, 54, 57
   16-foot, 54, 57, 145
   and force, 103, 112, 142, 15–53
   and tangent rails, 98, 181n6
   after-length, 63–64
   Bach, C. P. E., on, 83–84, 86
   Edinburgh stringing, 16, 64–65,
    153, 158
   for pedal-action, 3, 18–20
   Forkel on, 74
   gauges, 63–64
   good sound from, 95–96, 100–106,
    116, 128, 132, 144, 146
   Hass, 64–66, 68
   iron, 63
   Schweitzer on, 85
   speaking lengths, 63
   stringband, 56–57, 59
   tension, 61–63, 65, 67–68, 73, 96–
    97, 103
   triple-strung, 24
   Troeger on, 86
Stumpff, Heinrich, 18
Stuttgart, Germany, 21

tacit knowledge, 91–92, 157–58,
   180n2
tangents, 17–18, 53, 62, 63, 73, 75,
   83, 86, 96–98, 106, 112, 118,
   152–53
Taruskin, Richard, 4
technique 2, 36, 63, 68, 92–93, 97,
   101, 148, 156
   and rhetoric, 116–17
   Bach, C. P. E., 82–84
   Bach, J. S., 8, 13, 15, 52–53, 69–71,
    86–87, 105, 158
    Forkel on, 71–76, 100
    Griepenkerl on, 78–81
    reception of, 76–78
    Schweitzer on, 84–86

finger-based, 1, 62, 97–98, 118, 149
  pedal, 105–13
weight-transference, 62, 65, 67, 70–
  71, 103
  manual, 71, 79. 100
  pedal, 109, 111–12
tempo di buona, 99, 113
tempo di cattiva, 99, 113
Terry, Charles Sanford, 26–27
Thuringian organ, 63
touch, 159
  at the clavichord, 7, 53, 61, 72, 75,
    77–79, 84, 86–87, 95–96, 100,
    103–5, 149, 153
  at the forte-piano, 79
  at the harpsichord, 77–78, 83, 97
  at the organ, 75, 142, 148–50, 153,
    158
  at the piano, 85
  hardness of, 63–65, 68, 178n20
Treitler, Leo, 5–6
trochee, 136–37, 142, 145
Troeger, Richard, 86
tuning, 22–23, 27
  Chorton, 63
  Kammerton, 63

of materials, 67–68, 178n29,
  179n30

Überschreien, 61–62

van Eeeken, Henk, 154
van Oortmerssen, Jacques, 101,
  181n13
Verwolf, Dick, 9
vibrato, 61, 95
Virdung, Sebastian, 21–22, 24
  Musica getutscht, 21–22
Vogel, Harald, 2, 185n34
  North German Organ Academy, 2

Walther, Johann Gottfried, 13, 98–99,
  114, 117, 182n3
Watson Foundation, 2
Whitehead, Lance, 64
Williams, Peter, 45–47
Wolthersson, Gustaf Gabriel, 17, 19–
  20, 173n15

Yokota, Munetaka, 154

Zwey Claviere und Pedal, 35, 39, 46,
  130

Eastman Studies in Music

(ISSN 1071–9989)

The Poetic Debussy: A Collection of His Song Texts and Selected Letters (Revised Second Edition)
Edited by Margaret G. Cobb

Concert Music, Rock, and Jazz since 1945: Essays and Analytical Studies
Edited by Elizabeth West Marvin and Richard Hermann

Music and the Occult: French Musical Philosophies, 1750–1950
Joscelyn Godwin

"Wanderjahre of a Revolutionist" and Other Essays on American Music
Arthur Farwell, edited by Thomas Stoner

French Organ Music from the Revolution to Franck and Widor
Edited by Lawrence Archbold and William J. Peterson

Musical Creativity in Twentieth-Century China: Abing, His Music, and Its Changing Meanings (includes CD)
Jonathan P. J. Stock

Elliott Carter: Collected Essays and Lectures, 1937–1995
Edited by Jonathan W. Bernard

Music Theory in Concept and Practice
Edited by James M. Baker, David W. Beach, and Jonathan W. Bernard

Music and Musicians in the Escorial Liturgy under the Habsburgs, 1563–1700
Michael Noone

Analyzing Wagner's Operas: Alfred Lorenz and German Nationalist Ideology
Stephen McClatchie

The Gardano Music Printing Firms, 1569–1611
Richard J. Agee

"The Broadway Sound": The Autobiography and Selected Essays of Robert Russell Bennett
Edited by George J. Ferencz

Theories of Fugue from the Age of Josquin to the Age of Bach
Paul Mark Walker

The Chansons of Orlando di Lasso and Their Protestant Listeners: Music, Piety, and Print in Sixteenth-Century France
Richard Freedman

Berlioz's Semi-Operas: Roméo et Juliette and La damnation de Faust
Daniel Albright

The Gamelan Digul and the Prison Camp Musician Who Built It
Margaret J. Kartomi

"The Music of American Folk Song" and Selected Other Writings on American Folk Music
Ruth Crawford Seeger, edited by Larry Polansky and Judith Tick

Portrait of Percy Grainger
Malcolm Gillies and David Pear

Berlioz: Past, Present, Future
Edited by Peter Bloom

The Musical Madhouse (Les Grotesques de la musique)
Hector Berlioz
Translated and edited by Alastair Bruce
Introduction by Hugh Macdonald

The Music of Luigi Dallapiccola
Raymond Fearn

Music's Modern Muse: A Life of Winnaretta Singer, Princesse de Polignac
Sylvia Kahan

The Sea on Fire: Jean Barraqué
Paul Griffiths

"Claude Debussy As I Knew Him" and Other Writings of Arthur Hartmann
Edited by Samuel Hsu, Sidney Grolnic, and Mark Peters
Foreword by David Grayson

Schumann's Piano Cycles and the Novels of Jean Paul
Erika Reiman

Bach and the Pedal Clavichord: An Organist's Guide
Joel Speerstra

Bach and the Pedal Clavichord: An Organist's Guide

Friederich Griepenkerl, in his 1844 introduction to Volume 1 of the first complete edition of J. S. Bach's organ works, wrote: "Actually the six Sonatas and the Passacaglia were written for a clavichord with two manuals and pedal, an instrument that, in those days, every beginning organist possessed, which they used beforehand, to practice playing with hands and feet in order to make effective use of them at the organ. It would be a good thing to let such instruments be made again, because actually no one who wants to study to be an organist can really do without one."

What was the role of the pedal clavichord in music history? Was it a cheap practice instrument for organists or was Griepenkerl right? Was it a teaching tool that helped contribute to the quality of organ playing in its golden age? Most twentieth-century commentary on the pedal clavichord as an historical phenomenon was written in a kind of vacuum, since there were no playable historical models with which to experiment and from which to make an informed judgment.

At the heart of *Bach and the Pedal Clavichord: An Organist's Guide* are some extraordinary recent experiments from the Göteborg Organ Art Center (GOArt) at Göteborg University. The Johan David Gerstenberg pedal clavichord from 1766, now in the Leipzig University museum, was documented, reconstructed, then used for several years as a living instrument for organ students and teachers to experience. On the basis of these experiments and experiences, the book explores, in new and artful ways, Johann Sebastian Bach's keyboard technique, a technique preserved by his first biographer, J. N. Forkel (1802), and by Forkel's own student, Griepenkerl. It also sifts and weighs the assumptions and claims made for and against the clavichord and pedal clavichord over two and a half centuries: by Bach's son Carl Philipp Emanuel, by such noted Bach scholars as Walter Emery and Robert Marshall, and by sharp-eared music lovers, including one of the most perceptive (and one of the few from his era to have actually encountered a clavichord and recognized its unique qualities), George Bernard Shaw.

Joel Speerstra, an organist and clavichord player, is a Senior Researcher at the Göteborg Organ Center, Göteborg University, Sweden, and has taught at the University of Rochester's Eastman School of Music.

Hans Davidsson is Associate Professor of Organ at the Eastman School of Music, University of Rochester. He is also founder and General Artistic and Research Director of the Göteborg Organ Art Center (GOArt) at Göteborg University (Sweden), and a prominent musicologist and concertizing organist. In January 2004, he was awarded The King's Medal at the Royal Palace in Stockholm.

Praise for *Bach and the Pedal Clavichord: An Organist's Guide*:

"The first of its kind on this important subject. Authoritative scholarship combined with successful practical application makes Speerstra's work invaluable to all organists, pedagogues, instrument builders—indeed all those who are fascinated by the music of Bach."
>—David Higgs, Chair of the Organ Department,
>Eastman School of Music, University of Rochester

"For much of the twentieth century, the pedal clavichord was regarded as merely an inexpensive substitute instrument for the organist wishing to practice at home. Joel Speerstra—an experienced instrument maker who is also a performer/teacher and musicologist—understands the surviving historical instruments extraordinarily well and thus is in a position to show persuasively that the pedal clavichord was used as an instrument in its own right for both study and performance."
>—Gerhard Stradner, the former Director of the
>Collection of Ancient Musical Instruments,
>Kunsthistorisches Museum, Vienna (Austria)